Bibliography of published research of the
World Employment Programme

International Labour Bibliography No. 4

Bibliography of published research of the World Employment Programme

Seventh edition

International Labour Office Geneva

Seventh edition copyright © International Labour Organisation 1988

Publications of the International Labour Office enjoy copyright under Protocol 2 of the Universal Copyright Convention. Nevertheless, short excerpts from them may be reproduced without authorisation, on condition that the source is indicated. For rights of reproduction or translation, application should be made to the Publications Branch (Rights and Permissions), International Labour Office, CH-1211 Geneva 22, Switzerland. The International Labour Office welcomes such applications.

ISBN 92-2-106390-9

First published 1978
Seventh edition 1988

The designations employed in ILO publications, which are in conformity with United Nations practice, and the presentation of material therein do not imply the expression of any opinion whatsoever on the part of the International Labour Office concerning the legal status of any country, area or territory or of its authorities, or concerning the delimitation of its frontiers.
The responsibility for opinions expressed in signed articles, studies and other contributions rests solely with their authors, and publication does not constitute an endorsement by the International Labour Office of the opinions expressed in them.
Reference to names of firms and commercial products and processes does not imply their endorsement by the International Labour Office, and any failure to mention a particular firm, commercial product or process is not a sign of disapproval.

ILO publications can be obtained through major booksellers or ILO local offices in many countries, or direct from ILO Publications, International Labour Office, CH-1211 Geneva 22, Switzerland. A catalogue or list of new publications will be sent free of charge from the above address.

Printed in Switzerland

Table of Contents

Introduction	i
General publications on the World Employment Programme	1
ILO publications	1
Comprehensive employment planning	4
ILO publications	4
ILO works published by commercial and non-profit-making publishers.	14
Related books and articles	14
Manpower planning and labour market information systems	15
ILO publications	15
ILO works published by commercial and non-profit-making publishers	20
Basic needs and income distribution	21
ILO publications	21
ILO works published by commercial and non-profit-making publishers	31
Related books and articles	32
Labour market analysis and the informal sector	34
ILO publications	34
ILO works published by commercial and non-profit-making publishers	41
Related books and articles	42
Rural poverty, rural industrialisation and employment	43
ILO publications	43
ILO works published by commercial and non-profit-making publishers	56
Migration and urbanisation	59
ILO publications	59
ILO works published by commercial and non-profit-making publishers	66
Related books and articles	66
Population and employment	69
ILO publications	69
ILO works published by commercial and non-profit-making publishers	72
Related books and articles	73
Technology and employment	75
ILO publications	75
ILO works published by commercial and non-profit-making publishers	87
Related books and articles	88
Special employment programmes and vulnerable groups	89
ILO publications	89
ILO works published by commercial and non-profit-making publishers	94
Structural adjustment and the international division of labour	95
ILO publications	95
ILO works published by commercial and non-profit-making publishers	104
Related books and articles	104
Women	106
ILO publications	106
ILO works published by commercial and non-profit-making publishers	115
Related books and articles	116
Author Index	118
Country and Area Index	125

Introduction

This is the seventh edition of the WEP bibliography. It is complete up to December 1987. It differs from previous editions in that there is now only one section which includes all WEP publications, both those produced at ILO headquarters and those originating from WEP regional and subregional employment teams. All items issued before 1978, with the exception of important WEP documents, have been deleted.

The publications and documents contained in the bibliography are organised, by topic, into 12 chapters:

- General publications on the World Employment Programme

  This section includes a number of publications of two specific kinds. First are a number of official reports of the ILO to its own International Labour Conference which none the less discuss substantive issues and often serve as progress reports on work performed. Second are broad summary articles assessing the scope and impact of the activities of the World Employment Programme.

- Comprehensive employment planning

  Work in this field aims at assisting developing countries in the initiation, formulation, implementation and evaluation of broadly based policies to attain higher levels of employment as an integral part of overall socio-economic development planning and as a primary means of adequate growth and of alleviating poverty and satisfying basic needs.

- Manpower planning and labour market information systems

  Work in this field aims at helping developing countries to upgrade their capacity in manpower planning and labour market information, as a basis for appropriate decision-making in all matters relating to national, regional and local manpower and labour market issues.

- Basic needs and income distribution

  Since the basic-needs approach to development was endorsed by the World Employment Conference in 1976, a large number of studies have been undertaken to investigate both its overall feasibility and particular problems involved in its implementation. Country studies of basic-needs performance and of the factors constraining the achievement of higher levels of basic-needs satisfaction have been carried out. In the general field of income distribution, a large number of studies have been undertaken on issues concerned with the different types of income distribution and their relation to employment. Considerable attention has also been given to studies on instruments of government redistribution policy, such as government expenditure programmes and taxation, to questions of wealth distribution and redistribution and to the measurement and alleviation of poverty.

- Labour market analysis and the informal sector

  Documents under this heading describe research into the operation of the labour market, so as to assist in the design of adequate employment policies. Particular attention is given to the functions of the urban informal sector in selected large and medium-sized cities in Asia, Africa and Latin America. Generally speaking, the studies carried out fall into three categories: analysis of census data of informal sector units; results and conclusions of informal sector surveys; and formulation of a programme of action.

- Rural poverty, rural industrialisation and employment

    The main areas of research in this area are: quantification and analysis of the patterns, trends and characteristics of rural poverty; analysis and evaluation of alternative agrarian systems and rural development strategies with emphasis on labour absorption; assessment of the social costs and benefits of internal migration; studies of selected peasant organisations and mass participation in rural development. For the problems faced by women workers in rural areas, see the corresponding chapter on women. Work on rural industrialisation and employment has generated two sets of studies: the first focuses on the programmes and policies towards rural industries pursued in selected developing countries; and the second provides an in-depth analysis of rural small-scale industries in selected countries, generally based on field surveys.

- Migration and urbanisation

    Work in this field has focused on the process of urbanisation and the implications of urban development for employment generation in selected cities of the Third World. Work on migration is divided into two broad categories. The first investigates the implications for economic and social policy-making of international migration movements from low-income to high-income countries. It is primarily concerned with migration into Western Europe, the Arab States, and the southern Africa region. The second deals with questions of rural-urban and rural migration, both temporary and permanent; it includes the analysis of migration processes, the design of data collection surveys and the evaluation of policy.

- Population and employment

    The publications on population and employment cover the following themes. First, they include reports on and analyses of the Bachue series of economic-demographic models which are intended to improve analysis and policy evaluation in the field of population, employment and income distribution, based on system-wide approaches to these phenomena and their interactions. Second, they cover a number of specific relationships between population and employment, particularly studies on labour force participation, fertility, the impact of demographic change on wages and labour markets, and a number of other issues. The general disciplinary focus is one of applied economics. Related work is also included in other chapters, notably the chapters on migration and on women.

- Technology and employment

    Work in this field is concerned with technological choice and its social and economic ramifications in the agricultural, manufacturing and construction (roads and irrigation) sectors of the developing economy, as well as similar issues related to energy. The principal objectives of research carried out are:

(a) to identify alternative labour-intensive technologies which may be economically competitive in developing countries aspiring to fuller employment;

(b) to assess the scope for adapting technologies imported from the developed world;

(c) to assess the role of government policy in promoting domestic research, and the development and adaptation of technologies.

- Emergency employment schemes and special employment programmes

    In this field a number of studies are being undertaken concerning:

    (a) organisational, economic and technical aspects of emergency public works programmes, including youth programmes, aimed at alleviating unemployment and rural underemployment in developing countries;

    (b) steps to promote fuller utilisation of industrial capacity as a quick employment generating measure in developing countries;

    (c) steps taken in industrialised countries to cope with acute unemployment situations through emergency schemes.

    Research in the field of vulnerable groups has concentrated on three major issues. The first is the role of education systems in preparing young people for work, both in terms of skills developed and of attitudes created. The second issue concerns later job and career patterns associated with particular types and levels of education. The third issue is the interaction between family poverty and the child's need for education, which is often sacrificed in favour of child labour.

- Structural adjustment and the international division of labour

    Research undertaken in this field has primarily been concerned with analysing the effects of structural adjustment, of changes in international trade flows, and of transformations of the international division of labour on employment in both developing and developed countries. Results of recent work have been integrated into documents presented at the High-Level Meeting on Employment and Structural Adjustment. The latest studies published are the output of the second phase of the research project on employment, trade and north-south cooperation that deals with the effects on employment of the changing international trade flows in manufactures.

- Women

    The main areas of research in this field include: the impact of agricultural modernisation on women; the special situation of women workers in subsistence agriculture and wage employment; the stresses on women and poor families that arise from growing fuel scarcity; the growing phenomenon of separate male or female migration and the problems created for women, including the growth of female-headed households; the situation of women in home-based industries; the adoption of appropriate technologies to alleviate the work burden of rural women; the determinants of female labour force participation; inter-relationships between fertility and female employment; sex discrimination and sex segregation in labour markets; measurement of female work activities.

How to use the bibliography

Each chapter is divided as follows: ILO publications, ILO works published by commercial and non-profit making publishers and related books and articles. The ILO publications section is further divided into books and reports, articles in the *International Labour Review,* and working papers. All entries are listed in geographical and chronological order within their respective categories.

The bibliography contains an author index and a country and area index.

Documents available in more than one language are indicated by the first letter of the language.[1] Documents which are not available either because their contents are confidential or because they are out of print are marked with asterisks (*). Working papers available in microfiche form are identified by the letter "M" immediately following the serial number. A group or groups of three letters in square brackets at the end of an entry indicate the country or area under which the particular document is listed in the country and area index. Documents which do not deal specifically with any one country are not included in the index.

The following examples illustrate how to read an entry.

J. Doe: Employment and development in selected European countries (Geneva, ILO, 1980), vi + 100 pp. Sw.frs. 15. E*, F. [FRA, DEU, GBR] ISBN.....

The above publication exists in English and French (E, F); the English edition is out of print (E*); the document is listed in the country index under France [FRA], the Federal Republic of Germany [DEU], and the United Kingdom [GBR].

J. Doe: Employment forecasting techniques in France, May 1982 (WEP 5-51/WP.10). M. [FRA].

The above Working Paper exists in microfiche form and is listed under France [FRA] in the country index.

How to obtain documents listed in the bibliography

Priced items published by the ILO:
   from ILO Publications, International Labour Office,
   CH-1211 Geneva 22, Switzerland.

A complete catalogue is available on request.

Books published on behalf of the ILO by commercial publishing houses:
   from the publisher in question or your local bookseller.

Priced items published by the International Institute for Labour Studies:
   from the International Institute for Labour Studies,
   BP 6, CH-1211 Geneva 22, Switzerland.

Reports and working papers prepared by the **regional teams** can be obtained directly from them as follows:
   ARTEP: ILO/ARTEP, P.O. Box 643, New Delhi 110001, India.
   PREALC: PREALC, Casilla 618, Santiago de Chile.
   JASPA: JASPA, P.O. Box 2532, Addis Ababa, Ethiopia.
   SATEP: SATEP, P.O. Box 32181, Lusaka, Zambia.

Publications of the Labour and Population Team for the Middle East (LPME) are available for consultation at the ILO, Geneva.

WEP research working papers and all other documents may be requested directly from the Documentation Unit of the Employment and Development Department, International Labour Office, CH-1211 Geneva 22, Switzerland.

Working Papers are reproduced in limited numbers only, but many are available through a microfiche service. Divided into 16 subject series, the complete collection (1974-87) covers 518 volumes (Sw. frs. 4,050). Individual series can be obtained separately. Orders should be addressed to ILO Publications, International Labour Office, CH-1211 Geneva 22, Switzerland.

Publications emanating from the World Employment Programme are announced in International Labour Documentation, the abstracting bulletin produced by the ILO.

Retrospective searches can be made by the ILO using the LABORDOC data base; searches can also be arranged through ESA (Frascati, Italy), SDC (Santa Monica, United States), Télésystèmes Questel (Paris, France), Human Resource Information Network (Indianapolis, United States).

Notes:

1 E= English; F= French; S= Spanish; G= German; R= Russian; A= Arabic.

General publications on the World Employment Programme

ILO publications

Books and reports

- **General**

The World Employment Programme, Report of the Director-General (Part I) to the International Labour Conference, 53rd Session, Geneva, 1969 (Geneva, ILO, 1969), 151 pp. Sw. frs. 6. E, F, S*, G, R.

The World Employment Programme, Report IV, International Labour Conference, 56th Session, Geneva, 1971 (Geneva, ILO, 1971; 2nd impression, 1973), 86 pp. Sw. frs. 6. E, F, S, G, R.

Employment policy in the Second Development Decade. A United Nations family approach (Geneva, ILO, 1973), viii + 44 pp. Sw. frs. 8. E, F, S, G. ISBN 92-2-101004-X.

Time for transition. A mid-term review of the Second United Nations Development Decade. A mid-term review of progress in the attaining of the employment and income distribution objectives of the Second United Nations Development Decade (Geneva, ILO, 1975), vi + 84 pp. Sw. frs. 15. E*, F, S. ISBN 92-2-101301-4.

Tripartite World Conference on employment, income distribution and social progress and the international division of labour, Background papers (Geneva, ILO, 1976):

Volume I: *Basic needs and national employment strategies,* viii + 196 pp. Sw. frs. 22.50 ISBN 92-2-101583-1.
- D. Ghai and L. Emmerij: Foreword.
- P.J. Richards: "Poverty, unemployment and underemployment".
- M.J.D. Hopkins and H. Scolnik: "Basic needs, growth and redistribution: A quantitative approach".
- J.J. Stern: "Growth, redistribution and resource use".
- P.J. Richards: "Basic needs and national strategies: Developing countries".
- P. Kilby: "Appropriate technology at the national level": A survey".
- F.A. Mehta: "Employment, basic needs and growth strategy in India". [IND]
- G.E. Skorov and A.V. Danilov: "The USSR's experience of eliminating unemployment". [SUN]
- J.P. Mouly and R. Broadfield: "National strategies in industrialised market economy countries".

Volume II: *International strategies for employment,* viii + 228 pp. Sw. frs. 22.50. ISBN 92-2-101584-X.
- D. Ghai and L. Emmerij: Foreword.
- D.T. Healey: "Exports of manufactures and aid in relation to employment in developing countries".
- G. Fels and H.H. Glisman: "Some criteria for determining industries or sectors affected by the adjustment process".

- ICEM: "Transfer of qualified personnel to developing countries".
- J. Bhagwati: "The brain drain".
- M. Allal: "Trade in manufactures among developing countries".
- S. Gregory: "Adjustment assistance in Japan: A case study". [JPN]
- S. Zottos and B. Herman: "Adjustment assistance, the problem and its magnitude".
- S. Zottos: "Adjustment assistance in Sweden: A case study". [SWE]
- S. Zottos: "Adjustment assistance measures".
- UNCTAD: "The impact on employment of international policy measures in the field of trade and development".
- W.R. Böhning: "Migration from developing to high income countries".
- WFP: "Food aid in a "basic needs" development strategy: The role of World Food Programme".
- A.S. Bhalla and F. Stewart: "International action for appropriate technology".
- G. Helleiner: "Multinational corporations, manufactured exports and employment in less developed countries".

Employment, growth and basic needs: A one world problem. Report of the Director-General of the International Labour Office to the International Labour Conference (Geneva, ILO, 1978), vi + 178 pp. Sw. frs. 20. E, F, S, G, R. ISBN 92-2-100903-3.

R. Plant: *A short guide to the ILO World Employment Programme: A workers' education guide* (Geneva, ILO, 1982), 72 pp. Sw. frs. 10.* ISBN 92-2-103198-5.

Employment policy, Report VI (1), International Labour Conference, 69th Session, Geneva, 1983 (Geneva, ILO, 1983), 121 pp. Sw. frs. 20. E, F, S, G, R, A.

Employment policy, Report VI (2), International Labour Conference, 69th Session, Geneva, 1983 (Geneva, ILO, 1983), 104 pp. Sw. frs. 17.50. E, F, S, G, R, A.

The World Employment Programme: What it is, what it does (Geneva, ILO, 1984), 40 pp. E, F, S. ISBN 92-2-103663-4.

Employment and poverty in a troubled world. Report of a meeting of high-level experts on employment (Geneva, ILO, 1985), 55 pp. Sw. frs. 12.50. E, F, S. ISBN 92-2-100528-3.

World Employment Programme research in the 1980s (Geneva, ILO, 1985), vi + 103 pp. ISBN 92-2-105143-9.

Bibliography of published research of the World Employment Programme. (Geneva, ILO, 6th ed., 1986), vii + 177 pp. Sw. frs. 15. ISBN 92-2-105464-0.

Selected abstracts of WEP research work, No. 3 (Geneva, ILO, 1986), vii + 73 pp. ISBN 92-2-105764-X.

- Africa

G.M. Hamid: *The urgent need to reduce the employment dependency of BLS countries on the Republic of South Africa*. Paper submitted to the Government of Botswana (Lusaka, SATEP, 1980), ii + 23 pp. [BWA, LSO, SWZ, ZAF]

Articles in the International Labour Review

- General

J.P. Mayer: "The concept of the right to work in international standards and the legislation of ILO member States", Vol. 124, No. 2, Mar.-Apr. 1985.

Working papers

- Latin America and the Caribbean

Una nueva dimensión de la OIT: Interrelaciones entre empleo, población y distribución del ingreso (Santiago, PREALC), Sep. 1978 (No. 157).

Comprehensive employment planning

ILO publications

Books and reports

- General

A.S. Oberai: *Changes in the structure of employment with economic development* (Geneva, ILO, 1978; 2nd ed., 1981), 67 pp. Sw. frs. 7.50. ISBN 92-2-102773-2.

D.H. Freedman: *Employment: Outlook and insights*. A collection of essays on industrialised market economy countries (Geneva, ILO, 1979), vi + 148 pp. Sw. frs. 20. E, F. ISBN 92-2-102155-6.

Disarmament and Employment Research Programme. Progress Report, 1984-86 (Geneva, ILO, 1986), 27 pp. ISBN 92-2-105638-4.

- Africa

Towards self-reliance - Development, employment and equity issues in the United Republic of Tanzania (Addis Ababa, JASPA, 1978), 259 pp.* Sw. frs. 10. [TZA] ISBN 92-2-101996-9.

Emploi et développement au Cameroun: Perspectives sectorielles (Addis Ababa, JASPA, 1979), 169 pp. + tables. Sw. frs. 14. [CMR] ISBN 92-2-202111-8.

Options for a dependent economy: Development, employment and equity problems in Lesotho (Addis Ababa, JASPA, 1979), 316 pp.* Sw. frs. 14. [LSO] ISBN 92-2-102281-1.

Dynamique de l'emploi dans un système sahélien: Le Niger (Addis Ababa, JASPA, 1980), 301 pp. Sw. frs. 14. [NER] ISBN 92-2-202351-X.

Eléments pour une stratégie d'emploi dans les zones rurales au Bénin (Addis Ababa, JASPA, 1980). [BEN]

Review of the Employment Service Organisation in the Republic of Zambia (Addis Ababa, JASPA, 1980). [ZMB]

Review of the operation of the employment exchange in Monrovia and possible extension of employment service in Liberia (Addis Ababa, JASPA, 1980). [LBR]

Development, employment and equity issues in the United Republic of Tanzania - Report of a national seminar held from 21-25 July, 1980, by the Government of the United Republic of Tanzania, in collaboration with the University of Dar-es-Salaam and the ILO Jobs and Skills Programme for Africa (Addis Ababa, JASPA, 1981). [TZA]

Employment and income issues in Somalia - Report of a national seminar held from 17-21 August 1980 by the Government of Somalia in collaboration with the ILO's Jobs and Skills Programme for Africa (Addis Ababa, JASPA, 1981). [SOM]

Ensuring equitable growth - A strategy for increasing employment, equity and basic needs satisfaction in Sierra Leone (Addis Ababa, JASPA, 1981), xxxv + 314 pp. Sw. frs. 25. [SLE] ISBN 92-2-102776-7.

Le commerce inter-état et l'impact sur l'emploi dans les pays de l'UDEAC (Union douanière et économique des Etats de l'Afrique centrale (Addis Ababa, JASPA, 1981).

I. Livingstone: *Rural development, employment and incomes in Kenya*[1] (Addis Ababa, JASPA, 1981). [KEN] ISBN 92-2-102890-0.

Basic needs in danger. A basic needs oriented development strategy for the United Republic of Tanzania: Report to the Government of the United Republic of Tanzania by a JASPA mission (Addis Ababa, JASPA, 1982), xLiv + 418 pp. Sw. frs. 35. [TZA] ISBN 92-2-103256-6.

Pour une politique d'emploi au Sénégal: Esquisse d'une stratégie concertée et intégrée. Rapport présenté au Gouvernement de la République du Sénégal (Addis Ababa, JASPA, 1982), xxviii + 422 pp. US$ 19. [SEN] ISBN 92-2-202967-4.

B. Hansen and S. Radwan: *Employment opportunities and equity in a changing economy: Egypt in the 1980s: A labour market approach.* Report of an inter-agency team financed by the United Nations Development Programme and organised by the International Labour Office (Geneva, ILO, 1982), xviii + 294 pp. Sw. frs. 35. Arabic summary. [EGY] ISBN 92-2-102996-4.

Emploi et formation en Haute-Volta. Méthodes d'observation et de prévision. Rapport soumis au Gouvernement de la Haute-Volta par une mission d'assistance technique du PECTA (Addis Ababa, PECTA, 1983), 142 pp. [BFA]

Employment and development in Lesotho. Report of a national seminar organised by the Government of Lesotho in collaboration with JASPA and SATEP, 24 to 27 May, 1983 (Addis Ababa, JASPA, 1983), 229 pp. [LSO]

Employment and development issues in Sierra Leone. Report of a national seminar organised by the Government of Sierra Leone in collaboration with JASPA, Freetown, 12 to 16 July 1983 (Addis Ababa, JASPA, 1983), 229 pp. [SLE]

Employment opportunities and equity in Egypt. The technical papers of the ILO/UNDP comprehensive employment strategy mission to Egypt, 1980 (Geneva, ILO, 1983), Sw. frs. 25 (Set of 7 papers). [EGY] ISBN 92-2-102997-2.

No. 1 - M. Abdel-Fadil: *Informal sector employment in Egypt*;
No. 2 - Abdel-Fattah Nassef: *Demographic developments in Egypt, 1960-76*;
No. 3 - I.H. El-Issawy: *Employment inadequacy in Egypt*;
No. 4 - I.H. El-Issawy: *Labour force, employment and unemployment*;
No. 5 - G. Starr with the collaboration of M.A.F. Mongi: *Wages in the Egyptian formal sector*;
No. 6 - A. El Salmi: *Public sector management: An analysis of decision-making and employment policies and practices in Egypt*;*
No. 7 - H.A. Handoussa: *Public sector employment and productivity in the Egyptian economy.**

Increasing the efficiency of planning in Kenya: Concepts, methods and guidelines for reviewing performance and assessing impact. Report of a Government of Kenya/ILO Technical co-operation project (Geneva, ILO, 1983), 457 pp. [KEN] ISBN 92-2-103510-7.

Emploi d'abord au Bénin. Eléments de stratégies pour la priorité à l'emploi. Rapport présenté au Gouvernement de la République populaire du Bénin (Addis Ababa, JASPA, 1984), xxxix + 542 pp. Sw. frs. 52.80. [BEN] ISBN 92-2-203823-1.

Emploi, potentialités et priorités au Mali. Rapport présenté au Gouvernement du Mali par une mission du PECTA (Addis Ababa, JASPA, 1984), xix + 266 pp. US$ 9. [MLI] ISBN 92-2-203954-8.

Le défi de l'emploi pour le Rwanda. Problématique structurelle et stratégies proposées en vue du IIIe Plan quinquennal de développement 1982-1986 (Addis Ababa, JASPA, 1984), Lxv + 642 pp. Sw. frs. 38. [RWA] ISBN 92-2-203648.

Crise économique et perspectives de l'emploi dans une économie ouverte: Le cas du Togo. Rapport d'une mission globale d'emploi du PECTA au Togo en fév.-mars 1984. Vol. I: Rapport principal, (Addis Ababa, JASPA, 1985) x + 457 pp. US$ 19. [TOG] ISBN 92-2-205257-9.

Crise économique et perspectives de l'emploi dans une économie ouverte: Le cas du Togo. Rapport d'une mission globale d'emploi du PECTA au Togo en fév.-mars 1984. Vol. II: Contributions techniques et annexes statistiques (Addis Ababa, JASPA, 1985),iii + 352 pp. US$ 7. [TOG] ISBN 92-2-205258-7.

Crise écononomique et perspectives de l'emploi dans une économie ouverte: Le cas du Togo. Rapport d'une mission globale d'emploi du PECTA au Togo en fév.-mars 1984. Vol. III: Idées de projet (Addis Ababa, JASPA, 1985), ii + 178 pp. US$ 12. [TOG] ISBN 92-2-205259-5.

Employment promotion in the United Republic of Tanzania. Prospects in the rural and informal sectors (Addis Ababa, JASPA, 1986), iii + 107 pp. [TZA]

Réflexions pour une politique de l'emploi au Zaïre. Alternative pour les secteurs rural et non-structuré. Rapport d'une mission sectorielle d'emploi du PECTA présenté au Gouvernement du Zaïre (Addis Ababa, JASPA, 1986), xxxi + 570 pp. US$ 20.50. [ZAR] ISBN 92-2-205266-8.

Report of JASPA steering group meeting on priority employment policies and projects for Africa (Addis Ababa, JASPA, 1986), 43 pp. E, F.

The challenge of employment and basic needs in Africa. Essays in honour of S.B.L. Nigam and to mark the tenth anniversary of JASPA (Nairobi, Oxford University Press, 1986), xii + 379 pp. ISBN 0-19-572559-X.

Combating unemployment in Nigeria: Strategies and options (Addis Ababa, JASPA, 1987), v + 183 pp. [NGA] ISBN 92-2-105928-6.

Employment and economic reform: Towards a strategy for the Sudan. Report of a mission financed by the UNDP and organised by ILO/JASPA, Aug.-Sep. 1986 (Geneva, ILO, 1987), xvi + 172 pp. Sw. frs. 22.50. [SDN] ISBN 92-2-106221-X.

Generating employment and incomes in Somalia. Provisional report of an ILO/JASPA inter-disciplinary employment and project-identification mission to Somalia (Addis Ababa, JASPA, 1987), xxix + 417 pp. [SOM]

- Latin America and the Caribbean

Educación y empleo en América Latina. Investigation on Employment No. 10 (Santiago, PREALC, 1978.)

Employment in Latin America: Regional Employment Programme for Latin America and the Caribbean (PREALC) (New York, Praeger, 1978), 193 pp.

Opciones de políticas y creación de empleo productivo en México. Investigation on Employment No. 9 (Santiago, PREALC, 1978.) [MEX]

E. García D'Acuña and J. Mezzera: *El arancel externo común y la creación de empleo en el Grupo Andino.* Occasional papers No. 20 (Santiago, PREALC, 1978) *.

N.E. García: *Pequeña y gran industria: Generación de empleo y sectores claves: Un comentario.* Occasional papers No. 21 (Santiago, PREALC, Apr. 1978).*

E. Klein: *Employment in peasant economies.* Monograph No. 10 (Santiago, PREALC, Mar. 1978).

Mexico: La pequeña industria en una estrategia del empleo productivo. Investigation on Employment No. 17 (Santiago, PREALC, 1979.) [MEX]

L. Jarvis and E. Klein: *Generación de empleo y la conservación de los recursos naturales. Un programa para El Salvador.* Occasional papers No. 25 (Santiago, PREALC, July 1979). [SLV]

J. Tamblay: *Efecto ocupacional de la política de subsidio en la contratación adicional de mano de obra en Chile.* Monograph No. 14 (Santiago, PREALC, July 1979). [CHL]

R. Urmeneta: *El plan de empleo mínimo en Chile.* Monograph No. 13 (Santiago, PREALC, July 1979).* [CHL]

Políticas de empleo al alcance de los Ministerios del Trabajo. Investigation on Employment No. 19 (Santiago, PREALC, 1980.)

J.J. Buttari: *Unemployment in Latin America: Priority areas for international action in the 1980s.* Occasional papers No. 42 (Santiago, PREALC, Sep. 1981).

N.E. García: *Empleo manufacturero, productividad y remuneraciones, por tamaño de establecimiento (México 1965-76).* Monograph No. 18 (Santiago, PREALC, June 1981). [MEX]

N.E. García: *Incentivos, precios y empleo.* Occasional papers No. 43 (Santiago, PREALC, Sep. 1981). E, S.

V.E. Tokman: *Estrategia de desarrollo y empleo en los ochenta.* Occasional papers No. 39 (Santiago, PREALC, June 1981).

Planificación del empleo (Santiago, PREALC, 1982), x+306 pp. Sw. frs. 22. E, S. ISBN 92-2-102908-5.

V.E. Tokman: *Desarrollo desigual y absorción de empleo: América latina 1950-80.* Occasional papers No. 44 (Santiago, PREALC, Mar. 1982).

Empleo y salarios (Santiago, PREALC, 1983), xvi+126 pp. Sw. frs. 12. [PAN, URY, CHL] ISBN 92-2-303427-2.

B. Tomíc and R. González: *Municipio y Estado. Dimensiones de una relación clave.* (La reforma al gobierno y administración interiores en Chile). Monograph No. 27 (Santiago, PREALC/ISS, July 1983). [CHL]

El efecto empleo de la inversión pública. Investigation on Employment No. 23 (Santiago, PREALC, 1984). [PAN, ECU, BOL]

A. García: *Industrialización para el desarrollo equitativo.* Monograph No. 39 (Santiago, PREALC, Oct. 1984).

B. Tomíc: *Exámen crítico de tres intentos oficiales de planificación descentralizada y participativa.* Monograph No. 37 (Santiago, PREALC, Apr. 1984). [CRI, COL, CHL]

Más allá de la crisis. Trabajos presentados a la IV Conferencia Regional de Responsables de la Planificación del Empleo en América Latina y el Caribe, en San José, Costa Rica, 22-25 de octubre de 1984 (Santiago, PREALC, 1985), 484 pp. [CHL, BRA]

Más allá de la crisis (Santiago, PREALC, 1985), 165 pp. Sw. frs. 12. E,S. [CHL, BRA] ISBN 92-2-305025-1.

R. Echeverría: *Empleo público en América Latina.* Investigation on Employment No. 26 (Santiago, PREALC, 1985).

N.E. García and V.E. Tokman: *Acumulación, empleo y crisis.* Investigation on Employment No. 25 (Santiago, PREALC, 1985).

E. Klein and J. Wurgaft: *La creación de empleo en períodos de crisis.* Investigation on Employment No. 24 (Santiago, PREALC, 1985).

Modelos de empleo y política económica: Una decada de experiencias del PREALC (Santiago, PREALC, 1987), xiv+371 pp. US $8. [VEN, CHL, BRA, GTM, DOM, PER, JAM] ISBN 92-2-306303-5.

J. Wells: *Empleo en América Latina: Una búsqueda de opciones* (Santiago, PREALC, 1987), 194 pp. US$ 7. ISBN 92-2-306116-4.

- Asia

Employment planning and basic needs in Pakistan. Report of a national conference held in Islamabad (Bangkok, ARTEP, 1979). * [PAK]

Employment, resource mobilisation and basic needs through local-level planning (Bangkok, ARTEP, 1979). [LKA]

Employment and labour force in Asia (Bangkok, May 1980),60 pp.*ISBN 92-2-102380-X.

A.R. Khan and E. Lee: *Employment and development in Laos* (Bangkok, July 1980), 66 pp. Sw. frs. 5.25. [LAO] ISBN 92-2-102425-3.

Employment expansion through local resource mobilisation. Papers and proceedings of a workshop, Comilla, Bangladesh, 1-3 July 1981 (Bangkok, ARTEP, 1981), iv+145 pp. Sw. frs. 8.75. [BGD]

A.R. Khan, R. Islam and M. Huq: *Employment, income and the mobilisation of local resources - A study of two Bangladesh villages* (Bangkok, ARTEP, 1981), vii+149 pp. US$5.* [BGD] ISBN 92-2-102419-9.

R. Islam, A.R. Khan and E. Lee: *Employment and development in Nepal* (Bangkok, ARTEP, 1982), viii+124 pp. Sw. frs. 14. [NPL] ISBN 92-2-102742-2.

T. Maitra: *Expansion of employment through local resources mobilisation: Study of a cluster of villages in West Bengal, India* (Bangkok, ARTEP, 1982), xii+114 pp. Sw. frs. 8.75. [IND] ISBN 92-2-102745-7.

P. Phongpaichit in collaboration with P. Jaisaard, P. Chayaputi, S. Piriyarangsan and P. Vasuprasat: *Employment, income and the mobilisation of local resources in three Thai villages* (Bangkok, ARTEP, 1982), x + 138pp. Sw. frs. 8.75. [THA] ISBN 92-2-103280-9.

P. Wickramasekara: *Expansion of employment and income through local resource mobilisation: A study of two Sri Lankan villages* (Bangkok, ARTEP, 1983), iv+130 pp. Sw. frs. 8.75. [LKA] ISBN 92-2-103284-1.

Employment policy in Thailand. Papers and proceedings of a national seminar (Bangkok, ARTEP and the National Economic and Social Development Board, NESDB, 1984), vii+90 pp. [THA]

M. Arif, B. Ahmed, M. Jannisar: *Expansion of employment and income through local resource mobilisation. A study of three villages in Pakistan* (Bangkok, ARTEP, 1984), iii+121 pp. Sw. frs. 8.75. [PAK] ISBN 92-2-103682-0.

Bangladesh: Selected issues in employment and development (Bangkok, ARTEP, 1985), xxii+313 pp. [BGD]

Proceedings of the first meeting of the Asian employment planners, Bangkok, Thailand, 26-29 November 1985 (New Delhi, ARTEP, 1986), 37 pp. ISBN 92-2-105468-3.

G. Edgren: *Public services as a source of employment creation*. Paper prepared for the Second Meeting of Asian Employment Planners 24-26 November, 1987, New Delhi (New Delhi, ARTEP, 1987), 25 pp.

- OECD Countries

Employment and basic needs in Portugal. (Geneva, ILO, 1979), x + 248 pp. Sw. frs. 30. [PRT] ISBN 92-2-102203-X.

W. van Ginneken, in collaboration with M. Garzuel: *Unemployment in France, the Federal Republic of Germany and the Netherlands: A survey of trends, causes and policy options* (Geneva, ILO, 1982; 2nd impression, 1983), vii + 116 pp. Sw. frs. 17.50. [FRA, DEU, NLD] ISBN 92-2-103032-6

- Middle East.

Employment and manpower problems and policy issues in Arab countries: Proposals for the future. Papers and proceedings of a Regional Symposium held in Geneva, January 1983 (Geneva, ILO 1984), pp. 140. Sw. frs. 20. E, F. [LBN, SYR, JOR, IRQ, KWT, SDN, SOM, YEM, YMD, DZA, DJI, MRT, TUN] ISBN 92-2-103504-2.

Articles in the International Labour Review

- General

G. Standing: "The notion of voluntary unemployment", Vol. 120, No. 5, Sep.-Oct. 1981.

M.J.D. Hopkins: "Trends in employment in developing countries, 1960-80 and beyond", Vol. 122, No. 4, July-Aug. 1983.

G. Standing: "The notion of structural unemployment", Vol. 122, No. 2, Mar.-Apr. 1983.

Y. Sabolo: "Disarmament and employment: Background for a research programme", Vol. 122, No. 3, May-June 1983.

I. Thorsson: "Guns and butter: Can the world have both?", Vol. 122, No. 4, July-Aug. 1983.

M. Thee: "Swords into ploughshares: The quest for peace and human development", Vol. 122, No. 5, Sep.-Oct. 1983.

D.H. Freedman: "Employment and unemployment in the 1980s: Economic dilemmas and socio-political challenges", Vol. 123, No. 5, Sep.-Oct. 1984.

J.P. Mayer: "Regional employment development: The evolution of theory and practice", Vol. 123, No. 1, Jan.-Feb. 1984.

G. Standing: "The notion of technological unemployment", Vol. 123, No.2, Mar.-Apr. 1984.

K. Engelgardt: "Employment effects of disarmament on research and development personnel", Vol. 124, No. 2, Mar.-Apr. 1985.

J. Royer: "The long-term impact of disarmament policies: Some findings from an econometric model", Vol. 125, No. 3, May-June 1986.

P.J. Richards: "Preserving jobs under economic stabilisation programmes: Can there be an employment target?", Vol. 125, No. 4, July-Aug. 1986.

R. Zachmann: "Reduction of working time as a means to reduce unemployment: A microeconomic perspective", Vol. 125, No. 2, Mar.-Apr. 1986.

- Africa

B. Hansen and S. Radwan: "Employment planning in Egypt: An insurance policy for the future", Vol. 121, No. 5, Sep.-Oct. 1982. [EGY]

- Latin America and the Caribbean

E. García D'Acuña and J. Mezzera: "El arancel externo común y la creación de empleo en el Grupo Andino", Vol. 97, No. 1, Jan.-Mar. 1978.

P. Pommier: "The place of Mexico City in the nation's growth: Employment trends and policies", Vol. 121, No. 3, May-June 1982. [MEX]

V.E. Tokman: "The employment crisis in Latin America", Vol. 123, No. 5, Sep.-Oct. 1984.

- OECD Countries

D.H. Freedman: "Employment perspectives in industrialised market economy countries", Vol. 117, No. 1, Jan.-Feb. 1978.

J.P. Mayer: "La régionalisation des politiques d'emploi en Europe occidentale", Vol. 118, No. 4, July-Aug. 1979.

J.M. Mesa: "Short-time working or lay-offs? Experience from Canada and California", Vol. 123, No. 1, Jan.-Feb. 1984. [CAN, USA]

N. Ball: "Converting the workforce: Defence industry conversion in the industrialised countries", Vol. 125, No. 4, July-Aug. 1986.

G. Standing: "Meshing labour flexibility with security: An answer to British unemployment", Vol. 125, No. 1, Jan.-Feb. 1986. [GBR]

- East European Countries

V. Kondratiev: "Employment patterns and prospects in European socialist countries", Vol. 117, No. 3, May-June 1978.

A. Efremov: "The employment effects of disarmament in the USSR", Vol. 124, No. 4, July-Aug. 1985. [SUN]

Other articles

- General

M.J.D. Hopkins, R. van der Hoeven, J. Petit: "International development scenarios and employment", in *Labour and Society* (Geneva, IILS), Vol. 6, No. 2, Apr.-June 1981.

G. Standing: "Labour flexibility and employment", in *Social and Labour Bulletin* (Geneva, ILO), Nos. 3-4, Sep.-Dec. 1986.

- OECD Countries

D.H. Freedman: "Seeking a broader approach to employment and worklife in industrialised market-economy", in *Labour and Society* (Geneva, IILS), Vol. 8, No. 2, Apr.-June 1983.

Working papers

- General

S.A. Kuzmin: *Employment alternatives in global development scenarios. Part I: Dimensions of the employment problem in developing countries, 1970-2000*, Oct. 1980 (WEP 2-32/WP.23). M.

O.D.K. Norbye: *Research and action programme for least developed countries: Some tentative proposals*, Aug. 1980 (WEP 2-32/WP.22). M.

J. Reppy: *Labour use and productivity in military and non-military related industry*, Feb. 1986 (WEP 2-41/WP.2). ISBN 92-2-105454-3.

J. Royer: *The long-term employment impact of disarmament policies*, Feb. 1986 (WEP 2-41/WP.3). ISBN 92-2-105455-1.

P. Wilke and H. Wulf: *Manpower conversion in defence-related industry*, June 1986 (WEP 2-41/WP.4). ISBN 92-2-105615-5.

The conversion of manpower employed in the armaments industry and related actitivities: Report on the replies to an ILO questionnaire (October 1984) gathering information on disarmament and employment, Oct. 1987 (WEP 2-41/WP.6). ISBN 92-2-106287-2.

R. Zachmann: *Working time reductions as an employment generating tool: A survey*, July 1987 (WEP 2-43/WP.16). ISBN 92-2-106177-9.

- Africa

E.G. Rachidi and A. Agourram: *Problèmes et perspectives de développement regional et local au Maroc*, July 1980 (WEP 2-32/WP.21). M. [MAR]

G.M. Hamid: *Preliminary notes on the Lagos plan of action and the development of mineral industries in Africa* (Lusaka, SATEP), Mar. 1982.

F. Baffoe: *The role of the industrial sector in Lesotho: Its past, present and future contribution to general economic development and employment promotion* (Lusaka, SATEP), Feb. 1983. [LSO] ISBN 92-2-103658-8.

F. Lisk: *Labour and employment in Namibia: Current situation and post-independence prospects* (Lusaka, SATEP), Mar. 1986. [NAM] ISBN 92-2-105301-6.

E.M. Mhlanga: *The future outlook of employment prospects in South Africa and its impact on the Lesotho economy* (Lusaka, SATEP), Apr. 1986. [ZAF, LSO] ISBN 92-2-105387-3.

V. Jamal: *Somalia: Economics for an unconventional economy*, Dec. 1987 (WEP 10-6/WP.91) [SOM] ISBN 92-2-106363-1.

- Latin America and the Caribbean

Diagnosis, employment policies and planning and basic needs (Santiago, PREALC), Nov. 1978 (No. 162).

El problema del empleo en la región Andina: Elementos para un diagnóstico y una estrategia (Santiago, PREALC), June 1978 (No. 147). [BOL, ECU, PER, COL, VEN]

México: La pequeña industria en una estrategia de empleo productivo (Santiago, PREALC), Jan. 1978 (No. 120).* [MEX]

El Salvador: Proyectos de generación de empleos en el Corto Plazo, Tomo I y Tomo II (Santiago, PREALC), Jan. 1979 (No. 166).* [SLV]

Informe final del seminario sobre lineamientos de políticas de empleo en Centroamérica (Santiago, PREALC), June 1979 (No. 173).*

Integración económica y empleo: Algunos elementos para el caso centroamericano (Santiago, PREALC), Jan. 1979 (No. 167).

El impacto ocupacional de la inversión pública en Bolivia (Santiago, PREALC), Mar. 1980 (No. 182). [BOL]

Elasticidad de sustitución: Evaluación crítica e implicaciones para políticas de empleo en América Latina (Santiago, PREALC), Aug. 1980 (No. 192).

Empleo y salarios en Nicaragua (Santiago, PREALC), Sep. 1980 (No. 194). [NIC]

Essays on Brazilian growth, wages and poverty (Santiago, PREALC), July 1980 (No. 188). [BRA]

Honduras: El empleo en el Plan Nacional de Desarrollo 1979-1983 (Santiago, PREALC), Mar. 1980 (No. 181). [HND]

Industrialización y empleo: Identificación de sectores claves. (Primera parte: México y Colombia) (Santiago, PREALC), Aug. 1980 (No. 191). [MEX, COL]

La devolución del Canal de Panamá y su efecto sobre el empleo (Santiago, PREALC), Sep. 1980 (No. 195). [PAN]

Técnicas de planificación del empleo en América Latina y el Caribe (Santiago, PREALC), Sep. 1980 (No. 196).*

El criterio empleo en la evaluación de proyectos (Santiago, PREALC), Sep. 1981 (No. 209).*

El subempleo en América Latina: Evolución histórica y requerimientos futuros (Santiago, PREALC), Mar. 1981 (No. 198).

M.J.D. Hopkins: *An analysis of employment, underemployment and unemployment: The case of Colombia*, Nov. 1981 (WEP 2-32/WP.33). M. [COL]

Creación de empleo y efecto redistributivo del gasto e inversión pública. Ecuador 1980-84 (Santiago, PREALC), Mar. 1982 (No. 214). [ECU]

Empleo y planes de desarrollo 1970-1980 (Santiago, PREALC) Mar. 1982, (No. 212).

Sectorialización de modelos económico-demográficos: Una propuesta para Brasil (Santiago, PREALC), Mar. 1982 (No. 213). [BRA]

Efectos ocupacionales de los proyectos de inversión: Metodología y aplicación al caso de la promoción industrial en la República Argentina (Santiago, PREALC), Apr. 1983 (No. 224). [ARG]

Honduras: Situación y políticas de empleo en el corto plazo (Santiago, PREALC), July 1983 (No. 226). [HND]

Monetarismo global y respuesta industrial: El caso de Argentina (Santiago, PREALC), Dec. 1983 (No. 231). [ARG]

Costa Rica: Bases para una política de empleo en los años ochenta (Santiago, PREALC), Mar. 1984 (No. 235). [CRI]

Después de la crisis: Lecciones y perspectivas (Santiago, PREALC), Oct. 1984 (No. 250). E, S.

Determinantes estructurales y coyunturales de la producción en la industria manufacturera chilena: 1969-1983 (Santiago, PREALC), Sep. 1984 (No. 249). [CHL]

El perfil del desempleo en una situación de economía recesiva (Santiago, PREALC), Sep. 1984 (No. 248). [COL, CRI, CHL, VEN]

La creación de empleo en períodos de crisis (Santiago, PREALC), Oct. 1984 (No. 251).

Monetarismo global y respuesta industrial: El caso de Chile (Santiago, PREALC), Mar. 1984 (No. 232). [CHL]

Monetarismo global y respuesta industrial: El caso de Uruguay (Santiago, PREALC), Mar. 1984 (No. 233). [URY]

Políticas de vivienda y empleo (Santiago, PREALC), July 1984 (No. 244). [PAN, BOL, BRA, SLV, CHL]

Políticas del Ministerio de Trabajo y el empleo en una situación recesiva. El caso de Brasil (Santiago, PREALC), June 1984 (No. 243). [BRA]

Reactivación con transformación: El efecto empleo (Santiago, PREALC), Apr. 1984 (No. 238). [CHL]

Crisis del empleo en el grupo andino (Santiago, PREALC), Oct. 1985 (No. 271). [BOL, COL, ECU, PER, VEN]

Modelo de corto plazo y empleo. República Dominicana, 1983 (Santiago, PREALC), Feb. 1985 (No. 257). [DOM]

Reindustrialización: Una condición para el desarrollo (Santiago, PREALC), May 1985 (No. 264). [CHL]

Un modelo de política económica de corto plazo, empleo e ingresos: Perú, 1983 (Santiago, PREALC), Apr. 1985 (No. 261). [PER]

Creación de empleo productivo: Una tarea impostergable (Santiago, PREALC), Sep. 1986 (No. 280). S, E.

La crisis del empleo en America Latina (Santiago, PREALC), Dec. 1986 (No. 285).

La evolución del empleo formal e informal en el sector servicios latinoamericanos (Santiago, PREALC), Sep. 1986 (No. 279).

Políticas de ingresos y actores sociales (Santiago, PREALC), Sep. 1986 (No. 281). S,E.

Salarios reales y empleo bajo distintos regimenes macroeconómicos. Una aplicación para Chile y Brasil (Santiago, PREALC), July 1986 (No. 278). [CHL, BRA]

N.E. García: *A model for short term economic policy, employment and incomes Peru, 1983*, June 1986 (WEP 2-43/WP.6). [PER] ISBN 92-2-105634-4.

Acuerdo social para superar la crisis: Una perspectiva económica (Santiago, PREALC), Mar. 1987 (No. 294).

Ciclo económico, mercado de trabajo y pobreza. Gran Santiago 1969-1985 (Santiago, PREALC), July 1987 (No. 303). [CHL]

Estadísticas e indicadores socioeconómicos del istmo centroamericano. 1950-1980 (Santiago, PREALC), Mar. 1987 (No. 292). [GTM, PAN]

Nuevos antecedentes sobre la desindustrialización chilena (Santiago, PREALC), Oct. 1987 (Mo. 307). [CHL]

Pobreza y mercado de trabajo en el gran Santiago. 1969-1985 (Santiago, PREALC), June 1987 (No. 299). [CHL]

- Asia

S. Stavenuiter: *Quantitative techniques for employment planning: Applications to Indonesia's labour surplus economy*, June 1986 (WEP 2-43/WP.4). [IDN] ISBN 92-2-105614-7.

- OECD Countries

D.H. Freedman: *The contemporary work ethic in industrialised market economy countries*, Mar. 1978 (WEP 2-32/WP.10).

N. Ball: *Converting military facilities: Shared responsibilities and the need for planning*, Oct. 1983 (WEP 2-41/WP. 1). M. [GBR, USA, SWE] ISBN 92-2-105330.

J.P. Dunne: *The employment consequences of military expenditure: A comparative assessment*, Oct. 1986 (WEP 2-41/WP.5). [CAN, FRA, NOR, SWE, DEU, GBR, USA] ISBN 92-2-105765-8.

R.E. Kutscher: *Employment trends in the United States*, July 1987 (WEP 2-43/WP.15). [USA] ISBN 92-2-106101-9.

- Middle East

H.T. Azzam: *Development planning models in the Arab world: Problems and prospects* (Beirut, LPME), 1981 (W.P. 9), 50 pp. [EGY, TUN, SAU, SYR] ISBN 92-2-102583-7.

A. Benyoussef: *Employment, income and development planning in twenty Arab countries*, Dec. 1981 (WEP 2-32/WP.34) M.

C.E. Moujabber: *Service employment expansion in the Arab Region* (Beirut, LPME), Nov. 1981 (WP. 13). ISBN 92-2-102923-9

ILO works published by commercial and non-profit-making publishers.

- Africa

H. Rempel and W.J. House: *The Kenya employment problem* (Nairobi, Oxford University Press, 1978), xiv + 194 pp. [KEN]

- Latin America and the Caribbean

Dinámica del subempleo en América Latina (Santiago, PREALC/CEPAL, 1981).

M.J.D. Hopkins: *Alternatives to unemployment and underemployment. The case of Colombia* (Boulder, Colorado and London, Westview Press, 1985), xiv + 129 pp. [COL] ISBN 0-8133-0200-5.

Related books and articles

- General

P.K. Das: "Basic issues, macro policies and components of a programme of development" in *Industry and Development* (New York), No. 4, 1979.

J.A. Clark and R. van der Hoeven: "Industrialisation and employment in developed and developing countries", in *Methods for development planning: Scenarios, models and micro-studies* (Paris, UNESCO, 1981).

- Latin America and the Caribbean

M.J.D. Hopkins: "Respuestas contemporáneas al problema del empleo en Colombia", in *El Mundo - Documentos 44* (Medellin), May 1982, pp. 41-47. [COL]

- Asia

I.Z. Bhatty and L. Bérouti: " A development strategy for Afghanistan: Lessons of an employment policy mission", in *Pakistan Development Review* (Karachi), Vol XIX, No. 4, Winter 1980. [AFG]

Notes:

1 Also published as Rural development, employment and incomes in Kenya (Aldershot, Hampshire, Gower, 1986)

Manpower planning and labour market information systems

ILO publications

Books and reports

- **General**

Guidelines for the development of employment and manpower information programmes in developing countries. A practical manual (Geneva, ILO, 1979; 2nd impression, 1980), viii + 88 pp. Sw. frs. 12.50. E, A. [BRA, IND] ISBN 92-2-102176-9.

Strengthening manpower and employment information for decision making. A summary account of a new programme of technical co-operation. An ILO initiative supported by DANIDA, Japan, the Federal Republic of Germany and the Netherlands (Geneva, ILO, 1981), viii + 28 pp. E, F. ISBN 92-2-102816-X.

Employment and manpower information in developing countries: A training guide (Geneva, ILO, 1982), iv + 186 pp. Sw. frs. 15. E,F. ISBN 92-2-102985-9.

Labour market information through key informants. Report of an evaluation seminar conducted with the support of DANIDA (Geneva, ILO, 1982; 2nd impression, 1983), vi + 86 pp. Sw. frs. 10. ISBN 92-2-103082-2.

Report of the expert group meeting on assessment of manpower and training needs for the energy sector (Bangkok, ILO, 1982), 36 pp.

P. Duiker: *Manpower analysis for the energy sector: Some macro issues for discussion.* Report presented at the expert group meeting on assessment of manpower and training needs for the energy sector held in Bangkok, 1982 (Geneva, ILO, 1982), 19 pp. + annex.

O. Fulton, A. Gordon and G. Williams: *Higher education and manpower planning: A comparative study of planned and market economies.* A joint project undertaken by the ILO and the UNESCO European Centre for Higher Education (CEPES), (Geneva, ILO, 1982), viii + 128 pp. Sw. frs. 20. ISBN 92-2-102973-5.

Guidelines pool of labour market information reporting (Geneva, ILO, 1983), 20 pp. + annex.

Seminar on employment policies and labour market information for workers'organisations. Report of a seminar conducted by the ILO and the International Confederation of Free Trade Unions held in New Delhi, March 1983 (Geneva, ILO, 1983), 78 pp.

P. Duiker: *Manpower implications of accelerated energy resource development in developing countries.* Report presented at the United Nations technical energy group of the ACC task force on long-term development objectives, in New York, 1983 (Geneva, ILO, 1983), 23 pp.

W. Mason and L. Richter: *Reporting by key informants on labour markets. An operational manual* (Geneva, ILO, 1985), viii + 37 pp. Sw. frs. 12.50. ISBN 92-2-105109-2.

Major stages and steps in energy manpower analysis: A practical framework (Geneva, ILO, 1986), viii + 80 pp. Sw. frs. 15. ISBN 92-2-105246-X.

- Africa

Report on the ILO/ARLAC JASPA workshop on improvement of employment market information systems in English-speaking countries, Seychelles, May 1979 (Addis Ababa, JASPA, 1979).

Information sur le marché de l'emploi dans les pays de l'Afrique sahélienne. Projet d'evaluation exécuté avec le concours de la DANIDA (Geneva, ILO, 1981), xii + 118 pp. Sw. frs. 12.50. [MRT, SEN, MLI, BFA, NER, CPV] ISBN 92-2-202861-9.

Bilan et perspectives de la promotion humaine dans le cadre de la mise en valeur du bassin du fleuve Sénégal et création d'ateliers pédagogiques intégrés. Rapport soumis au Haut Commissariat général de l' OMVS par une mission technique du PECTA (Addis Ababa, JASPA, 1982), iv + 76 pp. [SEN]

Planification des ressources humaines et information sur le marché de l'emploi dans les pays non sahéliens d'Afrique francophone. Projet d'évaluation organisé conjointement par le BIT et l'OCAM avec le concours de la DANIDA (Geneva, ILO, 1982), xiv + 200 pp. Sw. frs. 15. [BEN, BDI, CMR, CAF, COG, CIV, GAB, TUN, ZAR, MAR, RWA, TGO] ISBN 92-2-203162-8.

La planification de la main-d'oeuvre, de l'emploi et des ressources humaines en Afrique francophone sub-saharienne. Bilans et perspectives à partir de l'experience vécue par neuf pays de l'Afrique sub-saharienne (Addis Ababa, JASPA, 1985). [BEN, CMR, COG, CIV, GAB, MLI, SEN, TGO, ZAR] ISBN 92-2-205251-X.

L'amélioration des systèmes d'information sur le marché de l'emploi dans les pays africains francophones. Rapport sur le séminaire régional tripartite OIT/DANIDA tenu à Abidjan du 3 au 7 février 1986 (Geneva, ILO, 1986), vi + 83 pp. [BEN, BFA, CMR, CAF, COG, CIV, GAB, MDG, MLI, MRT, RWA, SEN, ZAR]

Situation des ressources humaines en Guinée: Diagnostic et priorités d'action à court et à moyen termes. Rapport d'une mission sectorielle d'emploi du PECTA en République de Guinée (Addis Ababa, JASPA, 1986), vi + 28 pp. [GIN] ISBN 92-2-205946-8.

- Latin America and the Caribbean

Métodos alternativos de estimación de necesidades de formación. Investigation on Employment No. 14 (Santiago, PREALC, 1979). [ITA, BOL]

E. Klein: *Condicionantes de la subutilización y disponibilidad de la mano de obra.* Monograph No. 17 (Santiago, PREALC, Apr. 1981).

Participación laboral: Experiencias en Perú y Chile. Investigation on Employment No. 21 (Santiago, PREALC, 1982). * [PER, CHL]

N.E. García and M. Marfán: *Incidencia indirecta de la industria sobre el empleo.* Occasional papers No. 38, Rev. 1 (Santiago, PREALC, Nov. 1982).

N.E. García: *Industria manufacturera y empleo: América latina 1950-1980.* Occasional papers No. 49 (Santiago, PREALC, Sep. 1982).

B. Tomíc: *Descentralización y participación popular: La salud rural en Costa Rica.* Monograph No. 34 (Santiago, PREALC/ISS, Sep. 1983). [CRI]

Upgrading of labour market reporting systems in the Caribbean region. Report of the DANIDA/ILO Tripartite seminar held in Antigua, 20-24 May 1985 (Geneva, ILO, 1985), iv + 68 pp. [ATG, BLZ, GRD, GUY, JAM, KNA, LCA, VCT, TTO, SUR] ISBN 92-2-105377-6.

- **Asia**

The Asian HRD Planning Network. Proceedings of a technical workshop convened in Bangkok, 16-18 December 1986 to establish an Asian network of resource development planning institutes (New Delhi, n.d.), 13 pp.

Manpower assessment and planning projects in Asia. Situation, problems and outlook. A review conducted with the support of DANIDA and the Japanese Government (Geneva, ILO, 1978), 118 pp. Sw. frs. 12.50. [IND, PHL, JPN, NZL, LKA, THA] ISBN 92-2-101915-5.

Labour market information in Asia. Present issues and tasks for the future. Report of two workshops conducted with the support of the Federal Republic of Germany (Geneva, ILO, 1979; 2nd impression, 1980), vi + 116 pp. Sw. frs. 10. [IDN, KOR, SGP, HKG, BGD, IND, BUR, NPL, PAK, LKA, DEU, PHL, THA] ISBN 92-2-102168-8.

L. Richter: *Labour market information in developing countries.* A general review (Geneva, ILO, 1978; 2nd impression, 1980), 52 pp.* Sw. frs. 12.50. [IND] ISBN 92-2-101 950-0.

Manpower planning in Bangladesh - Projections, policies and planning with special reference to the second five-year plan - A report prepared for the Bangladesh Planning Commission (Bangkok, ARTEP, 1981). [BGD]

New developments in labour market information in nine Asian countries. National reports submitted to a study tour for Asian developing countries supported by the Japanese Government, 24 Sep.-7 Oct. 1980 (Geneva, ILO, 1981), vi + 106 pp. Sw. frs. 12.50. [BGD, IND, IDN, MYS, NPL, PAK, PHL, LKA, THA] ISBN 92-2-102809-7.

Information system for monitoring development indicators at district level: A demonstration exercise for Nuwara Eliya, Sri Lanka (Bangkok, ARTEP, 1982), vi + 76 pp. [LKA]

Employment and manpower planning. A manual for training in basic techniques (Bangkok, ARTEP, 1984), 87 pp.

R. Amjad (ed.): *Human resource planning. The Asian experience* (New Delhi, ARTEP, 1987), 323 pp. US$8. [THA, MYS, SGP, PHL, IDN, KOR, CHN, PAK, LKA, IND, BGD] ISBN 92-2-106033-0.

- **OECD Countries**

Labour market information for decision-making. The case of Japan. A study tour for Asian developing countries supported by the Japanese Government, 24 Sep.-7 Oct. 1980 (Geneva, ILO 1981), vi + 25 pp. Sw. frs. 25. [JPN] ISBN 92-2-102598-5.

- **Middle East**

Manpower assessment and planning projects in the Arab region. Current issues and perspectives. A review conducted with the support of UNDP (Geneva, ILO, 1979; 2nd impression, 1980), vi + 32 pp. Sw. frs. 10. ISBN 92-2-102173-4.

Articles in the International Labour Review

- **General**

L. Richter: "New sources of manpower information in developing countries", Vol. 117, No. 4, July-Aug. 1978.

R. Wéry: "Manpower forecasting and the labour market", Vol. 117, No. 3, May-June 1978.

L. Richter: "Manpower and employment information through key informants", Vol. 121, No. 4, July-Aug. 1982.

J.P. Mayer: "Workers' well-being and productivity: The role of bargaining", Vol. 122, No. 3, May-June 1983.

L. Richter: "Manpower planning in developing countries: Changing approaches and emphases", Vol. 123, No. 6, Nov.-Dec. 1984.

- Africa

D.H. Freedman: "Work in Nigeria: A cornerstone of meeting the needs of the people", Vol. 120, No. 6, Nov.-Dec. 1981. [NGA]

J-B. Célestin: "Manpower planning and labour market information in French-speaking Africa", Vol. 122, No. 4, July-Aug. 1983.

- Latin America and the Caribbean

E. Klein: "Determinants of manpower underutilisation and availability", Vol. 122, No. 2, Mar.-Apr. 1983.

- East European Countries

V. Kondratiev: "Labour resources and manpower policies in the Byelorussian SSR", Vol. 118, No. 6, Nov.-Dec. 1979. [BYS]

Working papers

- General

M.J.D. Hopkins, L. Crouch and S. Moreland: *MACBETH: A model for forecasting population, education, manpower, employment, underemployment and unemployment*, Sep. 1986 (WEP 2-43/WP.11). ISBN 92-2-105758-5.

S.I. Cohen: *Developments in the analysis and planning of labour and manpower*, Sep. 1986 (WEP 2-43/WP.12). ISBN 92-2-105757-7.

J. Vandemoortele: *Socio-economic analysis and planning within a social accounting framework*, June 1986 (WEP 2-43/WP.5). ISBN 92-2-105613-9.

- Africa

M. Diouf: *La planification régionale au Sénégal*, May 1981 (WEP 2-23/WP.99). [SEN]

L. Taylor: *Decentralised planning: A case study of Zambia*, Oct. 1982 (WEP 2-32/WP.43). [ZMB] ISBN 92-2-103272-8.

Tableaux analytiques de l'information sur l'emploi et la main-d'oeuvre dans douze pays d'Afrique francophone: Benin, Burkina Faso, Cameroun, Congo, Côte d'Ivoire, Gabon, Madagascar, Mali, Mauritanie, Rwanda, R. Centrafricaine, Sénégal (Addis Ababa, JASPA), May-June 1986.

- Latin America and the Caribbean

Bases para la planificación de los recursos humanos en Ecuador (Santiago, PREALC), 2 vols., June 1980 (No. 187). [ECU]

Ecuador: Requerimientos de ingenieros y tecnólogos en el Litoral 1980-90 (Santiago, PREALC), Mar. 1980 (No. 183). [ECU]

Situación ocupacional de los pobres (Santiago, PREALC), Sep. 1980 (No. 205).*

Empleo de mano de obra en las haciendas del Valle Central de Chile: VI Región 1965-1970-1976 (Santiago, PREALC), Apr. 1981 (No. 199). [CHL]

Problemas metodológicos de una encuesta rural en Chile y estructura del empleo (Santiago, PREALC), July. 1983 (No. 227). [CHL]

Lineamientos para un plan de recursos humanos en Guatemala (Santiago, PREALC), Apr. 1984 (No. 237). [GTM]

Lineamientos para un sistema de información sobre el mercado de trabajo para orientar la política de empleo en Brasil (Santiago, PREALC), Aug. 1984 (No. 245). [BRA]

Metodologías para evaluar los programas de inversiones y su impacto sobre el empleo (Santiago, PREALC), Sep. 1984 (No. 246). [NIC]

Human resources development from an employment perspective (Santiago, PREALC), May 1986 (No. 276).

Sistemas de información para el análisis del mercado de trabajo (Santiago, PREALC), June 1986 (No. 277)

- Asia

Evaluation of the Tambon development programme in Thailand (Bangkok, ARTEP), 1979. [THA]

D. Conyers: *Decentralised planning in Papua New Guinea*, Nov. 1981 (WEP 2-23/WP.107). [PNG]

Y.Y. Kueh: *Local level planning in China*, Nov. 1982 (WEP 2-32/WP.44). [CHN] ISBN 92-2-103274-4.

J. Wong: *Labour mobilisation in the Chinese commune system: A perspective from Guangdon* (Bangkok, ARTEP), Jan. 1982. [CHN]

R. Amjad and C. Colclough: *Manpower planning and employment issues in developing countries*, June 1986 (WEP 2-43/WP.7). [MYS] ISBN 92-2-105632-5.

R. Amjad: *Human resource planning: The Asian experience. An overview*. Asian Network of Human Resource Development Planning Institutes, Technical Workshop, Bangkok, 16-18 Dec. 1986 (New Delhi, ARTEP), 1986.

A. Chowdhury, C.H. Kirkpatrick and I. Islam: *Structural adjustment and human resources development in ASEAN*. Asian Network of Human Resource Development Planning Institutes, Technical Workshop, Bangkok, 16-18 Dec. 1986 (New Delhi, ARTEP), 1986

G. Edgren: *The HRD Network*. Asian Network of Human Resource Development Institutes, Technical Workshop, Bangkok, 16-18 Dec. 1986 (New Delhi, ARTEP), 1986.

A. Mitra: *Structural adjustment and human resources development*. Asian Network of Human Resource Development Planning Institutes, Technical Workshop, Bangkok, 16-18 Dec. 1986 (New Delhi, ARTEP), 1986.

R. Thamarajakshi: *Human resource development in Asian countries. An integrated approach*. Asian Network of Human Resource Development Planning Institutes, Technical Workshop, Bangkok, 16-18 Dec. 1986 (New Delhi, ARTEP), 1986.

- OECD Countries

R.G. Hollister, Jr.: *Aspects of governmental job-creation efforts in Western Europe and North America*, Sep. 1986 (WEP 2-43/WP.9). M. ISBN 92-2-105690-2.

M.-L. Caspar: *Le bilan des contrats emploi-formation en France, 1975-1985*, Oct. 1987 (WEP 2-43/WP.19). [FRA] ISBN 92-2-206263-9.

- East European Countries

V. Kondratiev: *Employment pattern and manpower planning in the Byelorussian Soviet Socialist Republic*, Dec. 1979 (WEP 2-34/WP.1). [BYS]

T. Beyazov, Y. Bozhilov and T. Avramov: *Employment patterns and manpower change in the People's Republic of Bulgaria*, July 1980 (WEP 2-34/WP.2). [BGR]

B. Popovic: *Some techniques for regionalised long-term planning of the size and structure of employment in Yugoslavia*. WEP workshop on quantitative techniques for employment planning and their implications for labour market analysis and data bases, 1986 (WEP 2-43/WP.10). [YUG] ISBN 92-2-105592-2.

- Middle East

H.T. Azzam: *Human resources planning: Methods and problems* (Beirut, LPME), 1981 (WP. 10), A. ISBN 92-2-102584-5.

ILO works published by commercial and non-profit-making publishers

- General

L. Richter: "Employment market information in developing countries - A plea for a practical approach" in *Manpower Journal* (New Delhi), Vol. XIV, No. 4, 1979.

L. Richter: "How to draw essential manpower and employment information from key informants?" in *Sri Lanka Labour Gazette* (Colombo), Vol. 30, No. 3, 1979.

L. Richter: "Beschäftigungsaspekte und-effekte integrierter ländlicher Entwicklungsprojekte" in *Integrierte Ländliche Entwicklung*, Herausgegeben von Theodor Dams, Entwicklung und Frieden, Materialien 8, Kaiser-Grünewald (München-Mainz), 1980.

L. Richter: "Arbeitsmarkt und Fachkräftebedarf in Entwicklungsländern" in *Arbeitsberichte und Materialien*, 5 Aspekte zukünftiger Reintegrations-förderung, Deutsches Institut für tropische und subtropische Landwirtschaft (Wirzenhauses), 1981.

Basic needs and income distribution

ILO publications

Books and reports

- General

G. Sheehan and M.J.D. Hopkins: *Basic needs performance*. An analysis of some international data (Geneva, ILO, 1979), vi + 138 pp.* Sw. frs. 17.50. ISBN 92-2-102113-0.

P.J. Richards and M.D. Leonor (eds.): *Target setting for basic needs: The operation of selected government services* (Geneva, ILO, 1982), viii + 130 pp. Sw. frs. 25. [IND, MDG, PHL, COL, HKG, ZMB] ISBN 92-2-102946-8.

J. Lecaillon, F. Paukert, C. Morrisson and D. Germidis: *Répartition du revenu et développement économique: Un essai de synthèse* (Geneva, ILO, 1983), ix + 208 pp. Sw. frs. 30. E, F. ISBN 92-2-203366-3.

W. van Ginneken and Jong-goo Park: *Generating internationally comparable income distribution estimates* (Geneva, ILO, 1984), 176 pp. Sw. frs. 25. ISBN 92-2-103666-9.

R.J. Szal and E. Thorbecke: *Food, nutrition and employment*. A review of ILO activities (Geneva, ILO, 1985), 33 pp. ISBN 92-2-105234-6.

- Africa

D. Ghai, M. Godfrey and F. Lisk: *Planning for basic needs in Kenya - Performance, policies and prospects*. (Geneva, ILO, 1979; 2nd impression, 1982), x + 168 pp. Sw. frs. 20. [KEN] ISBN 92-2-102171-8.

Evaluation du niveau de satisfaction des besoins de base dans les pays de l'Afrique de l'Ouest - Le cas du Sénégal (Addis Ababa, BIT/PECTA/CEAO, 1980). [SEN]

Evaluation du niveau de satisfaction des besoins de base dans les pays de l'Afrique de l'Ouest: Le cas de la Mauritanie (Addis Ababa, BIT/PECTA/CEAO, 1980). [MRT]

Evaluation du niveau de satisfaction des besoins de base: Le cas de la Côte-d'Ivoire (Addis Ababa, BIT/PECTA/CEAO, 1980). [CIV]

Evaluation du niveau de satisfaction des besoins de base: Le cas du Mali (Addis Ababa, BIT/PECTA/CEAO, 1980). [MLI]

Evaluation du niveau de satisfaction des besoins de base dans les pays de l'Afrique de l'Ouest - Rapport de synthèse (Addis Ababa, BIT/PECTA/CEAO, 1980).

L'emploi et la répartition des revenus dans la République gabonaise (Addis Ababa, JASPA, 1980). [GAB]

V. Jamal: *Incomes and inequality in Somalia* (Addis Ababa, JASPA, 1980). [SOM]

Basic needs in an economy under pressure. Findings and recommendations of an ILO/JASPA basic needs mission to Zambia (Addis Ababa, JASPA, 1981), xiii + 262 pp. Sw. frs. 25. [ZMB] ISBN 92-2-102683-3.

First things first - Meeting the basic needs of the people of Nigeria (Addis Ababa, JASPA, 1981), x + 256 pp. Sw. frs. 23. [NGA] ISBN 92-2-102682-5.

Wages and incomes in Somalia (with particular reference to the public sector) (Addis Ababa, JASPA, 1981). [SOM]

Disparités de revenus entre les villes et les campagnes au Bénin (Addis Ababa, JASPA, 1982), viii + 46 pp. [BEN]

Disparités de revenus entre les villes et les campagnes au Cameroun (Addis Ababa, JASPA, 1982), vi + 108 pp. [CMR]

Disparités de revenus entre les villes et les campagnes au Mali (Addis Ababa, JASPA, 1982), x + 94 pp. [MLI]

Disparités de revenus entre les villes et les campagnes au Sénégal (Addis Ababa, JASPA, 1982), x + 120 pp. [SEN]

Disparités de revenus entre les villes et les campagnes au Togo (Addis Ababa, PECTA, 1982), 140 pp. [TGO]

Disparités de revenus entre les villes et les campagnes en Côte-d'Ivoire (Addis Ababa, JASPA, 1982), viii + 60 pp. [CIV]

Disparités de revenus entre les villes et les campagnes en Haute-Volta (Addis Ababa, JASPA, 1982), viii + 49 pp. [BFA]

Disparités de revenus entre les villes et les campagnes en République populaire du Congo (Addis Ababa, JASPA, 1982), xiv + 86 pp. [COG]

Rural-urban gap and income distribution (A comparative sub-regional study): *The case of Ghana* (Addis Ababa, JASPA, 1982). [GHA] ISBN 92-2-103217-5.

Disparités de revenus entre les villes et les campagnes en Afrique noire francophone: Rapport de synthèse (Addis Ababa, JASPA, 1982), vi + 118 pp. [BEN, CMR, COG, CIV, BFA, MLI, SEN, TGO]

Rural-urban gap and income distribution (A comparative sub-regional study): *The case of Kenya* (Addis Ababa, JASPA, 1982). [KEN] ISBN 92-2-103211-6.

Rural-urban gap and income distribution (A comparative sub-regional study): *The case of Lesotho* (Addis Ababa, JASPA, 1982). [LSO] ISBN 92-2-103212-4.

Rural-urban gap and income distribution (A comparative sub-regional study): *The case of Liberia* (Addis Ababa, JASPA, 1982). [LBR] ISBN 92-2-103218-3.

Rural-urban gap and income distribution (A comparative sub-regional study): *The case of Nigeria* (Addis Ababa, JASPA, 1982). [NGA] ISBN 92-2-103213-2.

Rural-urban gap and income distribution (A comparative sub-regional study): *The case of Sierra Leone* (Addis Ababa, JASPA, 1982). [SLE] ISBN 92-2-103214-0.

Rural-urban gap and income distribution (A comparative sub-regional study): *The case of Somalia* (Addis Ababa, JASPA, 1982). [SOM] ISBN 92-2-103215-9.

Rural-urban gap and income distribution (A comparative sub-regional study): *The case of the United Republic of Tanzania* (Addis Ababa, JASPA, 1982). [TZA] ISBN 92-2-103216-7.

Rural-urban gap and income distribution (A comparative sub-regional study): *The case of Zambia* (Addis Ababa, JASPA, 1982). [ZMB] ISBN 92-2-103219-1.

Rural urban gap and income distribution (a comparative sub-regional study): Synthesis report of seventeen African countries (Addis Ababa, JASPA, 1984), v + 67 pp. (Expanded version of a report issued under the same title in 1982). ISBN 92-2-103786-X.

- Latin America and the Caribbean

N.E. García: *Necesidades básicas y crecimiento económico.* Occasional papers No. 27 (Santiago, PREALC, Oct. 1979).

G. Standing and R.J. Szal: *Poverty and basic needs: Evidence from Guyana and the Philippines* (Geneva, ILO, 1979), viii + 154 pp. Sw. frs. 15. [PHL, GUY] ISBN 92-2-102034-7.

V.E. Tokman: *Dinámica de los mercados de trabajo y distribución del ingreso en América Latina.* Occasional papers No. 26 (Santiago, PREALC, Aug. 1979).*

V.E. Tokman: *Empleo y distribución del ingreso en América Latina. Avance o retroceso?* Occasional papers No. 24 (Santiago, PREALC, Jan. 1979).

V.E. Tokman: *Pobreza urbana y empleo en América Latina: Lineas de acción.* Occasional papers No. 17 (Santiago, PREALC, July 1979), Rev.2.*

Asalariados de bajos ingresos y salarios mínimos en América Latina. Investigation on Employment No. 18 (Santiago, PREALC, 1980).

Necesidades esenciales y políticas de empleo en América Latina (Geneva, ILO, 1980), 137 pp. Sw. frs.15. ISBN 92-2-302417-X.

A. Uthoff: *Inversión en capital humano, empleo y distribución del ingreso, Gran Santiago 1969-1978.* Occasional papers No. 31 (Santiago, PREALC, May 1980). [CHL]

Empleo y necesidades básicas: Acceso a servicios urbanos y contratos públicos. Investigation on Employment No. 20 (Santiago, PREALC, 1981). [VEN, PER]

E. Dupré: *Empleo y distribución personal del ingreso: El caso de San Salvador.* Occasional papers No. 40 (Santiago, PREALC, June 1981). [SLV]

V. Vargas: *Salarios agrícolas en Chile en el periodo 1975-1981: Estudio de casos.* Monograph No. 24 (Santiago, PREALC, July 1982). [CHL]

Planificación para las necesidades básicas en América Latina. Monograph No. 29 (Santiago, PREALC/ISS, Aug. 1983).*

A. García (ed.): *El problema alimentario y nutricional en Chile: Diagnóstico y evaluación de políticas.* Monograph No. 33 (Santiago, PREALC/ISS, Sep. 1983). [CHL]

A. García: *La situación alimentaria en Costa Rica.* Monograph No. 31 (Santiago, PREALC/ISS, Sep. 1983). [CRI]

A. García: *Planificación alimentaria. Esquema metodológico para el análisis de experiencias en América Latina.* Monograph No. 28 (Santiago, PREALC, Aug. 1983).

A. García: *Un intento de planificación alimentaria integral: El Programa PAN-DRI de Colombia.* Monograph No. 35 (Santiago, PREALC/ISS, Sep. 1983). [COL]

B. Tomíc: *Necesidades básicas y participación popular: Opciones éticas y metodológicas.* Monograph No. 30 (Santiago, PREALC/ISS, Sep. 1983).

B. Tomíc: *Planificación participativa y descentralizada para las necesidades básicas.* Monograph No. 32 (Santiago, PREALC/ISS, Sep. 1983).

M. Castillo and A. García: *Una matriz de contabilidad social para Chile, 1977. Aspectos metodológicos y resultados.* Monograph No. 41 (Santiago, PREALC/ISS, Dec. 1984). [CHL]

H. Durán and S. Soza: *Consideraciones acerca del problema de la vivienda en América Latina.* Monograph No. 36 (Santiago, PREALC, Mar. 1984).

A. García: *Basic needs and the structure of production.* Monograph No. 38 (Santiago, PREALC, May 1984). [CHL]

A. Gutiérrez: *Ecuador: Salarios, empleo e ingresos - 1970-1982*. Monograph No. 45 (Santiago, PREALC/ISS, Dec. 1984). [ECU]

A. Gutiérrez: *Empleo y crecimiento en Ecuador 1970-1982: Tendencias recientes y lineamientos de política*. Monograph No. 44 (Santiago, PREALC/ISS, Dec. 1984). [ECU]

A. Gutiérrez: *Modelos del mercado de trabajo para la planificación de las necesidades básicas en Ecuador*. Monograph No. 46 (Santiago, PREALC/ISS, Dec. 1984). [ECU]

H. Szretter: *Ecuador: Nutrición y oferta de alimentos básicos*. Monograph No. 43 (Santiago, PREALC/ISS, Dec. 1984). [ECU]

D. Benavente: *A medio morir cantando*. 13 testimonios de cesantes (Santiago, PREALC, 1985), 286 pp. [CHL] ISBN 92-2-305393-5.

A. Gutiérrez: *Mercado de trabajo y necesidades básicas en Ecuador*. Monograph No. 48 (Santiago, PREALC/ISS, May 1985). [ECU]

H. Szretter: *Mexico: Las necesidades básicas de alimentación*. Monograph No. 47 (Santiago, PREALC/ISS, Jan. 1985). [MEX]

Buscando la equidad. Planificación para la satisfacción de las necesidades basicas. (Santiago, PREALC, 1986), xiii + 205 pp. US$ 7. ISBN 92-2-305762-0.

J. Rodriguez and J. Wurgaft: *La protección social a los desocupados en América latina*. Investigation on Employment No. 28 (Santiago, PREALC, 1987). ISBN 92-2-306006-0.

- Asia

A. Rudra: *The basic needs concept and its implementation in Indian development planning* (Bangkok, ARTEP, Dec. 1978; 2nd edition, 1981), 82 pp. US $2. [IND] ISBN 92-2-102044-4.

Planning for basic needs and mobilisation of resources (Bangkok, ARTEP, 1980), 286 pp. US$5. [NPL]

P.J. Richards and W. Gooneratne: *Basic needs, poverty and government policies in Sri Lanka*. (Geneva, ILO, 1980; 2nd impression, 1981), vi + 176 pp. Sw. frs. 17.50. E, Sinhala version. [LKA] ISBN 92-2-102316-8.

The basic needs approach to Indian planning - Proceedings and papers of a seminar in Trivandrum, India - July 21-22, 1980 (Bangkok, ARTEP, 1981), 78 pp. Sw. frs. 5.25. [IND]

Employment and basic needs in Nepal: A preliminary analysis of problems and policies (Bangkok, ARTEP, 1982), x + 194 pp. [NPL]

Fighting poverty: Asia's major challenge (New Delhi, ARTEP, 1986), 40 pp. US$5. ISBN 92-2-103944-7.

- OECD Countries

W. Beckerman in collaboration with W. van Ginneken, R.J. Szal and M. Garzuel: *Poverty and the impact of income maintenance programmes in four developed countries, case studies of Australia, Belgium, Norway and Great Britain* (Geneva, ILO, 1979), ix + 90 pp. Sw. frs. 17.50. E, F. [AUS, BEL, NOR, GBR] ISBN 92-2-102064-9.

D. Hsieh: *Fiscal measures for poverty alleviation in the United States* (Geneva, ILO, 1979), iv + 160 pp. Sw. frs. 20. [USA] ISBN 92-2-102107-6.

Articles in the International Labour Review

- **General**

N. Rao Maturu: "Nutrition and labour productivity", Vol. 118, No. 1, Jan.-Feb. 1979.

A. Bequele and D.H. Freedman: "Employment and basic needs: An overview", Vol. 118, No. 3, May-June 1979.

E.P. Mach: "Selected issues on health and employment", Vol. 118, No. 2, Mar.-Apr. 1979.

P.J. Richards: "Housing and employment", Vol. 118, No. 1, Jan.-Feb. 1979.

R.J. Szal: "Popular participation, employment and the fulfilment of basic needs", Vol. 118, No. 1, Jan.-Feb. 1979.

W. van Ginneken, L. Join-Lambert and J. Lecaillon: "Persistent poverty in the industrial market economies", Vol. 118, No. 6, Nov.-Dec. 1979.

P.J. Richards: "Target setting for basic needs services: Some possible approaches", Vol. 120, No. 5, Sep.-Oct. 1981.

M.J.D. Hopkins and R. van der Hoeven: "Basic-needs planning and forecasting: Policy and scenario analysis in four countries", Vol. 121, No. 6, Nov.-Dec. 1982.

- **Africa**

F. Lisk and R. van der Hoeven: "Measurement and interpretation of poverty in Sierra Leone", Vol. 118, No. 6, Nov.-Dec. 1979. [SLE]

A. Bequele and R. van der Hoeven: "Poverty and inequality in Sub-Saharan Africa", Vol. 119, No. 3, May-June 1980.

D. Ghai: "Basic needs: From words to action, with illustrations from Kenya", Vol. 119, No. 3, May-June 1980. [KEN]

T. Alfthan: "Industrialisation in the Ivory Coast: Impact on employment and basic-needs satisfaction", Vol. 121, No. 6, Nov.-Dec. 1982. [CIV]

R. van der Hoeven: "Zambia's economic dependence and the satisfaction of basic needs", Vol. 121, No. 2, Mar.-Apr. 1982. [ZMB]

- **Latin America and the Caribbean**

W. van Ginneken: "Socio-economic groups and income distribution in Mexico", Vol. 118, No. 3, May-June 1979. [MEX]

R. van der Hoeven: "Employment, basic needs and industrialisation: Some reflections on the Lima target", Vol. 119, No. 4, July-Aug. 1980. [PER]

- **Asia**

R. Hsia and L. Chau: "Industrialisation and income distribution in Hong Kong", Vol. 117, No. 4, July-Aug. 1978. [HKG]

I. Ahmed and J.G. Laarman: "Technologies for basic needs: The case of Philippine forestry", Vol. 117, No. 4, July-Aug. 1978. [PHL]

S. Radwan and T. Alfthan: "Household surveys for basic needs: Some issues", Vol. 117, No. 2, Mar.-Apr. 1978. [PHL]

C.P. Holtsberg: "Effects of a new feeder road on employment and income distribution: A case study in Thailand", Vol. 118, No. 2, Mar.-Apr. 1979. [THA]

I. Ahmed and D.H. Freedman: "Access to rural factor markets, technological change and basic needs: Evidence from Bangladesh", Vol. 121, No. 4, July-Aug. 1982. [BGD]

Other articles

- Asia

R.J. Szal: "Emerging trends in income distribution in Korea and their implications for future planning", in *Labour and Society* (Geneva), Vol. 6, No. 4, Oct.-Dec. 1981. [KOR]

Working papers

- General

D. Curtis, K. Davey, A. Hughes and A. Shepherd: *Popular participation in decision-making and the basic needs approach to development: Methods, issues and experiences*, June 1978 (WEP 2-32/WP.12). M.

M.J.D. Hopkins and O.D.K. Norbye: *Meeting basic human needs: Some global estimates*, July 1978 (WEP 2-32/WP.13). M.

J.P. Mouly and S.A. Kuzmin: *Five essays on the basic needs approach*, May 1978 (WEP 2-32/WP.11). M.

A.K. Sen: *Three notes on the concept of poverty,*[1] Jan. 1978 (WEP 2-23/WP.65). M.

G. Sheehan and M.J.D. Hopkins: *Basic needs performance: An analysis of some international data,*[2] Jan. 1978 (WEP 2-32/WP.9).

I. Adelman and P. Whittle: *Static and dynamic indices of income inequality*, June 1979 (WEP 2-23/WP.74). M.

W. van Ginneken: *Comparable income distribution data for Mexico (1968), United Kingdom (1979) and the Federal Republic of Germany (1974)*, Sep. 1981 (WEP 2-23/WP.105). [MEX, DEU, GBR]

T. Alfthan: *Basic needs satisfaction in ILO member States. Presentation and analysis of national responses to a world enquiry*, Apr. 1979 (WEP 2-32/WP.16). M.

M.J.D. Hopkins and R. van der Hoeven: *Economic and social factors in development: A socio-economic framework for basic needs planning (a contribution to the United Nations Third Development Decade)*, July 1979 (WEP 2-32/WP.19). M.

S.A. Kuzmin: *Policy inter-actions within an integrated (basic needs-oriented) development strategy*, June 1979 (WEP 2-32/WP.18). M.

M.D. Leonor, Jr.: *Dimensions and targets in basic education (an illustrative exercise in assessing the fulfilment of education as a basic need)*, Oct. 1979 (WEP 2-23/WP.78). M.

P.J. Richards: *Some distributional issues in planning for basic needs health care*, June 1979 (WEP 2-23/WP.75). M.

S. Radwan and T. Alfthan: *Household surveys for poverty studies: Some guidelines*, May 1979 (WEP 2-32/WP.17). M.

A. Singh: *The "basic needs" approach to development and the significance of Third World industrialisation*, Feb. 1979 (WEP 2-32/WP.15). M. [CHN, PER]

J. James: *Product choice and poverty: A study of the inefficiency of low-income consumption and the distributional impact of product changes*, May 1980 (WEP 2-23/WP.88). M.

A. Kuyvenhoven: *Technology, employment and basic needs in leather industries in developing countries*, Aug. 1980 (WEP 2-22/WP.65). M.

N. Fergany: *Monitoring the condition of the poor in the Third World: Some aspects of measurement*, Dec. 1981 (WEP 10-6/WP.52). M.

M.J.D. Hopkins and R. van der Hoeven: *Modelling economic and social factors in development*, Nov. 1981 (WEP 2-32/WP.32). M. [IND, KEN, BRA, COL]

H. Lydall: *Effects of alternative measurement techniques on the estimation of the inequality of income*, June 1981 (WEP 2-23/WP.100).

R. Rietschin: *Les déterminants de la satisfaction des besoins essentiels et leur impact*, Mar. 1981 (WEP 2-32/WP.24). M.

R.C. Sinha, S.P. Siha, G.P. Mishra and G. Pingle: *Implications of a basic needs strategy for the edible-oil industry*, July 1981 (WEP 2-23/WP.102 - WEP 2-22/WP.84).

J. Pickford: *Human waste disposal in urban areas*, [3] July 1982 (WEP 2-32/WP.39). M. ISBN 92-2-103182-9.

J. Skolka: *Economic growth, structure of the economy and distribution of income*, Jan. 1983 (WEP 2-32/WP.45). ISBN 92-2-103326-0.

E. Ghani: *The effects of devaluation on employment and poverty in developing countries*, Nov. 1984 (WEP 2-32/WP.57). [PER, IDN] ISBN 92-2-103976-5.

J. Skolka: *The influence of basic needs policies on sectoral value added shares in input-output tables*, July 1984 (WEP 2-32/WP.55). ISBN 92-2-103912-9.

S.V. Sethuraman: *Basic needs and the informal sector: The case of low-income housing in developing countries*, Jan. 1985 (WEP 2-19/WP. 35). ISBN 92-2-205013-1.

- Africa

M.J.D. Hopkins: *Somalia and basic needs: Some issues*, Jan. 1978 (WEP 2-32/WP.8). M. [SOM]

R.J. Szal, in collaboration with M. Garzuel: *Income inequality and fiscal policies in Botswana*, Apr. 1979 (WEP 2-23/WP.73). M. [BWA]

R. van der Hoeven: *Meeting basic needs in a socialist framework: The example of the United Republic of Tanzania*, July 1979 (WEP 2-32/WP.20). M. [TZA]

K. Korayem: *The impact of the elimination of food subsidies on the cost of living in Egypt's urban population*, Aug. 1980 (WEP 2-23/WP.9l). [EGY]

M. Turok and B. Sanyal: *Lusaka housing project: A critical overview of low-cost housing in Zambia*, Sep. 1980 (WEP 2-23/WP.92). M. [ZMB]

V. Jamal: *Nomads, farmers and townsmen: Incomes and inequality in Somalia* (Addis Ababa, JASPA), 1981. [SOM] ISBN 92-2-102897-6.

V. Jamal: *Rural-urban gap and inequality in Kenya* (Addis Ababa, JASPA), 1981. [KEN] ISBN 92-2-102895-X.

V. Jamal: *Rural-urban gap and inequality in Nigeria* (Addis Ababa, JASPA), 1981. [NGA] ISBN 92-2-102894-1.

V. Jamal: *Rural-urban gap in the United Republic of Tanzania* (Addis Ababa, JASPA), 1981. [TZA] ISBN 92-2-102896-8.

M. Ourabah: *Industrialisation, emploi et besoins essentiels en Algérie*, May. 1981 (WEP 2-32/WP.27). [DZA]

R.K. Srivastava and I. Livingstone: *Growth and distribution: The case of Mozambique*, Mar. 1981 (WEP 10-6/WP.45). [MOZ]

J. Trouvé and C. Bessat: *Satisfaction des besoins essentiels et l'impact de l'organisation économique et sociale: Deux études de cas en Afrique*, June 1981 (WEP 2-32/WP.26). M. [BFA, BDI]

R. van der Hoeven: *A socio-economic framework for basic needs planning: A Kenya case study*, June 1981 (WEP 2-32/WP.28). M. [KEN]

T. Alfthan: *Industrialisation, employment and basic needs: The case of the Ivory Coast*, July 1982 (WEP 2-32/WP.40). M. [CIV] ISBN 92-2-103192-6.

J. Vandemoortele and R. van der Hoeven: *Income distribution and consumption patterns in urban and rural Kenya by socio-economic groups*, May 1982 (WEP 2-32/WP.38). M. [KEN] ISBN 92-2-103161-6.

J. Vandemoortele: *The public sector and the basic-needs strategy in Kenya: The experience of the seventies*, Jan. 1983 (WEP 2-32/WP.46). M. [KEN] ISBN 92-2-103359-7.

W. van Ginneken: *Incomes and wages in Namibia* (Lusaka, SATEP), Jan. 1986 [NAM] ISBN 92-2-105302-4.

- Latin America and the Caribbean

Bolivia: Informe sobre el uso de las estadísticas salariales para el estudio de la distribución del ingreso (Santiago, PREALC), July 1978 (No. 149). [BOL]

Crédito, empleo y distribución del ingreso: El caso de Bolivia (Santiago, PREALC), July 1978 (No. 151). [BOL]

Diferenciales de remuneraciones y coexistencia de establecimientos de distinto tamaño: México 1965-75 (Santiago, PREALC), Sep. 1978 (No. 155). [MEX]

Perú: Estrategia de desarrollo y grado de satisfacción de las necesidades básicas (Santiago, PREALC), May 1978 (No. 127). [PER]

F. Bourguignon: *General equilibrium analysis of the Colombian income distribution: Applications to rural development, wage and income policies*, June 1978 (WEP 2-23/WP.68). M. [COL]

R.J. Szal: *The distribution of the benefits of growth: Basic needs in the Philippines,*[4] Jan. 1978 (WEP 2-32/WP.7). [PHL]

Planning for basic needs in Latin America. Final Report, Bogotá : Workshop Seminar (Santiago, PREALC), May 1979 (No. 171).* [COL]

W. van Ginneken: *Basic needs in Mexico: Analysis and policies*, July 1979 (WEP 2-23/WP.76). M. [MEX]

Criterios y metodologías para la satisfacción de necesidades básicas (Santiago, PREALC), July 1980 (No. 190).

Empleo y distribución del ingreso en Venezuela (Santiago, PREALC), Sep. 1980 (No. 193). [VEN]

Panamá: Estrategia de necesidades básicas y empleo (Santiago, PREALC), July 1980 (No. 189). [PAN]

C. Bunge: *Basic needs in Panama: The health sector*, Apr. 1980 (WEP 2-23/WP.87). M. [PAN]

Estructura y evolución salarial en el sector industrial moderno en Chile (Santiago, PREALC), May 1981 (No. 201). [CHL]

H. Banguero: *Colombia 2000: A framework for population, employment, growth, income distribution and essential human needs planning*[5], Oct. 1981 (WEP 2-32/WP.31). M [COL]

M.J.D. Hopkins: *A socio-economic framework for basic needs planning: A Brazil case study*, June 1981 (WEP 2-32/WP.30). M. [BRA]

Industrialización y necesidades básicas en América latina (Santiago, PREALC), Oct. 1982 (No. 219). E, S. [CRI]

Remuneraciones, precios e importaciones de bienes, Ecuador, 1982[6] (Santiago, PREALC), Sep. 1982 (No. 217). [ECU]

Producción de alimentos básicos y empleo en el istmo centroamericana (Santiago, PREALC), Aug. 1983 (No. 229). [GTM, SLV, HND, NIC, CRI, PAN]

Venezuela: Empleo e ingresos en el corto plazo. Tomo I y Tomo II (Santiago, PREALC), Mar. 1983 (No. 221). [VEN]

Ecuador: Aspectos redistributivos de la política económica, 1979-1983 (Santiago, PREALC), Sep. 1984 (No. 247). [ECU]

Salarios e inflación. Argentina 1970-1983 (Santiago, PREALC), Apr. 1984 (No. 239). [ARG]

J. Córdova: *La estratégia de satisfacción de las necesidades esenciales y la política de industrialización de alimentos en México*, Apr. 1984 (WEP 2-32/WP.54). [MEX] ISBN 92-2-303870-7.

Panamá: Evolución y estructura de los salarios (Santiago, PREALC), June 1985 (No. 267). [PAN]

Política de ingresos y actores sociales (Santiago, PREALC), Dec. 1985 (No. 273). [ARG, COL]

Un indice de la escala única de remuneraciones del sector público chileno: 1974-86 (Santiago, PREALC), Mar. 1987 (No. 293). [CHL]

- Asia

P.J. Alailima: *Fiscal incidence in Sri Lanka*, Aug. 1978 (WEP 2-23/WP.69). M. [LKA]

S.M. Fine: *Fiscal and macro-economic policies for employment promotion and better income distribution in Indonesia* (Bangkok, ARTEP), 1978. [IDN]

C.P. Holtsberg: *The Cha-am Road, employment and income distribution effects of rural road construction*, Apr. 1978 (WEP 2-23/WP.66). M. [THA]

J.G. Maton and M. Garzuel: *Redistribution of income, patterns of consumption and employment: The case study for Malaysia,*[7] Oct. 1978 (WEP 2-23/WP.71). M. [MYS]

J. Skolka and M. Garzuel: *Income distribution by size, employment and the structure of the economy: A case study for the Republic of Korea,*[7] May 1978 (WEP 2-23/WP.67). M. [KOR]

Ng Gek-Boo: *Mass participation and basic needs satisfaction: The Chinese approach*, Jan. 1979 (WEP 2-32/WP.14). M. [CHN]

W. Gooneratne: *Land tenure and government policies and income distribution in Sri Lanka,*[8] Sep. 1979 (WEP 2-23/WP.77). M. [LKA]

A.P. Gupta: *The poor, the non-poor and the taxes they pay in India: A state-wise study*, Nov. 1979 (WEP 2-23/WP.79). M. [IND]

G.B. Rodgers: *Approaches to the analysis of poverty*, May 1979 (WEP 2-21/WP.71). M. [LKA]

F. Paukert, J. Skolka and J.G. Maton: *Income distribution by size, structure of the economy and employment: A comparative study for four Asian countries,*[7] Mar. 1979 (WEP 2-23/WP.72). M. [PHL, IRN, KOR, MYS]

T.M. Vinod Kumar and Jatin De: *Basic needs and the provision of government services: An area study of Ranaghat block in West Bengal*, Feb. 1980 (WEP 2-23/WP.85). M. [IND]

A.P. Gupta: *Who benefits from government expenditures in India?*, June 1980 (WEP 2-23/WP.90). M. [IND]

K. Griffin and A. Saith: *The pattern of income inequality in rural China* (Bangkok, ARTEP), July 1980. [CHN]

A.P. Gupta: *Poverty and unemployment in India: Is there light at the end of the tunnel?*, Sep. 1981 (WEP 2-23/WP.104). [IND]

C.P. Holtsberg: *Income distribution implications of the Thai rice price policy*, Jan. 1980 (WEP 2-23/WP.83). M. [THA]

M. Krongkaew: *The distribution of and access to basic health services in Thailand*, Sep. 1980 (WEP 2-23/WP.93). M. [THA]

M. Ahmed and A. Ahmad: *Provision and distribution of selected public goods and services in India*, June 1981 (WEP 2-23/WP.101). [IND]

C.U. Chiswick: *The distribution of income in Thailand*, Feb. 1981 (WEP 2-23/WP.97). [THA]

J.G. Krishnayya, K.N.S. Nair, B. Joshi, V. Phaneendhrudu and S. Chatterji: *India basic needs: A socio-economic and demographic simulation model*, Mar. 1981 (WEP 2-32/WP.25). M. [IND]

G.H. Pieris: *Basic needs and the provision of government services in Sri Lanka*, Jan. 1982 (WEP 2-32/WP.35). M. [LKA] ISBN 92-2-103017-2.

G.H. Pieris: *Basic needs and the provision of government services in Sri Lanka: A case study of Kandy District, Part II*, May 1982 (WEP 2-32/WP.36). M. [LKA] ISBN 92-2-103045-8.

T.S. Papola and R.C. Sinha: *The impact of income redistribution on technology and employment in the metal utensils sector of India*,[9] Apr. 1982 (WEP 2-22/WP.94). [IND] ISBN 92-2-103153-5.

F.F. Rivera, V. Molina and O. Ringor: *Self-help basic housing in a Philippine rice-farming village*, Oct. 1983 (WEP 2-32/WP.53). M. [PHL] ISBN 92-2-103599-9.

E. Gutkind: *Towards basic needs policies in development planning*, Jan. 1983 (WEP 2-32/WP.47). M. [LKA] ISBN 92-2-103358-9.

A. Singh: *Industrialisation, employment and basic needs in a fast-growing agrarian state: A study of the Indian Punjab*, Jan. 1983 (WEP 2-32/WP.48). M. [IND] ISBN 92-2-103381-3.

V.S. Vyas, A.P. Bhatt and S.M. Shah: *Decentralised planning in India*, Sep. 1983 (WEP 2-32/WP.52). M. [IND] ISBN 92-2-103598-0.

P. Alailima: *Fiscal incidence in Sri Lanka, 1973 and 1980*, Nov. 1984 (WEP 2-32/WP.56). [LKA] ISBN 92-2-103962-5.

B. Hewavitharana: *Industrialisation, employment and basic needs: The case of Sri Lanka*, Feb. 1986 (WEP 2-32/WP.60). [LKA] ISBN 92-2-105426-8.

T. Larhed: *Employment, wages and income distribution in Malaysia* (New Delhi, ARTEP), Dec. 1987. [MYS] ISBN 92-2-106038-1.

- OECD Countries

W. Beckerman: *Estimates of poverty in Italy in 1975*, Sep. 1978 (WEP 2-23/WP.70). M. [ITA]

W. Beckerman: *Estimates of poverty in Greece, 1974*, Dec. 1979 (WEP 2-23/WP.80). M. [GRC]

T.K. Chowdhury: *Consumer information from public and private sources: Some Canadian results*, Dec. 1979 (WEP 2-23/WP.82). M. [CAN]

W. Beckerman: *The impact of income maintenance payments on poverty in Ireland, 1973*, Aug. 1981 (WEP 2-23/WP.103). [IRL]

W. Beckerman: *The impact of income maintenance programmes on poverty in Canada, 1975*, Mar. 1981 (WEP 2-23/WP.98). [CAN]

M.M. Silva: *Emploi, besoins essentiels et industrialisation au Portugal*, June 1981 (WEP 2-32/WP.29). M. [PRT]

P. Sicherl: *A dynamic analysis of regional disparities in Yugoslavia*, Jan. 1980 (WEP 2-23/WP.84). M. [YUG]

ILO works published by commercial and non-profit-making publishers

- General

H. Leibenstein: *Inflation, income distribution and X-efficiency theory* (London, Croom Helm, 1980), 122 pp. ISBN 0-06-494169-8.

F. Paukert, J. Skolka and J.G. Maton: *Income distribution, structure of economy and employment - the Philippines, Iran, the Republic of Korea and Malaysia* (London, Croom Helm, 1981), 170 pp. [PHL, IRN, KOR, MYS] ISBN 0-7099-2006-7.

A.K. Sen: *Poverty and famines: An essay on entitlement and deprivation* (Oxford, Clarendon Press, 1981), xii + 258 pp. [IND, BGD, ETH] ISBN 0-19-828426-8.

M.J.D. Hopkins and R. van der Hoeven: *Basic needs in development planning* (Aldershot, Hampshire, Gower, 1983), xvii + 184 pp. ISBN 0-566-00626-X.

P.J. Richards and A.M. Thomson (eds.): *Basic needs and the urban poor: The provision of communal services* (London, Croom Helm, 1984), 276 pp. ISBN 0-7099-2281-7.

F. Lisk (ed.): *Popular participation in planning for basic needs. Concepts, methods and practices* (Aldershot, Hampshire, Gower, 1985), ix + 277 pp. [CHN, TZA, KEN, BGD] ISBN 0-566-00979-X.

- Latin America and the Caribbean

M. Carnoy, in collaboration with J. Lobo, A. Toledo and J. Velloso: *Can educational policy equalise income distribution in Latin America?* (Farnborough, Hampshire, Saxon House, 1979), ix + 110 pp. [MEX, BRA, CHL, CUB, PER] ISBN 0-566-00255-8.

A. Foxley, E. Aninat and J.P. Arellano: *Redistributive effects of government programmes: The Chilean case.* [10] (Oxford, Pergamon Press Ltd., 1979), viii + 240 pp. [CHL] ISBN 0-08-023130-6.

W. van Ginneken: *Socio-economic groups and income distribution in Mexico.* Preface by F. Paukert[11] (London, Croom Helm, 1980), 238 pp. [MEX] ISBN 0-7099-0167-4.

In search of equity. Planning for the satisfaction of basic needs in Latin America (Aldershot, Hampshire, Gower, 1987), xvi + 249 pp. ISBN 0-566-05537-6.

- Asia

R. Hsia and L. Chau: *Industrialisation, employment and income distribution. A case study of Hong Kong* (London, Croom Helm, 1978), 206 pp. [HKG] ISBN 0-85664-684-9

P.J. Richards and M.D. Leonor: *Education and income distribution in Asia* (London, Croom Helm, 1981), 190 pp. [PHL, IND, LKA, THA] ISBN 0-7099-2201-9.

P.J. Richards (ed.): *Basic needs and government policies in Thailand* (Singapore, Maruzen Asia, 1982), x + 182 pp. [THA] ISBN 962-220-225-X.

- OECD Countries

Emprego e necessidades básicas em Portugal (Lisbon, Instituto de Pesquisa social Damiao de Góis, Presidencia da República, 1985), 173 pp. [PRT]

Related books and articles

- General

I. Adelman, M.J.D. Hopkins, S. Robinson, G.B. Rodgers and R. Wéry: "A comparison of two models for income distribution planning", in *Journal of Policy Modelling* (New York), Vol. 1, No. 1, Jan. 1979.

R.J. Szal: "Operationalising the concept of basic needs", in *Pakistan Development Review* (Karachi), XIX (3), Autumn 1980.

H. Lubell and S.V. Sethuraman: "Low income settlement improvement through income and employment generation and integrated housing programme", in UNCHS (Habitat): *The residential circumstances of the urban poor in developing countries* (New York, 1981).

M.J.D. Hopkins and R. van der Hoeven: "Survey - Policy analysis in a socio-economic model of basic needs applied to four countries", in *Journal of Policy Modelling* (New York), Vol. 4, No. 3, 1982.

M.J.D. Hopkins and R. van der Hoeven: "Economic and social factors in development: A socio-economic framework for basic needs planning", in S.I. Cohen, P.A. Cornelisse, R. Teekens and E. Thorbecke (eds.): *The modelling of socio-economic planning processes* (Aldershot, Hampshire, Gower, 1984).

S.V. Sethuraman: "Basic needs and the informal sector. The case of low-income housing in developing countries", in *Habitat International* (Oxford, United Kingdom), Vol. 9, No. 3/4, 1985.

- Latin America and the Caribbean

H. Banguero (ed.): *Colombia 2000. Estrategias de desarrollo para satisfacer las necesidades humanas esenciales en Colombia* (Bogotá, Universidad de los Andes, CEDE, 1982), 326 pp. [COL]

A. de Villamil, B. Guerrero, H. Banguero and M.J.D. Hopkins: *Colombia hasta el año 2000* (Bogotá, Asociación de exalumnos de la Universidad de los Andes, 1982), 169 pp. [COL]

- Asia

J. James: "The employment effects of an income redistribution: A test for aggregation bias in the Indian sugar processing industry", in *Journal of Development Economics* (Amsterdam), Vol. 7, 1980. [IND]

International Council on Social Welfare: *The urban dead-end? Pattern of employment among slum-dwellers* (Bombay, Somaiya Publications, 1983). [IND]

Notes:

[1] Reprinted in A.K. Sen: Poverty and famines: An essay on entitlement and deprivation (Oxford, Clarendon Press, 1981).

[2] Reprinted in G. Sheehan and M.J.D. Hopkins: Basic needs performance. An analysis of some international data (Geneva, ILO, 1979).

3 Also published in P.J. Richards and A.M. Thomson(eds.): Basic needs and the urban poor: The provision of communal services (London, Croom Helm, 1984).

4 Reprinted in G. Standing and R. Szal: Poverty and basic needs: Evidence from Guyana and the Philippines (Geneva, ILO, 1979)

5 Also published as a book: H. Banguero (ed.): Colombia 2000: Estrategias de desarrollo para satisfacer las necesidades humanas esenciales en Colombia - Colección debates CEDE No. 4 (Bogotá, Universidad de Los Andes, 1982).

6 Also published in: Política salarial, inflación y restricción externa (Santiago, PREALC, 1987).

7 Reprinted in F. Paukert, J. Skolka and J. Maton: Income distribution, structure of economy and employment - the Philippines, Iran, the Rep. of Korea and Malaysia (London, Croom Helm, 1981).

8 Reprinted in P.J. Richards and W. Gooneratne: Basic needs, poverty and government policies in Sri Lanka (Geneva, ILO, 1980).

9 Published in W. van Ginneken and C. Baron (eds.): Appropriate products, employment and technology. Case studies on consumer choice and basic needs in developing countries (London, Macmillan, 1984).

10 Also published as Las desigualdades económicas y la acción del Estado (Mexico City, Fondo de Cultura Económica, 1980), 272 pp.

11 Also published as Los grupos socioeconómicos y la distribución del ingreso en México (Mexico City, Fondo de Cultura Económica, 1985).

Labour market analysis and the informal sector

ILO publications

Books and reports

- **General**

Rural small industries and non-farm employment. A progress report on research and operational activities (Geneva, ILO, forthcoming), ii + 42 pp. ISBN 92-2-106347-X.

S.V. Sethuraman (ed.): *The urban informal sector in developing countries - Employment, poverty and environment* (Geneva, ILO, 1981), xii + 226 pp. Sw. frs. 35. [SLE, NGA, LKA, BRA, IDN, PHL, ARG] ISBN 92-2-102591-8.

M. Allal and E. Chuta: *Cottage industries and handicrafts: Some guidelines for employment promotion* (Geneva, ILO, 1982), xiv + 202 pp. Sw. frs. 20. [SLE, IND] ISBN 92-2-103029-6.

Cottage industries, handicrafts and non-farm employment. A progress report on research and operational activities. Progress report no. 1 of the Technology and Employment Branch (Geneva, ILO, 1984), 23 pp. ISBN 92-2-103816-5.

E. Chuta and S.V. Sethuraman (eds.): *Rural small-scale industries and employment in Africa and Asia.* A review of programmes and policies (Geneva, ILO, 1984), x + 160 pp. Sw. frs. 25. [KEN, TZA, CHN, NGA, IND, PAK, LKA] ISBN 92-2-103513-1.

- **Africa**

Assistance au secteur non structuré à Dakar: Le problème de l'accès à une technologie appropriée (Dakar, JASPA, 1979). [SEN]

F.R. Banugire: *Uganda's development patterns - An historical and prospective analysis* (Addis Ababa, JASPA, 1979). [UGA]

Employment, incomes and production in the informal sector in the Gambia (Addis Ababa, JASPA, 1980). [GMB]

Propositions pour une politique globale de développement de la petite entreprise à Ouagadougou (Addis Ababa, JASPA, 1980). [BFA]

Colloque sur l'acquisition des qualifications et l'emploi dans le secteur non structuré urbain d'Afrique francophone BIT/OCAM (Addis Ababa, JASPA, 1981).

Secteur informel et emploi en République populaire du Congo: Une vue d'ensemble. Rapport soumis au Gouvernement de la République populaire du Congo par une mission d'assistance technique du PECTA (Addis Ababa, JASPA, 1982), viii + 76 pp. [COG]

The urban informal sector in Zambia: A programme for action (Lusaka, SATEP, 1982), viii + 72 pp. [ZMB]

G. Nihan and E. Demol, with the collaboration of A.A. Tabi: *Le secteur non-structuré "moderne" de Yaoundé (République-unie du Cameroun)* (Geneva, ILO, 1982), xiii + 198 pp. Sw. frs. 22.50. [CMR] ISBN 92-2-202902-X.

A.A. Tabi, J.M. Gern and P. Mandeng: *Recherche sur l'emploi et la formation au Cameroun*. Rapport d'enquête et analyse des données sur les entreprises modernes (Yaoundé, Division des Ressources humaines, Ministère de l'Economie et du Plan, République-unie du Cameroun/BIT, 1982), vii + 176 pp. [CMR]

I. El-Bagir, J. Dey, A. Abdel Gadir Ali, T. Barnett, J. Ghosh and A. Wagner: *Labour markets in the Sudan*. A study carried out within the framework of the ILO/UNHCR Project on Income Generating Activities for Refugees in Eastern and Central Sudan (Geneva, ILO, 1984), x + 224 pp. Sw. frs. 27.50. [SDN] ISBN 92-2-103749-5.

Informal sector in Africa (Addis Ababa, JASPA, 1985), 137 pp. Sw. frs. 16. ISBN 92-2-103785-1.

Le secteur non structuré d'Antsirabe: Analyse typologique, facteurs de blocage et perspectives de promotion des activités du bois, construction métallique, garages et réparations (Addis Ababa, JASPA, 1985), vii + 71 pp. [MDG] ISBN 92-2-205256-0.

Le secteur non structuré de Mahajanga: Analyse typologique, facteurs de blocage et perspectives de promotion des activités du bois, construction métallique, garages et réparations (Addis Ababa, JASPA, 1985), v + 114 pp. [MDG] ISBN 92-2-205254-4.

Le secteur non structuré de Toamasina: Analyse typologique, facteurs de blocage et perspectives de promotion des activités du bois, construction métallique, garages et réparations et pêche (Addis Ababa, JASPA, 1985), xi + 187 pp. [MDG] ISBN 92-2-205255-2.

A.A. Aboagye: *An analysis of Dar-es-Salaam's informal sector survey* (Addis Ababa, JASPA, 1985), 76 pp. + annexes. [TZA] ISBN 92-2-105239-7.

K.M. Gozo: *Le secteur non structuré à Djibouti*. Caractéristiques des entreprises et de la main-d'oeuvre du secteur. Contribution à l'emploi et la formation des revenus (Addis Ababa, JASPA, 1985), xiv + 188 pp. [DJI] ISBN 92-2-205240-4.

K.M. Gozo: *Le secteur non structuré de Kinshasa*. Caractéristiques des entreprises et de la main-d'oeuvre. Potentialités d'emploi et de distribution de revenu. Contribution à une mission sectorielle d'emploi au Zaïre (Addis Ababa, PECTA, 1985), iii + 72 pp. [ZAR] ISBN 92-2-100538-0.

K.M. Gozo: *Le secteur non structuré urbain d'Antananarivo: Nouvelles priorités sectorielles* (Addis Ababa, JASPA, 1985), vi + 175 pp. [MDG] ISBN 92-2-205103-3.

A.A. Aboagye: *Informal sector employment in Kenya. A survey of informal sector activities in Nairobi, Kisumu and Mombasa* (Addis Ababa, JASPA, 1986), vii + 117 pp. + annexes. [KEN] ISBN 92-2-105557-4.

A.A. Aboagye: *Informal sector in Lilongwe. A survey of informal activities in garages, metal fabricating, tinsmithing and woodworking* (Addis Ababa, JASPA, 1986), vii + 125 pp. [MWI] ISBN 92-2-105410-1.

C. Maldonado avec la collaboration de J. Capt et E. Demol: *Petits producteurs urbains d'-Afrique francophone*. Analyse et politiques d'appui. Etude comparative à Bamako, Lomé, Nouakchott et Yaoundé (Geneva, ILO, 1987), xvii + 258 pp. Sw. frs. 30. [MLI, TGO, TCD, CMR] ISBN 92-2-206196-9.

- **Latin America and the Caribbean**

Comercio informal en una comuna de Santiago. Investigation on Employment No. 11 (Santiago, PREALC, 1978). [CHL]

La ampliación de turnos en la industria chilena. Investigation on Employment No. 8 (Santiago, PREALC, 1978). [CHL]

Sector informal: Funcionamiento y políticas (Santiago, PREALC, 1978), 369 pp. Sw. frs. 22.50. [MEX, SLV, CHL, ECU, JAM] ISBN 92-2-301903-6.

N.E. García: *Microindustrias en el sector manufacturero de México*. Occasional papers No. 23 (Santiago, PREALC, July 1978).* [MEX]

P. Meller: *Enfoques sobre demanda de trabajo: Relevancia para América Latina*. Investigation on Employment No. 12 (Santiago, PREALC-CIEPLAN, 1978).*

Identificación de sectores claves para la generación de empleo: Metodologías alternativas. Investigation on Employment No. 15 (Santiago, PREALC, 1979).

N.E. García and M. Marfán: *La interpretación operacional de la noción de encadenamientos*. Occasional papers No. 33 (Santiago, PREALC, Nov. 1980).

E. Klein: *Diferenciación social: Tendencias del empleo y los ingresos agrícolas*. Occasional papers No. 28 (Santiago, PREALC, Mar. 1980). [BRA, CHL, SLV, PER]

D. Lehmann: *Proletarización, movimientos sociales y reforma agraria. De las teorías de ayer a la práctica de mañana*. Occasional papers No. 29 (Santiago, PREALC, Mar. 1980).

J. Ramos: *Capital market segmentation, underemployment and income distribution*. Monograph No. 16 (Santiago, PREALC, Sep. 1980).

J. Ramos: *Segmentación del mercado de capital y empleo*. Occasional papers No. 35 (Santiago, PREALC, Nov. 1980).

V.E. Tokman: *Growth, underemployment and income distribution*. Occasional papers No. 30, Rev. 1. (Santiago, PREALC, Aug. 1980).

V.E. Tokman: *Influencia del sector informal urbano sobre la desigualdad económica*. Monograph No. 15 (Santiago, PREALC, Aug. 1980). E, S.

El sector informal urbano y la formación profesional. Occasional papers No. 36 (Santiago, PREALC, Mar. 1981).

N.E. García and M. Marfán: *Un marco analítico para la estimación de encadenamientos de empleo*. Occasional papers No. 41 (Santiago, PREALC, July 1981). [BRA]

C. Piña: *Sector informal: Estrategias ocupacionales y orientaciones ideológicas*. Monograph No. 20 (Santiago, PREALC, July 1981). [CHL]

J. Ramos: *Inversión en capital humano y la oferta de trabajo*. Occasional papers No. 37 (Santiago, PREALC, Mar. 1981).

A. Uthoff: *Changes in earnings inequality and labour market segmentation*. Monograph No. 21 (Santiago, PREALC, Aug. 1981).

Mercado de trabajo en cifras. 1950-1980 (Santiago, PREALC, 1982), xix + 180 pp. Sw. frs. 16. ISBN 92-2-302971-6.

N.E. García and M. Marfán: *Estructuras industriales y eslabonamientos de empleo*. Monograph No. 26 (Santiago, PREALC, Dec. 1982).

N.E. García: *Absorción creciente con subempleo persistente: América latina 1950-80*. Occasional papers No. 48 (Santiago, PREALC, June 1982).

M.A. Ropert: *Sindicatos y salarios reales en la industria chilena 1979-1981*. Monograph No. 25 (Santiago, PREALC, Sep. 1982). [CHL]

Movilidad ocupacional y mercados de trabajo (Santiago, PREALC, 1983), x + 263 pp. Sw. frs. 17.50. [BRA, BOL, CHL, ARG] ISBN 92-2-303605-4.

H.C. Haan: *El sector informal en Centroamérica*. Investigation on Employment No. 27 (Santiago, PREALC, 1985).

Cambio y polarización ocupacional en Centroamérica. Ponencias del Coloquio Subregional sobre la Repercusión de la Crisis Económica en los Mercados Laborales Centroamericanos, Ciudad de Panamá, octubre de 1985 (Santiago, PREALC, 1986), 174 pp. [CRI, SLV, GTM, HND, NIC, PAN]

Imagenes del trabajo. 4° Concurso internacional de arte: El empleo o El empleo o su carencia 1986 (Santiago, PREALC, 1987), 78 pp. ISBN 92-2-305897-X.

Política salarial, inflación y restricción externa (Santiago, PREALC, 1987), x + 180 pp. US$ 7. [ECU, VEN, GTM, CRI, ARG, BRA] ISBN 92-2-306175-X.

J. Mezzera: *Credito y capacitación para el sector informal*. Investigation on Employment No. 29 (Santiago, PREALC, 1987). ISBN 92-2-306227-6.

A. Touraine: *Actores sociales y sistemas políticos en América Latina* (Santiago, PREALC, 1987), xv + 256 pp. US$ 8. ISBN 92-2-305887-2.

- Asia

S.V. Sethuraman in collaboration with P. Bangasser: *Rural small industries and employment in Sri Lanka: Results of a sample survey*. Rural industrialisation and employment project, technical report no. 1 (Geneva, ILO, 1983), 80 pp. + appendices. [LKA] ISBN 92-2-103639-1.

- OECD Countries

G. Standing: *Unemployment and labour market flexibility. The United Kingdom* (Geneva, ILO, 1986), xi + 147 pp. Sw. frs. 30. [GBR] ISBN 92-2-105291-5.

Articles in the International Labour Review

- General

R. Anker and C. Hein: "Why Third World urban employers usually prefer men", Vol. 124, No. 1, Jan.-Feb. 1985.

- Africa

G. Nihan and R. Jourdain: "The modern informal sector in Nouakchott", Vol. 117, No. 6, Nov.-Dec. 1978. [MRT]

G. Nihan, E. Demol and C. Jondoh: "The modern informal sector in Lomé", Vol. 118, No. 5, Sep.-Oct. 1979. [TGO]

E. Chuta and C. Liedholm: "Employment growth and change in Sierra Leone small-scale industry: 1974-80", Vol. 121, No. 1, Jan.-Feb. 1982. [SLE]

E. Demol and G. Nihan: "The modern informal sector in Yaoundé",[1] Vol. 121, No. 1, Jan.-Feb. 1982. [CMR]

- Asia

A. Stretton: "Circular migration, segmented labour markets and efficiency: The building industry in Manila and Port Moresby", Vol. 122, No. 5, Sep.-Oct. 1983. [PHL, PNG]

S.V. Sethuraman: "The informal sector in Indonesia: Policies and prospects", Vol. 124, No. 6, Nov.-Dec. 1985. [IDN]

R. Anker, M.E. Khan and R.B. Gupta: "Biases in measuring the labour force. Results of a methods test survey in Uttar Pradesh, India", Vol. 126, No. 2, Mar.-Apr. 1987. [IND]

A.T.M. Nurul Amin: "The role of the informal sector in economic development. Some evidence from Dhaka, Bangladesh", Vol. 126, No. 5, Sep.-Oct. 1987. [BGD]

Working Papers

- **General**

M. Carton: *La formation dans le secteur non-structuré*, Sep. 1980 (WEP 2-33/WP.18).

G. Standing: *A labour status approach to labour statistics*, Aug. 1983 (WEP 2-21/WP.139). M. ISBN 92-2-103558-1.

G.B. Rodgers *Labour markets, labour processes and economic development: Some research issues*, Sep. 1985 (WEP 2-43/WP. 1). ISBN 92-2-105288-5.

S.V. Sethuraman: *Basic needs and the informal sector: The case of low-income housing in developing countries*, Jan. 1985 (WEP 2-19/WP. 35). ISBN 92-2-205013-1.

G. Standing: *Labour flexibility: Towards a research agenda*, Apr. 1986 (WEP 2-43/WP.3). ISBN 92-2-105538-8.

- **Africa**

Coût des facteurs de production et tarif douanier au Sénégal: Leur incidence sur le développement de l'industrie et de l'emploi (Addis Ababa, JASPA), 1978. [SEN]

E. Demol: *Analyse des résultats du recensement du secteur non-structuré de Lomé, République du Togo*, 1978 (WEP 2-33/Doc.6). M. [TGO]

D.A. Fowler: *The informal sector of Freetown (Sierra Leone)*, [2] Apr. 1978 (WEP 2-19/WP.26) M. [SLE]

O.J. Fapohunda: *The informal sector of Lagos: An inquiry into urban poverty and employment*, [2] Aug. 1978 (WEP 2-19/WP.32). [NGA]

R. Jourdain: *Analyse des résultats du recensement du secteur non-structuré de la ville de Bamako, République du Mali*, 1978 (WEP 2-33/Doc.8)*. M. [MLI]

G. Nihan, in collaboration with D. Viry and R. Jourdain: *Le secteur non-structuré "moderne" de Nouakchott, République islamique de Mauritanie - Rapport d'enquête et analyse des résultats*, 1978 (WEP 2-33/Doc.4). M. [MRT]

G. Nihan, in collaboration with R. Jourdain and E. Demol: *Le secteur non-structuré "moderne" de Nouakchott, République islamique de Mauritanie: Resumé des résultats et propositions pour une contribution au développement de son potentiel de formation et d'emploi*, 1978 (WEP 2-33/Doc.5)*. M. [MRT]

G. Nihan, M. Carton, E. Demol and C. Jondoh: *Le secteur non-structuré "moderne" de Lomé, République togolaise - Esquisse des résultats de l'enquête et programme d'action*, 1978 (WEP 2-33/Doc.13). M. [TGO]

G. Nihan, with the collaboration of E. Demol, D. Viry and C. Jondoh: *Le secteur non-structuré "moderne" de Lomé, République du Togo - Rapport d'enquête et analyse des résultats*, 1978 (WEP 2-33/Doc.11). M. [TGO]

B. Balkenhol: *Small contractors: Untapped potential or economic impediment? Some observations on the construction industry in Cameroon, Niger and Sierra Leone*, Apr. 1979 (WEP 2-22/WP.48). M. [CMR, SLE, NER]

G. Nihan, M. Carton and H. Sidibé: *Le secteur non-structuré "moderne" de Bamako, République du Mali: Esquisse des résultats de l'enquête et propositions pour un programme d'action*, 1979 (WEP 2-33/Doc.15)*. M. [MLI]

G. Nihan, R. Jourdain and H. Sidibé: *Le secteur non-structuré "moderne" de Bamako, République du Mali: Synthèse des résultats de l'enquête*, 1979 (WEP 2-33/Doc.14)*. [MLI]

Secteur non-structuré "moderne": Une première synthèse à partir de l'étude de cinq villes, Sep. 1980 (WEP 2-33/WP.17). [MRT, TGO, MLI, CMR, RWA]

G. Nihan and E. Demol, with the collaboration of A.A. Tabi: *Le secteur non-structuré "moderne" de Yaoundé, République unie du Cameroun - Rapport d'enquête et analyse des résultats,* [1] Sep. 1980 (WEP 2-33/Doc.16). [CMR]

G. Nihan and M. Carton: *Le secteur non-structuré "moderne" de Kigali - République du Rwanda - Propositions pour un programme d'action*, Jan. 1980 (WEP 2-33/Doc.19). [RWA]

G. Nihan, with the collaboration of D. Viry and J. Schwartz: *Le secteur non-structuré de Kigali, République du Rwanda: Rapport d'enquête et analyse des résultats*, Sep. 1980 (WEP 2-33/Doc.10). [RWA]

A.A. Suliman: *Some technological issues of informal sector industries in Khartoum*, July 1980 (WEP 2-22/WP.62). M. [SDN]

A. Kamya: *Factors affecting efficiency in the informal sector in Lusaka and Kitwe* (Lusaka, SATEP), Nov. 1981. [ZMB]

J.M. Mulwila and R.K. Mushota: *The legal framework within which the informal sector functions in Zambia* (Lusaka, SATEP), Nov. 1981. [ZMB]

U.K. Olsson: *Trade policies and their impact on the informal sector in Zambia: Some issues* (Lusaka, SATEP), Sep. 1981. [ZMB]

H.C. Haan: *Some characteristics of informal sector businessmen in Lusaka and Kitwe, Zambia* (Lusaka, SATEP), July 1982. [ZMB]

H.C. Haan: *The structure of manufacturing industry in Zambia and its implications for the development of the informal sector* (Lusaka, SATEP), Aug. 1982. [ZMB]

T. Mkandawire: *The informal sector in the labour reserve economies of Southern Africa; with special reference to Zimbabwe* (Lusaka, SATEP), 1984. [ZWE] ISBN 92-2-103705-3.

W.J. House: *The state of human resources, conditions of employment and determinants of incomes and poverty in Southern Sudan: Evidence from the urban Juba informal economy*, May 1985 (WEP 2-21/WP. 149). [SDN] ISBN 92-2-105144-7.

C. Maldonado: *Programme d'appui au secteur non-structuré urbain d'Afrique francophone (1ère phase). Premier rapport d'avancement des activités du programme* (Feb. 1982 - Jan. 1983), Aug. 1985 (WEP 2-33/Doc. 22). ISBN 92-2-205207-6.

J.C. Woillet: *L'artisanat urbain au Mali: Eléments pour une politique de l'artisanat*, Aug. 1985 (WEP 2-33/Doc. 21). [MLI] ISBN 92-2-205271-4.

A. Barampama: *A l'écoute des artisans du secteur non structuré de Kigali. Résultats d'une recherche-action participative*, 1986 (WEP 2-33/Doc. 25). [RWA] ISBN 92-2-205491-1.

A. Carrizo: *Les micro-entreprises à Ouagadougou: Analyse et stratégie de développement*, Nov. 1986 (WEP 2-19/WP.38). [BFA] ISBN 92-2-205664-7.

F. Mbali: *The growth of black trade unionism in South Africa, its role in influencing changes in wage differentials with special reference to the mining industry* (Lusaka, SATEP), May 1986. [ZAF] ISBN 92-2-105343-1.

M. Penouil and J-P. Lachaud: *Le secteur informel et la marche du travail en Afrique noire francophone*, Apr. 1986 (WEP 2-19/WP.37). ISBN 92-2-205521-7.

- **Latin America and the Caribbean**

Análisis sobre el proceso de subcontratación en el sector linea blanca en Chile (Santiago, PREALC), Sep. 1978 (No. 159). [CHL]

Efectos del codigo del trabajo sobre el empleo, la productividad, los costos y la inversión en Panamá (Santiago, PREALC), Aug. 1978 (No. 156).* [PAN]

Empleo, distribución del ingreso y necesidades básicas en América Latina (Santiago, PREALC), June 1978 (No. 148).* [ARG, BRA, COL, CRI, CHL, HND, MEX, PER, URY, VEN]

La situación del empleo de los recursos humanos en las regiones de colonización del ITCO (Costa Rica) (Santiago, PREALC), May 1978 (No. 125). [CRI]

La situación ocupacional en Centroamérica y Panamá (Santiago, PREALC), Aug. 1978 (No. 153).* [PAN]

Tipo de cambio, empleo y pobreza: El caso de Bolivia (Santiago, PREALC), July 1978 (No. 152). [BOL]

Archivo de datos ocupacionales sobre América Latina y el Caribe (Santiago, PREALC), May 1979 (No. 168).

Archivo de datos sobre Bolivia (Santiago, PREALC), May 1979 (No. 169). [BOL]

Entrevistas en profundidad a empresas y trabajadores del sector informal en la reparación de automóviles (Santiago, PREALC), July 1979 (No. 175). [CHL]

Centroamérica y Panamá: Archivo de datos ocupacionales en el sector industrial (Santiago, PREALC), Oct. 1980 (No. 206).* [PAN]

Los trabajadores por cuenta propia en Santiago (Santiago, PREALC), Mar. 1980 (No. 184). [CHL]

Necesidades de capacitación de los trabajadores por cuenta propia en Santiago (Santiago, PREALC), Apr. 1980 (No. 186). [CHL]

Panamá: Instrumentos de incentivo al desarrollo industrial y su efecto en el empleo (Santiago, PREALC), Feb. 1980 (No. 179). [PAN]

Panamá: Segmentación del mercado de trabajo: Información estadística básica (Santiago, PREALC), Sep. 1982 (No. 216). [PAN]

Efectos ocupacionales de la inversión pública. Proposiciones metodólogicas y su aplicación a algunas experiencias en Brasil (Santiago, PREALC), Oct. 1983 (No. 230). [BRA]

Costa Rica: Características de las microempresas y sus dueños, (Santiago, PREALC) Nov. 1984 (No. 253). [CRI]

La actividad comercial de los mercados persas de Santiago. Efectos sobre el empleo y los ingresos, (Santiago, PREALC) May 1984 (No. 240). [CHL]

Panamá: Situación y perspectivas del empleo en el sector informal urbano, (Santiago, PREALC) Mar. 1984 (No. 236). [PAN]

Barreras institucionales de entrada al sector informal en la ciudad de Mexico (Santiago, PREALC), Mar. 1985 (No. 258). [MEX]

Barreras institucionales de entrada al sector informal en Lima metropolitana (Santiago, PREALC), Jan. 1985 (No. 255). [PER]

Enfoques alternativos sobre el mercado del trabajo: Un examen de los modelos neoclásico, keynesiano, neomarxista y de segmentación (Santiago, PREALC), Nov. 1985 (No. 272).

The urban informal sector and labour market information systems (Santiago, PREALC), Oct. 1986 (No. 283).

R. Infante and G. García-Huidobro: *Studies on labour market modelling and employment planning in Central America*, June 1986 (WEP 2-43/WP.8). [GTM, VEN, BRA] ISBN 92-2-105720-8.

La microempresa en la rama de la confección. Estudios de casos en la ciudad de Lima (Santiago, PREALC), Apr. 1987 (No. 295). [PER]

Modelos de capital humano y segmentacion: Quienes obtienen retornos superiores? (Santiago, PREALC), Sep. 1987 (No. 306).

Notes on segmented labour markets in urban areas (Santiago, PREALC), Feb. 1987 (No. 289). E,S.

Pobreza y mercado de trabajo en cuatro paises: Costa Rica, Venezuala, Chile y Peru (Santiago, PREALC), Oct. 1987 (No. 309). [CRI, VEN, CHL, PER]

Poverty and labour market in Costa Rica (Santiago, PREALC), Feb. 1987 (No. 288) [CRI].

- Asia

G.M. Jurado and J.S. Castro: *The informal sector in the greater Manila area, 1976: An overview,* [2] Aug. 1978 (WEP 2-19/WP.34) M. [PHL]

H. Moir: *The Jakarta informal sector,* [3] June 1978 (WEP 2-19/WP.31) M. [IDN]

Y.A. Panditrao: *Development and transfer of technology in village industries in India: Experiences of the Khadi and village industries commission*, July 1982 (WEP 2-37/WP.10). [IND] ISBN 92-2-103156-X.

A.N. Bose: *Intersectoral linkage in a comprehensive area development approach: The case of West Bengal*, Apr. 1983 (WEP 2-37/WP. 11). [IND] ISBN 92-2-103482-8.

I.Z. Bhatty: *Policies for promoting small scale industries: A framework for analysis* (Bangkok, ARTEP), 1984. ISBN 92-2-103686-3.

Kirloskar Consultants: *Technology adaptation in plastic processing industry in the informal sector: A case study in India*, Jan. 1985 (WEP 2-19/WP. 36). [IND] ISBN 92-2-105025-4.

- OECD Countries

B. Harrison and B. Bluestone: *The dark side of labour market "flexibility": Falling wages and growing income inequality in America*, Oct. 1987 (WEP 2-43/WP.17). [USA] ISBN 92-2-106264-3.

- Middle East

H.T. Azzam: *Labour market structure in Saudi Arabia* (Beirut, LPME), 1980 (WP. 1), 40 pp. [SAU] ISBN 92-2-102501-2.

W.J. House: *Labour market segmentation and labour policies in Cyprus: Some empirical evidence* (Beirut, LPME), 1980 (WP.5), 39 pp. [CYP] ISBN 92-2-102512-8.

W.J. House: *Labour market segmentation: Evidence from Cyprus,* [4] May 1982 (WEP 2-21/WP.117). M. [CYP] ISBN 92-2-103110-1.

ILO works published by commercial and non-profit-making publishers

- Africa

E. Chuta and C. Liedholm: *Employment and growth in small-scale industry. Empirical evidence and policy assessment from Sierra Leone* (London, Macmillan, 1985), x + 265 pp. [SLE] ISBN 0-333-38788-0.

- Latin America and the Caribbean

R. Cortázar, A. Foxley and V.E. Tokman: *Legados del monetarismo: Argentina y Chile* (Buenos Aires, Ediciones Solar, 1984), 146 pp. [ARG, CHL] ISBN 950-9086-14-2.

Cambio y polarización ocupacional en Centroamérica (Costa Rica, EDUCA, 1986), 202 pp. [CRI, SLV, GTM, HND, NIC, PAN] ISBN 92-2-305432-X.

México: La pequeña industria en una estrategia de empleo productivo (México, Dirección del Empleo, 1978).* [MEX]

- Asia

Marga Institute: *The informal sector of Colombo City (Sri Lanka)* (Colombo, Marga Publications, 1978), x + 155 pp. [LKA]

Related books and articles

- General

G. Nihan: "Le secteur non-structuré: Signification, aire d'extension du concept et application expérimentale", in *Revue Tiers-Monde* (Paris), Tome XXI, No. 82, Apr.-June 1980.

- Africa

G. Le Boterf: "Les apprentis dans le projet d'appui au secteur non-structuré urbain de Bamako (éléments d'une recherche participative et propositions pour l'action)", in *Genève-Afrique* (Geneva, IUED), Vol. XXII, No. 1, 1984. [MLI]

Notes:

1 Summary of G. Nihan, E. Demol with the collaboration of A.B. Tabi: Le secteur non-structuré "moderne" de Yaoundé, République-unie du Cameroun (Geneva, ILO, 1982).

2 A shorter version of this paper is included in: S.V. Sethuraman (ed.): The urban informal sector in developing countries - Employment, poverty and environment (Geneva, ILO, 1981)

3 Superseded by H. Moir: Jakarta informal sector. Monograph series (Jakarta, National Institute of Economic and Social Research, Indonesian Institute of Sciences, 1979).

4 Also published in R. Anker and C. Hein (eds.): Sex inequalities in urban employment in the Third World (London, Macmillan, 1986).

Rural poverty, rural industrialisation and employment

ILO publications

Books and reports

- **General**

The participation of the rural poor in development. Releasing the creative energies of rural workers (Geneva, ILO, n.d.), 55 pp. E, F, S. ISBN 92-2-105285-0.

Poverty and employment in rural areas of the developing countries (ACRD IX/1979/II). Advisory Committee on Rural Development (Ninth Session, Geneva, ILO, 27 Nov.-6 Dec. 1979), 56 pp. Sw. frs. 15. E*, F, S.

Profiles of rural poverty. A popularised version of *Poverty and landlessness in rural Asia*, with additional material on Africa and Latin America. (Geneva, ILO, 1979), viii + 50 pp. Sw. frs. 7.50. [BGD, IND, MYS, CHN] ISBN 92-2-102142-4.

Review of ILO rural development activities since 1974 (ACRD IX/1979/I). Advisory Committee on Rural Development (Ninth Session, Geneva, ILO, 27 Nov.-6 Dec. 1979), 52 pp. Sw. frs. 15. E*, F, S.

Rural employers' and workers' organisations and participation (ACRD IX/1979/III), Advisory Committee on Rural Development (Ninth Session, Geneva, ILO, 17 Nov.-6 Dec. 1979), 56 pp. Sw. frs. 15. E, F, S.

I.J. Barwell and J.D.G.E. Howe: *Appropriate transport facilities for the rural sector in developing countries* (Geneva, ILO, Jan. 1979), ii + 80 pp.

D. Ghai, E. Lee, J. Maeda and S. Radwan: *Overcoming rural under-development.* Proceedings of a workshop on alternative agrarian systems and rural development, Arusha, the United Republic of Tanzania, 4-14 Apr. 1979 (Geneva, ILO, 1979), vi + 98 pp. Sw. frs. 12.50. [TZA] ISBN 92-2-102149-1.

Promotion of employment and incomes for the rural poor, including rural women, through non-farm activities (ACRDX/1983/II). Advisory Committee on Rural Development (Tenth Session, Geneva, ILO, 22 Nov.-1 Dec. 1983), 132 pp. Sw. frs. 17.50. E,F,S. ISBN 92-2-103506-9.

Review of ILO rural development activities since 1979 (ACRD X/1983/I). Advisory Committee on Rural Development (Tenth Session, Geneva, ILO, 22 Nov.-1 Dec. 1983), ii + 62 pp. Sw. frs. 12.50. E,F,S. ISBN 92-2-103505-0.

Rural labour markets and employment policies: Issues relating to labour utilisation, remuneration and the position of women (ACRD X/1983/III). Advisory Committee on Rural Development (Tenth Session, Geneva, ILO, 22 Nov.-1 Dec. 1983), iii + 92 pp. Sw. frs. 15. E,F,S. ISBN 92-2-103507-7.

Selected list of books, reports and major documents and articles concerning rural development published or sponsored by the ILO from May 1979 to April 1983 (ACRD X/1983/I (Supplement). Advisory Committee on Rural Development (Tenth Session, Geneva, ILO, 22 Nov.-1 Dec. 1983), 42 pp.

Md.A. Rahman: *Participatory organisations of the rural poor.* Introduction to an ILO Programme (Geneva, ILO, 1984) [IND] ISBN 92-2-103716-9.

P. Oakley and D. Marsden: *Approaches to participation in rural development* (Geneva, ILO, 1984; 4th impression, 1987), x + 91 pp. Sw. frs. 15. E, F, S. [NPL, IND, ETH, BRA] ISBN 92-2-103594-8.

Review of ILO rural development activities since 1983 (PACRD/1/1985/I). Panel of the Advisory Committee on Rural Development (Geneva, ILO, 1985), 43 pp. Sw. frs. 10. E,F,S. ISBN 92-2-105312-1.

Selection of two technical items for discussion at the Eleventh Session of the Advisory Committee on Rural Development in 1987 (PACRD/1/1985/II). Panel of the Advisory Committee on Rural Development (Geneva, ILO, 1985), 16 pp. Sw. frs. 6. E,F,S. ISBN 92-2-105313-X.

The challenge of rural poverty. A progress report on research and technical co-operation concerning rural employment, agrarian institutions and policies. (Geneva, ILO, 3rd ed., 1985), iii + 53 pp. E,F,S. ISBN 92-2-100531-3.

Strategies for promoting rural employment. Report on an international seminar on rural employment promotion strategies. (Geneva, ILO, 1987), 73 pp. [CHN] ISBN 92-2-105937-5.

- Africa

Rural development: Options for Namibia. Proceedings of a workshop held in Lusaka, 5-15 October 1983. Compiled by Iq. Ahmed (Geneva, ILO, n.d.), 49 pp. [NAM]

Z. Svejnar: *Employment and technology in African agriculture and industry* (Addis Ababa, JASPA, 1978).

D. Baytelman: *La agricultura en Cabo Verde y la satisfacción de las necesidades básicas de sus habitantes* (Geneva, ILO, 1979). [CPV]

J. de Veen: *The rural access roads programme: Appropriate technology in Kenya* (Geneva, ILO, 1980; 3rd impression, 1984), viii + 168 pp. Sw. frs. 20. E,F. [KEN] ISBN 92-2-102204-8.

R. Dumont, C. Reboul and M. Mazoyer: *Pauvreté et inégalités rurales en Afrique de l'Ouest francophone* (Haute-Volta, Sénégal, Côte-d'Ivoire) (Geneva, ILO, 1981), xiii + 78 pp. Sw. frs. 15. [SEN, CIV, BFA] ISBN 92-2-202700-0.

W. Keddeman: *Rural development and employment in Africa - A review of JASPA reports and priorities for future action* (Addis Ababa, JASPA, 1981).

Manpower demand and supply in the agricultural sector of member states of the Mano River union (Addis Ababa, JASPA, 1982), x + 156 pp. [SEN]

Eléments pour une stratégie d'emploi dans les zônes rurales au Togo. Rapport d'une mission du PECTA présenté au Gouvernement du Togo (Addis Ababa, JASPA, 1983), 80 pp. [TGO]

D. Ghai and S. Radwan (eds.): *Agrarian policies and rural poverty in Africa* (Geneva, ILO, 1983; 2nd impression, 1985), x + 312 pp. Sw. frs. 27.50. [KEN, CIV, MWI, BWA, NGA, MOZ, SOM, ZMB, GHA] ISBN 92-2-103100-4.

An assessment of the rural labour markets in the Sudan (Addis Ababa, JASPA, 1984), ii + 60 pp. [SDN]

Labour use and productivity and technological change in African smallholder agriculture: The case of Gambia (Addis Ababa, JASPA, 1985), x + 204 pp. [GMB] ISBN 92-2-105039-4.

Labour use and productivity and technological change in African smallholder agriculture: The case of Ghana (Addis Ababa, JASPA, 1985), viii + 134 pp. [GHA] ISBN 92-2-92-2-105041-6.

Labour use and productivity and technological change in African smallholder agriculture: The case of Sudan (Addis Ababa, JASPA, 1985), v + 1 50 pp. [SDN] ISBN 92-2-105076-9.

Labour use and productivity and technological change in African smallholder agriculture: The case of Uganda (Addis Ababa, JASPA, 1985), iv + 175 pp. [UGA] ISBN 92-2-105105-6.

Labour use and productivity and technological change in African smallholder agriculture: The case of Zimbabwe (Addis Ababa, JASPA, 1985), ii + 75 pp. [ZWE] ISBN 92-2-105042-4.

Politiques de développement rural en Afrique. Impacts sur l'emploi et les revenus. Cas de Madagascar (Addis Ababa, JASPA, 1985), vi + 140 pp. [MDG] ISBN 92-2-205253-6.

Politiques de développement rural en Afrique. Impacts sur l'emploi et les revenus. Cas du Gabon (Addis Ababa, JASPA, 1985), iv + 110 pp. [GAB] ISBN 92-2-205252-8

Report of joint inter-agency mission on the preparatory work for the establishment of an African regional network for agricultural tools and equipment. Sudan, Ethiopia, the United Republic of Tanzania, Zambia, Botswana, and Kenya, Jan.-Mar. 1985 (Geneva/Rome, ILO/FAO, 1985), xii + 114 pp. [BWA, SDN, ETH, TZA, ZMB, KEN] ISBN 92-2-105212-5.

M. Fafchamps: *Labour use and productivity and technological change in African smallholder agriculture. A case study of Northern Nigeria* (Addis Ababa, JASPA, 1985), iv + 50 pp. [NGA] ISBN 92-2-105075-1.

M. Fafchamps: *Labour use and productivity and technological change in African smallholder agriculture. Synthesis report* (Addis Ababa, JASPA, 1985), iii + 114 pp. ISBN 92-2-105040-8.

Iq. Ahmed (ed.): *Rural development: Options for Namibia after independence*. Selected papers and proceedings of a workshop organised by the ILO, SWAPO, and UNIN, Lusaka, Zambia, 5-15 October 1983 (Geneva, ILO, 1985), vi + 154 pp. Sw. frs. 20. [BWA, NAM, ZMB, ZWE, TZA, AGO] ISBN 92-2-103853-X.

J.D. Rogers: *Patterns of rural development and impact on employment and incomes (A comparative sub-regional study): Synthesis report* (Addis Ababa, JASPA, 1985), iv + 118 pp. [LBR, SLE, TZA, MWI, KEN, ETH, SDN, SOM] ISBN 92-2-105038-6.

J.D. Rogers: *Patterns of rural development and impact on employment and incomes (A comparative sub-regional study): The case of Ethiopia* (Addis Ababa, JASPA, 1985), 88 pp. [ETH] ISBN 92-2-105037-8.

J.D. Rogers: *Patterns of rural development and impact on employment and incomes (A comparative sub-regional study): The case of Kenya* (Addis Ababa, JASPA, 1985), iv + 107 pp. [KEN] ISBN 92-2-105063-7.

J.D. Rogers: *Patterns of rural development and impact on employment and incomes (A comparative sub-regional study): The case of Liberia* (Addis Ababa, JASPA, 1985), v + 101 pp. [LBR] ISBN 92-2-105033-5.

J.D. Rogers: *Patterns of rural development and impact on employment and incomes (A comparative sub-regional study): The case of Sierra Leone* (Addis Ababa, JASPA, 1985), iv + 109 pp. [SLE] ISBN 92-2-105064-5.

J.D. Rogers: *Patterns of rural development and impact on employment and incomes (A comparative sub-regional study): The case of Somalia* (Addis Ababa, JASPA, 1985), 103 pp. [SOM] ISBN 92-2-105036-X.

J.D. Rogers: *Patterns of rural development and impact on employment and incomes (A comparative sub-regional study): The case of Sudan* (Addis Ababa, JASPA, 1985), iii + 79 pp. [SDN] ISBN 92-2-105032-7.

Excess manufacturing capacity and farm equipment needs in Kenya. Paper and proceedings of a national workshop on farm tools and equipment technology, basic needs and employment, Nairobi, Kenya, 15-18 October 1985 (Geneva, ILO, 1986), vii + 117 pp. Sw. frs. 17.50. [KEN] ISBN 92-2-105484-5.

Initiatives for farm equipment programmes in Botswana: Improving co-ordination. Papers and proceedings of a national workshop on farm tools and equipment technology, basic needs and employment, Gaborone, Botswana, 3-5 December 1985 (Geneva, ILO, 1986), vii + 113 pp. Sw. frs. 20. [BWA] ISBN 92-2-105485-3.

Promotion de l'emploi rural et développement des PME/PMI au Cameroun. Rapport soumis au Gouvernment du Cameroun par une mission d'assistance technique BIT/PECTA (Addis Ababa, JASPA, 1986), xxv + 159 pp. US$7. [CMR] ISBN 92-2-205722-8.

J. Greer and E. Thorbecke: *Food poverty and consumption patterns in Kenya* (Geneva, ILO, 1986), xii + 170 pp. Sw. frs. 20. [KEN] ISBN 92-2-105374-1.

Coping with technological dualism in the farm equipment sector of the Sudan. Papers and proceedings of national workshop on farm tools and equipment technology, basic needs and employment, Khartoum, Sudan, 12-14 November 1985 (Geneva, ILO, 1987), vii + 97 pp. Sw. frs. 20. [SDN] ISBN 92-2-105481-0.

In quest of agricultural mechanisation policy and strategies in the United Republic of Tanzania. Papers and proceedings of a national workshop on farm tools and equipment technology, basic needs and employment, Dar es Salaam, 8-10 October 1985 (Geneva, ILO, 1987), vii + 69 pp. Sw. frs. 12.50. [TZA] ISBN 92-2-105482-9.

- Latin America and the Caribbean

E. García D'Acuña: *Heterogeneous rural labour market and employment*. Monograph No. 11 (Santiago, PREALC, June 1978).

C. Olavarría: *La asignación de tierras en Chile (1973-1976), sus efectos en el empleo agrícola*. Monograph No. 9 (Santiago, PREALC, Mar. 1978). [CHL]

Economía campesina y empleo (Santiago, PREALC, 1981), xvi + 326 pp. Sw. frs. 22. [BRA, PER, VEN, ARG, PRY, CHL, BOL, ECU, COL] ISBN 92-2-302549-4.

A. Hintermeister: *El empleo agrícola en una estructura en transformación: El caso de Nicaragua*. Occasional papers No. 46 (Santiago, PREALC, Mar. 1982). [NIC]

A. Hintermeister: *Modernización de la agricultura y pobreza rural en Guatemala*. Occasional papers No. 45 (Panama, PREALC, Apr. 1982). [GTM]

B. Tomíc: *Participación popular y desarrollo en la base*. Monograph No. 40 (Santiago, PREALC, Oct. 1984).

- Asia

P.K. Bardhan, A. Vaidyanathan, Y. Alagh, G.S. Bhalla and A. Bhadurai: *Labour absorption in Indian agriculture: Some exploratory investigations* (Bangkok, ARTEP/ILO, Nov. 1978). * [IND] ISBN 92-2-102023-1.

Y. Hara: *Labour absorption in Asian agriculture: Japanese experience* (Bangkok, ARTEP, 1978; 2nd impression, 1981). [JPN]

S. Ishikawa: *Labour absorption in Asian agriculture*, An "issues" paper (Bangkok, ARTEP, 1978; 2nd impression, 1981), 109 pp. US$8. [TWN, CHN, JPN] ISBN 92-2-101986-1.

Employment expansion in Indian agriculture - Proceedings of a national seminar held in Bangalore (Bangkok, ARTEP, 1979). * [IND]

Employment expansion in Asian agriculture: A comparative analysis of South-Asian countries (Bangkok, ARTEP, Mar. 1980), vii + 292 pp.* [BGD, PAK, LKA] ISBN 92-2-102344-3.

Labour absorption in agriculture: The East Asian experience (Bangkok, ARTEP, July 1980), 286 pp. US$5.* [JPN, TWN, CHN] ISBN 92-2-102426-1.

I. Ahmed: *Technological change and agrarian structure* - A study of Bangladesh (Geneva, ILO, 1981), xvi + 136 pp. Sw. frs. 15. [BGD] ISBN 92-2-102543-8.

K. Griffin and A. Saith: *Growth and equality in rural China* (Bangkok, ARTEP, 1981), x + 166 pp. Sw. frs. 17.50. [CHN] ISBN 92-2-102427-X.

A.R. Khan and E. Lee: *The expansion of productive employment in agriculture: The relevance of the East Asian experience for developing Asian countries* (Bangkok, ARTEP, 1981).

Md.A. Rahman: *Sarilakas: A pilot project for stimulating grass-roots participation in the Philippines*. Technical co-operation. Evaluation report (Geneva, ILO, 1983), 44 pp.* [PHL] ISBN 92-2-103466-6.

W. Gooneratne (ed.): *Labour absorption in rice-based agriculture: Case studies from South-East Asia* (Bangkok, ARTEP, 1982), xvi + 182 pp. Sw. frs. 8.75. [IDN, THA, PHL] ISBN 92-2-102747-3.

S. Ishikawa, S. Yamada and S. Hirashima: *Labour absorption and growth in agriculture - China and Japan* (Bangkok, ARTEP, 1982), viii + 102 pp. Sw. frs. 14. [CHN, JPN] ISBN 92-2-102744-9.

Landlessness in Upper Northern Thailand (Bangkok, ARTEP and ALRO (Agricultural Land Reform Office, Government of Thailand), 1983), 190 pp. [THA]

A.R. Khan and E. Lee: *Agrarian policies and institutions in China after Mao*. (Bangkok, ARTEP, 1983), viii + 128 pp. Sw. frs. 14. [CHN] ISBN 92-2-103281-7

Employment and income generation in agriculture in the district of Hambantota, Sri Lanka (Bangkok, ARTEP, 1984), 92 pp. [LKA].

W. Gooneratne and D. Wesumperuma (eds.): *Plantation agriculture in Sri Lanka. Issues in employment and development* (Bangkok, ARTEP, 1984), xiv + 257 pp. Sw. frs. 14. [LKA]

Group-based savings and credit for the rural poor. Papers and proceedings of a workshop held in Bogra (Bangladesh), 6-10 November 1983. Panel on People's Participation of the ACC Task Force on Rural Development (Geneva, ILO, 1984), xii + 126 pp. Sw. frs. 17.50. [BGD, IND, PAK, LKA, PHL, NPL, THA] ISBN 92-2-103891-2.

A.R. Khan and E. Lee (eds.): *Poverty in rural Asia* (Bangkok, ARTEP, 1984), xii + 276 pp. Sw. frs. 22. [PAK, IND, LKA, NPL, BGD, THA, IDN] ISBN 92-2-103286-8.

V.M. Rao, G.H. Peiris and S. Tilakaratne: *Planning for rural development. The experience of the district integrated rural development programme of Sri Lanka* (Bangkok, ARTEP, 1984), ii + 118 pp. US$ 5. [LKA]

D.J.C. Forsyth: *Mechanisation of sugar harvesting in Fiji* (Geneva, ILO, 1985) [FJI]

R. Islam (ed.): *Strategies for alleviating poverty in rural Asia* (Bangkok, Bangladesh Institute of Development Studies, Dhaka/ARTEP, 1985), xii + 315 pp. Sw. frs. 17.50. [BGD, IND, NPL, PAK, LKA] ISBN 92-2-103398-2.

Rural development in the Vientiane province. A report to the Government of the Lao People's Democratic Republic (New Delhi, ARTEP, 1986), i + 132 pp. [LAO]

The impact of economic liberalisation on the small scale and rural industries of Sri Lanka. A report prepared for the Ministry of Rural Industrial Development, Government of Sri Lanka (New Delhi, ARTEP, 1986), iv + 60 pp. [LKA]

S. Hirashima and M. Muqtada: *Hired labour and rural labour markets in Asia. Studies based on farm-level data* (New Delhi, ARTEP, 1986), 180 pp. US$ 8. [BGD, PAK, PHL, THA] ISBN 92-2-105475-6.

Rural industries and employment in Sri Lanka. A report prepared by the Ministry of Rural Industrial Development, Government of Sri Lanka (New Delhi, ARTEP, 1987), xiii + 95 pp. [LKA]

R. Islam: *Adjustment in small and cottage industries: The role of technology.* Paper prepared for the Second Meeting of Asian Employment Planners 24-26 November, 1987, New Delhi (New Delhi, ARTEP, 1987), 26 pp.

R. Islam: *Rural industrialisation and employment in Asia* (New Delhi, ARTEP, 1987), 327 pp. US$ 8. [BGD, IND, NPL, PHL, LKA, THA, JPN, KOR, TWN, CHN] ISBN 92-2-106031-4.

Articles in the International Labour Review

- General

A. Dawson: "Suggestions for an approach to rural development by foreign aid programmes", Vol. 117, No. 4, July-Aug. 1978.

P. Kilby and P. Bangasser: "Assessing technical co-operation: The case of rural industry", Vol. 117, No. 3, May-June 1978.

E. Lee: "Changing approaches to rural development", Vol. 119, No. 1, Jan.-Feb. 1980.

B. Agarwal: "Agricultural mechanisation and labour use: A disaggregated approach", Vol. 120, No. 1, Jan.-Feb. 1981.

G.A. Edmonds: "Towards more rational rural road transport planning", Vol. 121, No. 1, Jan.-Feb. 1982.

B.H. Kinsey and I. Ahmed: "Mechanical innovations on small African farms: Problems of development and diffusion", Vol. 122, No. 2, Mar.-Apr. 1983.

P. Egger: "Banking for the rural poor: Lessons from some innovative saving and credit schemes", Vol. 125, No. 4, July-Aug. 1986.

- Africa

D. Wilcock and E. Chuta: "Employment in rural industries in Eastern Upper Volta", Vol. 121, No. 4, July-Aug. 1982. [BFA]

- Latin America and the Caribbean

A. Guichaoua and J. Majeres: "Agrarian structure, technology and employment: Agricultural development in Chile, 1955-65", Vol. 120, No. 5, Sep.-Oct. 1981. [CHL]

R.H. Wood: "Tractor mechanisation and employment on larger private Mexican farms", Vol. 122, No. 2, Mar.-Apr. 1983. [MEX]

- Asia

I. Ahmed and D.H. Freedman: "Access to rural factor markets, technological change and basic needs: Evidence from Bangladesh", Vol. 121, No. 4, July-Aug. 1982. [BGD]

A.S. Oberai and H.K.M. Singh: "Migration, production and technology in agriculture: A case study in the Indian Punjab", Vol. 121, No. 3, May-June 1982. [IND]

Working Papers

- **General**

Md.A. Rahman: *Research on participation of the poor in development*, Dec. 1978 (WEP 10/WP.4).* M.

R. Weitz, D. Pelley and L. Applebaum: *Employment and income generation in new settlement projects*, Nov. 1978 (WEP 10/WP.3).* M.

D. Ghai, E. Lee and S. Radwan: *Rural poverty in the Third World: Trends, causes and policy reorientations*, May 1979 (WEP 10-6/WP.23)*. M.

Md.A. Rahman: *Transition to collective agriculture and peasant participation - North Vietnam, the United Republic of Tanzania and Ethiopia*, Jan. 1980 (WEP 10/WP.9).* M. [ETH, TZA, VNM]

D. Ghai: *Income distribution and labour utilisation under different agrarian systems*, Nov. 1980 (WEP 10-6/WP.39)*. M. [NPL, KOR, TZA, CHN, VNM]

V.W. Ruttan: *Institutional factors affecting the generation and diffusion of agricultural technology: Issues, concepts and analysis*, Oct. 1980 (WEP 2-22/WP.67). M.

J.D.G.E. Howe: *Criteria for rural road planning*, Nov. 1981 (WEP 2-23/WP.108).

J.D.G.E. Howe: *The impact of rural roads on poverty alleviation: A review of the literature*, Nov. 1981 (WEP 2-23/WP.106).

P.J. Richards, M.A. El-Hawary, T.Y. El-Reedy, P.K. Thomas, J.D.G.E. Howe and J. Hugh Jones: *Rural roads and poverty alleviation: An introduction and four country studies*, Aug. 1982 (WEP 2-32/WP.41). [NPL, EGY, IND, BWA, THA] ISBN 92-2-103209-4.

S.D. Biggs and E.J. Clay: *Generation and diffusion of agricultural technology: A review of theories and experiences*, Aug. 1983 (WEP 2-22/WP.122). M. ISBN 92-2-103579-4.

F. Fluitman: *The socio-economic impact of rural electrification in developing countries: A review of evidence*, Nov. 1983 (WEP 2-22/WP.126). M. ISBN 92-2-103660-X.

Md.A. Rahman: *The theory and practice of participatory action research*, Aug. 1983 (WEP 10/WP.29)*. M. [IND, LKA, BGD, COL] ISBN 92-2-103574-3.

M. Arda: *The new international economic order and rural development*, Nov. 1984 (WEP 10-6/WP.66). ISBN 92-2-103957-9.

A.K.N. Reddy: *The energy and economic implications of agricultural technologies: An approach based on the technical options for the operations of crop production*, June 1985 (WEP 2-22/WP. 149). M. ISBN 92-2-105214-1.

A. Bhaduri: *Employment and livelihood: The nature of the labour process in the formulation of rural development policy*, Feb. 1986 (WEP 10-6/WP.78). ISBN 92-2-105408-X.

A. Errington: *Rural employment trends and issues in market industrialised countries*, Nov. 1987 (WEP 10-6/WP.90). ISBN 92-2-106336-4.

A.K. Ghose: *Agriculture-industry terms of trade and distributive shares in a developing economy*, Jan. 1987 (WEP 10-6/WP.81). ISBN 92-2-105900-6.

- **Africa**

A. Abate and T. Teklu: *Land reform and peasant associations in Ethiopia - A case study of two widely differing regions*,[2] Oct. 1979 (WEP 10/WP.8)*. M. [ETH]

C. Colclough and P. Fallon: *Rural poverty in Botswana - Dimensions, causes and constraints*, July 1979 (WEP 10-6/WP.26)*. M. [BWA]

A. Abate and F.G. Kiros: *Agrarian reform, structural changes and rural development in Ethiopia*, Sep. 1980 (WEP 10-6/WP.37)*. [ETH]

A. Bequele: *Poverty, inequality and stagnation - The Ghanaian experience*, May 1980 (WEP 10-6/WP.33).* [GHA]

E. Chuta: *A preliminary appraisal of rural industrialisation policies and programmes in Nigeria*, Apr. 1980 (WEP 2-37/WP.4)*. M. [NGA]

Ch. Elliot: *Equity and growth - Unresolved conflict in Zambian rural development policy*, Jan. 1980 (WEP 10-6/WP.30). [ZMB]

D. Ghai and S. Radwan: *Growth and inequality: Rural development in Malawi. 1964-1978*, July 1980 (WEP 10-6/WP.35). [MWI]

W.J. House and T. Killick: *Social justice and development policy in Kenya's rural economy*, Jan. 1980 (WEP 10-6/WP.31). [KEN]

B.H. Kinsey: *Farm equipment innovations, agricultural growth and employment in Zambia*, [6] Aug. 1980 (WEP 2-22/WP.64). M. [ZMB]

E. Lee: *Export-led rural development: The Ivory Coast*, Jan. 1980 (WEP 10-6/WP.32). [CIV]

B.P. Mramba: *Rural industrialisation in the United Republic of Tanzania: A preliminary assessment*, Mar. 1980 (WEP 2-37/WP.2)*. M. [TZA]

G. Muchri: *Farm equipment innovation for small holders in semi arid Kenya: A conceptual and empirical analysis*, [6] Oct. 1980 (WEP 2-22/WP.76). M. [KEN]

G. Norcliffe, D. Freeman and N. Miles: *Rural industrialisation policies and programme in Kenya*, Feb. 1980 (WEP 2-37/WP.1)*. M. [KEN]

J. Trouvé: *Rural industrialisation in French-speaking Black Africa: Policies, achievements, and problems*, [3] July 1980 (WEP 2-37/WP.6(E)). M. (WEP 2-37/WP.8(F)) ISBN 92-2-102476-8.

P. Collier: *Oil and inequality in rural Nigeria*, Feb. 1981 (WEP 10-6/WP.44)*. [NGA]

B.F. Johnston: *Farm equipment innovations and rural industrialisation in Eastern Africa: An overview*, [6] July 1981 (WEP 2-22/WP.80). [KEN, TZA, UGA] ISBN 92-2-102836-4.

V. Jamal: *Nomads and farmers: Incomes and poverty in rural Somalia* (Addis Ababa, JASPA), 1981. [SOM] ISBN 92-2-102893-3.

M.J. Dorling: *National research systems and the generation and diffusion of innovations: The horticultural industry in Kenya*, June 1982 (WEP 2-22/WP.95). M. [KEN] ISBN 92-2-103169-1.

M. Fafchamps: *Les politiques de développement rural et leur efficacité: Réflexions sur la réalité Africaine* (Addis Ababa, JASPA), Jan. 1982.

A.W. Shepherd and A.M. El Neima: *Popular participation in decentralised water supply planning: A case study on the Western district of Northern Kordofan Province, Sudan*, Oct. 1982 (WEP 2-32/WP.42). [SDN] ISBN 92-2-103266-3.

G.H.R. Chipande: *Labour availability and smallholder agricultural development: The case of Lilongwe land development programme (Malawi)*, Sep. 1983 (WEP 10-6/WP. 61). M. [MWI] ISBN 92-2-103587-5.

P. Collier: *Contractual constraints upon the processes of labour exchange in rural Kenya*, Aug. 1983, (WEP 10-6/WP.59). M. [KEN] ISBN 92-2-103571-9.

D. Ghai and L. Smith: *Food policy and equity in sub-Saharan Africa: Rural employment policy research programme*, Aug. 1983 (WEP 10-6/WP.55). ISBN 92-2-103544-1.

A. Djeflat: *The socio-economic impact of rural electrification in Algeria*, Nov. 1985 (WEP 2-22/WP. 157). [DZA] ISBN 92-2-105414-4.

H. Tabatabai: *Food crisis and development policies in sub-saharan Africa*, July 1985 (WEP 10-6/WP. 72). M. ISBN 92-2-105210-9.

W.J. House and K.D. Philips-Howard: *Population and poverty in rural Southern Sudan: A case study of the Acholi area*, Nov. 1986 (WEP 2-21/WP.155). [SDN] ISBN 92-2-105815-8.

P. Collier: *Oil shocks and food security in Nigeria*, Sep. 1987 (WEP 10-6/WP.86). [NGA] ISBN 92-2-106205-8.

D. Ghai: *Successes and failures in growth in Sub-Saharan Africa: 1960-82*, Mar. 1987 (WEP 10-6/WP.83). ISBN 92-2-105965-0.

R.J. Szal: *An agrarian crisis in Madagascar?*, July 1987 (WEP 10-6/WP.84). [MDG] ISBN 92-2-105839-5.

- Latin America and the Caribbean

El régimen cooperativo en la producción industrial de azúcar en Tucuman (Santiago, PREALC), Nov. 1978 (No. 160).* [ARG]

Estructura agraria y empleo en el Nordeste del Brasil (Santiago, PREALC), May 1978 (No. 146). [BRA]

Tecnología, empleo y distribución de ingresos en la industria azucarera de la República Dominicana (Santiago, PREALC), Sep. 1978 (No. 158).* [DOM]

M. Mora y Araiyo and D. Orlansky: *Cambio technológico y empleo en la producción agroindustria de azúcar en Tucuman*, Oct. 1978 (WEP 2-22/WP.38). [ARG]

P. Peek: *Agrarian change and rural emigration in Latin America*, Aug. 1978 (WEP 10-6/WP.22)*. M.

Diagnóstico de las estadísticas y bibliografía sobre el empleo rural en Centroamérica y Panamá (Santiago, PREALC), July 1979 (No. 174). [PAN]

Distribución del ingreso, migraciones y colonización: Una alternativa para el campesinado boliviano (Santiago, PREALC), July 1979 (No. 176). [BOL]

Guatemala: Estacionalidad y subempleo en el sector agropecuario (Santiago, PREALC), Oct. 1980 (No. 207).* [GTM]

C. Kay: *The agrarian reform in Peru: An assessment*, Nov. 1980 (WEP 10-6/WP.41). [PER]

S. Roca with the collaboration of M. Bachrach and J. Servat: *Participatory processes and action of the rural poor in Anta: Peru*, Sep. 1980 (WEP 10/WP.12). [PER]

S. Roca: *La forma de organización cooperativa en la producción de azúcar: El caso peruano*, Nov. 1980 (WEP 10-6/WP.40). M. [PER]

J.I. Stallmann and J.W. Pease: *Rural industrialisation policy in Honduras*, Sep. 1980 (WEP 2-37/WP.7). M. [HND] ISBN 92-2-102490-3.

Small farmers and agricultural workers in Chile (Santiago, PREALC), Sep. 1981 (No. 210). [CHL]

S. Gomez: *Participation experiences in the countryside: A case study in Chile*, May 1981 (WEP 10/WP.20)*. M. [CHL]

C. Edquist: *Technical change in sugar cane harvesting: A comparison of Cuba and Jamaica (1958-1980)*, July 1982 (WEP 2-22/WP.96). [CUB, JAM] ISBN 92-2-103193-4.

L. Castillo and D. Lehmann: *Agrarian reform and structural change in Chile: 1965-1979*, Jan. 1982 (WEP 10-6/WP.53). M. [CHL] ISBN 92-2-102976-X.

P. Peek: *Agrarian reforms and rural development in Nicaragua (1979-81)*, Mar. 1982 (WEP 10-6/WP.51). M. [NIC] ISBN 92-2-103081-4.

La evolución de la pobreza rural en Honduras (Santiago, PREALC), Mar. 1983 (No. 223). [HND]

La evolución de la pobreza rural en Panamá (Santiago, PREALC), Mar. 1983 (No. 222). [PAN]

S. Commander and P. Peek: *Oil exports, agrarian change and the rural labour process: The Ecuadorian sierra in the 1970s*, Nov. 1983 (WEP 10-6/WP. 63). M. [ECU] ISBN 92-2-103627-8.

A. Figueroa: *Rural labour markets in Peru: A study of labour exchange*, Aug. 1983 (WEP 10-6/WP.58). M. [PER] ISBN 92-2-103570-0.

R. Pinnock and C. Elton: *Rural poverty in Panama: Trends and structural causes*, Sep. 1983 (WEP 10-6/WP.60). M. [PAN] ISBN 92-2-103581-6.

C.D. Deere and M. Diskin: *Rural poverty in El Salvador: Dimensions, trends and causes*, Feb. 1984 (WEP 10-6/WP.64). [SLV] ISBN 92-2-103704-5.

A. Hintermeister: *Rural poverty and export farming in Guatemala*, Oct. 1984 (WEP 10-6/WP. 71). [GTM] ISBN 92-2-105024-5.

P. Peek and C. Raabe: *Rural equity in Costa Rica: Myth or reality*, Oct. 1984 (WEP 10-6/WP.67). [CRI] ISBN 92-2-103966-8.

P. Peek: *Agrarian reform and poverty alleviation: The recent experience in Nicaragua*, Oct. 1984 (WEP 10-6/WP 69). [NIC] ISBN 92-2-100533-X.

P. Peek: *Agrarian structure and rural poverty: The case of Honduras*, Sep. 1984 (WEP 10-6/WP.68). [HND]

P. Peek: *Rural poverty in Central America: Dimensions, causes and policy alternatives*, Nov. 1984 (WEP 10-6/WP. 70). ISBN 92-2-100541-0.

El impacto heterogeneo de la modernización agrícola sobre el mercado del trabajo (Santiago, PREALC), Apr. 1985 (No. 260).

Estructura agraria, mercado de trabajo y población rural en Guatemala (Santiago, PREALC), Feb. 1985 (No. 256). [GTM]

Guatemala: Pobreza rural y crédito agrícola al campesino (Santiago, PREALC), June 1985 (No. 266). [GTM]

Inestabilidad y complementariedad de las ocupaciones rurales en Guatemala (Santiago, PREALC), Aug. 1985 (No. 269). [GTM]

A. de Janvry, E. Sadoulet and L. Wilcox: *Rural labour in Latin America*, June 1986 (WEP 10-6/WP.79). [CHL, SLV, BRA, MEX, PER] ISBN 92-2-105589-2.

C.A. Smith: *Survival strategies among rural smallholders and petty commodity producers: A case study of western Guatemala*, Jan. 1986 (WEP 10-6/WP. 77). [GTM] ISBN 92-2-105407-1.

G. Castro de Rezende: *Food production, income distribution and prices: Brazil 1960-80*, Nov. 1987 (WEP 10-6/WP.89). [BRA] ISBN 92-2-106323-2.

F. Homem de Melo: *Export-oriented agricultural growth: The case of Brazil*, Sep. 1987 (WEP 10-6/WP.87). [BRA] ISBN 92-2-106222-8.

- Asia

Ng Gek-Boo: *Operation and control of individual economic activities in collective agriculture: The case of China*, June 1978 (WEP 10-6/WP.19). [CHN]

Teng-Hui Lee, Hsi Huang Che and Yueh-eh-Chen: *Labour absorption in Taiwan agriculture* (Bangkok, ARTEP), 1978. [TWN]

P.K. Bardhan: *Aspects of the rural labour market in West Bengal: An analysis of household survey data, 1972-73*, Mar. 1978 (WEP 10-6/WP.15).* M. [IND]

A.R. Khan: *The Comilla model and the integrated rural development programme of Bangladesh: An experiment in co-operative capitalism,* [7] July 1978 (WEP 10-6/WP.20). [BGD]

E.H. Lee: *Egalitarian peasant farming and rural development: The case of South Korea,* [7] Apr. 1978 (WEP 10-6/WP.16). [KOR]

A. Rudra: *Organisations of agriculture for rural development: The Indian Case,* [7] May 1978 (WEP 10-6/WP.17).* [IND]

J. Sigurdson: *The changing pattern of intersectoral technological linkages in the rural machinery industry in China,* [1] Jan. 1979 (WEP 2-22/WP.45) M. [CHN]

Ng Gek-Boo: *Grass-root management in rural China: The workpoint system of the people's communes*, July 1979 (WEP 10-6/WP.25)*. M. [CHN]

A. Bhaduri: *Agricultural co-operatives in North Vietnam,* [2] Mar. 1979 (WEP 10/WP.6)* M. [VNM]

A.K. Ghose: *Short-term changes in income distribution in poor agrarian economies: A study of famines with reference to the Indian sub-continent*, Oct. 1979 (WEP 10-6/WP.28). M. [IND]

M. Hossain, R.A. Mahmood and Q.K. Ahmad: *Participatory development efforts in rural Bangladesh - A case study of experiences in three areas,* [2] Feb. 1979 (WEP 10/WP.5)*. [BGD]

M.H. Khan: *Sind Hari Committee, 1930-1970: A peasant movement?,* [2] May 1979 (WEP 10/WP.7). M. [PAK]

N. Ahmad: *Peasant struggle in a feudal setting. A study of the determinants of the bargaining power of tenants and small farmers in five villages of district Attock, Pakistan*, July 1980 (WEP 10/WP.11)*. [PAK]

A.K. Ghose: *Agrarian reform in West Bengal: Objectives, achievements and limitations*, May 1980 (WEP 10-6/WP.34). [IND]

D.B. Gupta: *Government policies and programmes of rural industrialisation with special reference to the Punjab region in Northern India* [3] (Geneva, ILO, 1984). June 1980 (WEP 2-37/WP.5) M. [IND] ISBN 92-2-102465-2.

R.C. Sinha: *Rural industrialisation in China in a historical perspective*, Mar. 1980 (WEP 2-37/WP.3)*. M. [CHN]

National Council of Applied Economic Research: *Transport technology for the rural areas: India*, July 1981 (WEP 2-22/WP.83). [IND] ISBN 92-2-102826-7.

C. Bot: *Employment and incomes in sugar cane cultivation in Thailand* (Bangkok, ARTEP), 1981. [THA]

A.S. Oberai and H.K.M. Singh: *Migration and technological change in agriculture: Results of a case study in the green revolution belt of India*, Oct. 1981 (WEP 2-21/WP.111). M. [IND] ISBN 92-2-102919-0.

P.V. Paranjape, V. Kanhere, N. Sathe, S. Kulkarni and S. Gothoskar: *Grass-roots self-reliance in Shramic Sanghatana Dhulia district, India*, 1981 (WEP 10/WP.22)*. M. [IND]

K.N. Raj and M. Tharakan: *Agrarian reform in Kerala and its impact on the rural economy - A preliminary assessment*, Sep. 1981 (WEP 10-6/WP.49). [IND]

J.D. Smith: *Transport technology and employment in rural Malaysia*, Dec. 1981 (WEP 2-22/WP.88). [MYS] ISBN 92-2-102960-3.

Lim Teck Ghee and Tan Phaik Leng: *Grass-roots self-reliance initiatives in Malaysia: A case study of Kampung Batu's struggle for land*, Jan. 1982 (WEP 10/WP.25)*. M. [MYS] ISBN 92-2-103025-3.

A.S. Bhalla: *Rural industrialisation and new economic policies in Hunan (China)*, May 1982 (WEP 2-37/WP.9). [CHN] ISBN 92-2-103166-7.

M. Hossein: *Conscientising rural disadvantaged peasants in Bangladesh: Intervention through group action: A case study of Proshika*, June 1982 (WEP 10/WP.27)*. [BGD] ISBN 92-2-103195-0.

N.N. Luu: *Institutional factors and technological innovation in North Vietnamese agriculture*, Aug. 1982 (WEP 2-22/WP.98). M. [VNM] ISBN 92-2-103208-6.

R.B. Ocampo: *Rural transport in the Philippines: Jeepneys, trimobiles and other simple modes in two Bibol towns*, Nov. 1982 (WEP 2-22/WP.102). M. [PHL] ISBN 92-2-103312-0.

A. Rudra: *Extraeconomic constraints on agricultural labour: Results of an intensive survey in some villages near Santiniketan, West Bengal* (Bangkok, ARTEP), Aug. 1982. [IND] ISBN 92-2-102743-0.

S. Tilakaratna: *Grass-roots self-reliance in Sri Lanka: Organisations of betel and coir yarn producers*, Jan. 1982 (WEP 10/WP.24).* M. [LKA] ISBN 92-2-103014-8.

C. Bot: *Mechanisation and employment in Thai paddy cultivation* (Bangkok, ARTEP), 1983. [THA] ISBN 92-2-103283-3.

K. Bardhan: *Economic growth, poverty and rural labour markets in India: A survey of research*, Mar. 1983 (WEP 10-6/WP.54). [IND] ISBN 92-2-103403-8.

A.K. Ghose: *The new development strategy and rural reforms in post-Mao China*, Sep. 1983 (WEP 10-6/WP.62). M. [CHN] ISBN 92-2-103622-7.

H.M.G. Herath: *Role of rural institutions in the diffusion of agricultural innovations in Sri Lanka*, Jan. 1983 (WEP 2-22/WP.109). [LKA]

M. Muqtada and M. Mustafa Alam: *Hired labour and rural labour market in Bangladesh. An analysis of farm level data* (Bangkok, ARTEP), 1983. [BGD] ISBN 92-2-103288-4.

S. Mukhopadhyay: *Factors affecting agricultural research and technology: A case study of India*, June 1983 (WEP 2-22/WP.120). M. [IND] ISBN 92-2-103499-2.

P.H. Prasad and G.B. Rodgers: *Class, caste and landholding in the analysis of the rural economy*, Aug. 1983 (WEP 2-21/WP.140). M. [IND] ISBN 92-2-103562-X.

G.B. Rodgers *Poverty ten years on: Incomes and work among the poor of rural Bihar*, May 1983 (WEP 2-21/WP 130). M. [IND] ISBN 92-2-103491-7.

Chee Peng Lim: *The socio-economic impact of rural electrification in Malaysia*, Nov. 1984 (WEP 2-22/WP.135). [MYS] ISBN 92-2-100495-3.

Q.K. Ahmad, K.M. Rahman, K.Md.N. Islam and Md.E. Ali: *Technology adaptation and employment in the agricultural tools and equipment industry of Bangladesh*, Nov. 1984 (WEP 2-22/WP.134). [BGD] ISBN 92-2-103961-7.

G. Hart: *Agrarian labour arrangements and structural change: Lessons from Java and Bangladesh*, Mar. 1984 (WEP 10-6/WP.65). [IDN, BGD]

M. Hossain: *Employment generation through cottage industries. Potentials and constraints: The case of Bangladesh* (Bangkok, ARTEP), 1984. [BGD] ISBN 92-2-103687-1.

Differentiation among the rural poor and its bearing on solidarity and organisational development. A study of five locations in India, June 1985 (WEP 10/WP. 36). [IND] ISBN 92-2-105129-3.

N. Bandyopadhyaya and associates: *Evaluation of land reform measures in West Bengal. A report* (Bangkok, ARTEP), June 1985. [IND]

S. Chandra Mishra: *Technological adaptation and employment in the small-scale farm machinery industry: Uttar Pradesh, India*, Oct. 1985 (WEP 2-22/WP. 156). [IND] ISBN 92-2-105304-0.

R. Islam and Md.A. Rahman: *Agrarian change, labour contracts and interlinked transactions in labour, land and credit in rural Bangladesh. A study with micro-level data* (Bangkok, ARTEP), June 1985. [BGD] ISBN 92-2-103942-0.

M.A. Jabbar: *Commercialisation of agricultural equipment generated by R and D system in Bangladesh*, Sep. 1985 (WEP 2-22/WP. 155). [BGD] ISBN 92-2-105299-0.

W. Mahmud and S. Mahmud: *Age-sex aspects of the food and nutrition problem in rural Bangladesh*, Oct. 1985 (WEP 10-6/WP.74). M. [BGD] ISBN 92-2-105292-3.

C. Rammanohar Reddy: *Rural labour market in Varhad: A case study of agricultural labourers in rain-fed agriculture in India*, Oct. 1985 (WEP 10-6/WP. 75). [IND] ISBN 92-2-105317-2.

I. Rajaraman: *Returns to labour in developing country agriculture: India*, Nov. 1985 (WEP 10-6/WP. 76). M. [IND] ISBN 92-2-105361-X.

V.R. Reddy, F. Kasryno and M. Siregar: *Diffusion and commercialisation of technology prototypes rice post harvest in Indonesia*, Apr. 1985 (WEP 2-22/WP. 143). M. [IDN] ISBN 92-2-105105-4.

S. Tilakaratna: *The animator in participatory rural development: Some experiences from Sri Lanka*, Dec. 1985 (WEP 10/WP. 37). [LKA] ISBN 92-2-105418-7.

National Council of Applied Economic Research (NCAER): *Socio-economic impact of rural electrification in India*, Oct. 1986 (WEP 2-22/WP.171). [IND] ISBN 92-2-105761-5.

D. Bandyopahyay: *A study on poverty alleviation in rural India through special employment creation programmes* (New Delhi, ARTEP), Sep. 1986. [IND] ISBN 92-2-105472-1.

T.S. Papola: *Rural industrialization and agricultural growth: A case study on India*[4] (New Delhi, ARTEP), July 1986. [IND] ISBN 92-2-105471-3.

A. Saith: *Contrasting experiences in rural industrialisation: Are the East Asian successes transferable?*[A] (New Delhi, ARTEP), Sep. 1986. [KOR, TWN, JPN] ISBN 92-2-105473-X.

G.M. Bautista: *The impact of agricultural changes on the rural labour market in the Philippines* (New Delhi, ARTEP), Mar. 1987. [PHL] ISBN 92-2-105772-0.

A.K. Ghose: *Trends and fluctuations in rural poverty in India: An explanatory framework and some conclusions*, Nov. 1987 (WEP 10-6/WP.88). [IND] ISBN 92-2-106307-0.

G. Hart: *The mechanisation of Malaysian rice production: Will petty producers survive?*, Mar. 1987 (WEP 10-6/WP.82). [MYS] ISBN 92-2-105961-8.

S. Ray: *Returns to rural labour in Asia*, Sep. 1987 (WEP 10-6/WP.85). [KOR, BGD, IDN, MYS, PAK, THA, PHL, LKA] ISBN 92-2-106153-1.

P. Wickramasekara: *Labour absorption in Asian agriculture: A review* (New Delhi, ARTEP), May 1987. [JPN, CHN] ISBN 92-2-105776-3.

- OECD Countries

C. Keyder: *The social structure and the labour market in Turkish agriculture*, Aug. 1983 (WEP 10-6/WP.57). M. [TUR] ISBN 92-2-103569-7.

- Middle East

H. Katouzian: *The agrarian question in Iran*, May 1981 (WEP 10-6/WP.47). [IRN]

M.J. Dorling and S. Mutlu: *Commercialisation of new indigenous technology in Jordanian agriculture*, July 1985 (WEP 2-22/WP. 150). M. [JOR] ISBN 92-2-105211-7.

ILO works published by commercial and non-profit-making publishers

- General

I.Z. Bhatty: *Technological change and employment: A study of plantations*. (New Delhi, Macmillan Press of India Ltd., 1978), xii + 222 pp. [IND] ISBN 0-33390-240-8.

A.R. Berry and W.R. Cline: *Agrarian structure and productivity in developing countries* (Baltimore, Johns Hopkins University Press, 1979), x + 248 pp. [IND, BRA, COL, PHL, PAK, MYS] ISBN 0-8018-2190-8.

D. Ghai, A.R. Khan, E. Lee and S. Radwan (eds.): *Agrarian systems and rural development* (London, Macmillan Press Ltd., 1979), xvi + 376 pp. [IND, KOR, BGD, EGY, GUY, TZA, CHN, CUB] ISBN 0-333-27343-5.

C. Harvey, J. Jacobs, G. Lamb and B. Schaffer: *Rural employment and administration in the Third World*. Development methods and alternative strategies. (Farnborough, Hampshire, Saxon House, 1979), x + 112 pp. ISBN 0-566-00261-2.

A. Bhaduri and Md.A. Rahman (eds.): *Studies in rural participation* (New Delhi, Oxford and IBH Publishing Co., 1982), vii + 229 pp. [TZA, VNM, ETH, PAK, PNG, BGD, IND, CHL]

A.K. Ghose (ed.): *Agrarian reform in contemporary developing countries* (London, Croom Helm; New York, St. Martin's Press, 1983), 364 pp. [IND, ETH, PER, CHL, IRN, NIC] ISBN 0-7099-1312-5.

J.D.G.E. Howe and P.J. Richards (eds.): *Rural roads and poverty alleviation* (London, Intermediate Technology Publications, 1984), 192 pp. [EGY, IND, THA, BWA, NPL] ISBN 0-946668-05-2.

I. Barwell, G.A. Edmonds, J.D.G.E. Howe and J. de Veen: *Rural transport in developing countries* (London, Intermediate Technology Publications, 1985), 145 pp. [MYS, IND, NGA, KEN, KOR, PHL, WSM, TZA, BGD] ISBN 0-946688-80-X.

The design and manufacture of animal-drawn carts. Prepared for the ILO and the United Nations Centre for Human Settlements (London, Intermediate Technology Publications, 1986), x + 72 pp. ISBN 0-946688-52-4.

- Africa

I. Ahmed and B.H. Kinsey (eds.): *Farm equipment innovations in Eastern and Central Southern Africa* (Aldershot, Hampshire, Gower, 1984), xvii + 345 pp. [KEN, TZA, SDN, MWI, UGA, ZMB] ISBN 0-566-00697-9.

P. Collier, S. Radwan and S. Wangwe, with A. Wagner: *Labour and poverty in rural the United Republic of Tanzania. Ujamaa and rural development in the United Republic of Tanzania* (Oxford, Clarendon Press, 1986), 143 pp. [TZA] ISBN 0-19-828531-0.

D. Ghai and L.D. Smith: *Agricultural prices, policy, and equity in Sub-Saharan Africa* (Boulder, Colorado, Lynne Rienner Publishers, 1987), ix + 173 pp. ISBN 1-55587-005-8.

- Latin America and the Caribbean

Medición del empleo y de los ingresos rurales (Santiago, CEPAL, 1982).

O. Fals Borda: *Conocimiento y poder popular: Lecciones con campesinos de Nicaragua, México y Colombia* (Bogotá, Siglo Veintiuno Editores, 1985), 177 pp. [NIC, MEX, COL] ISBN 958-606-003-9.

- Asia

A.N. Bose: *Calcutta and rural Bengal: Small sector symbiosis* (Calcutta, Minerva Associates Publications Pvt., 1978), vii + 172 pp., table. [IND]

A.R. Khan and D. Ghai: *Collective agriculture and rural development in Soviet Central Asia* (London, Macmillan Press Ltd., 1979), xi + 120 pp. ISBN 0-333-27094-0.

Md.A. Rahman (ed.): *Grass-roots participation and self-reliance: Experiences in South and South-East Asia* (New Delhi, Oxford and IBH Publishing Co., 1984), viii + 215 pp. [PAK, MYS, IND, PHL, NPL, LKA, BGD]

Related books and articles

- General

L. Richter: "Integrated rural development - Training for effective implementation" in *Training for Agricultural and Rural Development* (Rome), 1978.

L. Richter: "Integrierte ländliche entwicklung als neues internationales Gemeinschaftsprogramm" in *Zeitschrift für Ausländische Landwirtschaft* (Berlin), 17. Jahrgang, Heft 4, Oct.-Dec. 1978.

D. Ghai and S.V. Sethuraman: "Expanding rural employment opportunities: Some policy alternatives" in *Increasing Agricultural Production for the Benefit of the Rural Poor - A Workshop Report* (Rome, International Fund for Agricultural Development, 1979).

L. Richter: "Integrierte ländliche Entwicklungsstrategie - Die Ausführungsorgane müssen gestärkt werden" in *Entwicklung und Ländlicher Raum* (Frankfurt), 13. Jahrgang, Heft 2, Mar.-Apr. 1979.

Md.A. Rahman: " Transition to collective agriculture and peasant participation - North Vietnam, the United Republic of Tanzania and Ethiopia", [5] in *Bangladesh Development Studies* (Dacca), Vol. 7, No. 3, Monsoon 1979. [VNM, TZA, ETH]

L. Richter: "Integrated rural development - A false turning?", in *Quarterly Journal of International Agriculture* (Berlin), Vol. 19, No. 3, July-Sep. 1980.

R.J. Szal: "Aspects of the International Labour Organization's work for rural development", in *World Agriculture* (Paris), Vol. 24, No. 3, 1980.

- Africa

P.W. Dunkel: "Arbeit und Einkommen auf dem Lande - Vier Studien in Afrika", in *Entwicklung und Ländlicher Raum* (Frankfurt), Sep.-Oct. 1979.

- Asia

A.R. Khan and D. Ghai: "Collective agriculture in Soviet Central Asia", in *World Development* (Oxford), Vol. 7, No. 4/5, 1979.

E. Lee: "Egalitarian peasant farming and rural development: The case of South Korea", in *World Development* (Oxford), Vol. 7, No. 4/5, 1979. [KOR]

I. Ahmed: "Labour use in dynamic agriculture: Evidence from Punjab", in *Economic and Political Weekly* (Bombay) Vol. XVI, No. 13, Nov. 1981. [IND]

M. Farbman: "Rural agrarian employment and land relationship and income inequality in India", in *Contributions to Asian Studies* (Leiden), Vol. XIII, 1981. [IND]

G.B. Rodgers and J. Rodgers: "Incomes and work among the poor of rural Bihar, 1971-81", in *Economic and Political Weekly* (Bombay), Vol. XIX, No. 13, Review of Agriculture, Mar. 1984. [IND]

Notes:

1 A revised version appears in S. Watanabe (ed.): Technology, marketing and industrialisation: Linkages between large and small enterprises (New Delhi, Macmillan India, 1983).

2 Reprinted in A. Bhaduri and Md. A. Rahman (eds.): Studies in rural participation (New Delhi, Oxford and IBH Publishing Co., 1982).

3 Reprinted in E. Chuta and S.V. Sethuraman (eds.): Rural small-scale industries and employment in Africa and Asia (Geneva, ILO, 1984).

4 Published in: R. Islam: Rural industrialisation and employment in Asia (New Delhi, 1987), 327 pp.

5 Also published in Human Features (New Delhi), Winter 1980.

6 Published in I. Ahmed and B.H. Kinsey (eds.): Farm equipment innovations in Eastern and Central Southern Africa (Aldershot, Hampshire, Gower, 1984).

7 Reprinted in Poverty and landlessness in rural Asia (Geneva, ILO, 1977).

Migration and urbanisation

ILO publications

Books and reports

- **General**

R.E. Bilsborrow: *Surveys of internal migration in low-income countries: Issues of survey and sample design*[1] (Geneva, ILO, 1981), iv + 164 pp. ISBN 92-2-102625-6.

R.E. Bilsborrow: *Surveys of internal migration in low-income countries: The need for and content of community-level variables*[1] (Geneva, ILO, 1981), iv + 64 pp. E, F. ISBN 92-2-102738-4.

A.S. Oberai: *Demographic and social information in migration surveys: Analytical significance and guidelines for data collection.* (Geneva, ILO, 1981), vi + 52 pp. E, F. ISBN 92-2-102638-8.

A.S. Oberai: *Migration, production and technological change: Analytical issues and guidelines for data collection and analysis* (Geneva, ILO, 1981), iv + 82 pp. ISBN 92-2-102830-5.

G. Standing: *Income transfers and remittances: A module for migration surveys* (Geneva, ILO, 1981), viii + 84 pp. E, F. ISBN 92-2-102755-4.

G. Standing: *Migrants and the labour process: A module for migration surveys*[1] (Geneva, ILO, 1981), xii + 140 pp. E, F. ISBN 92-2-102640-X.

G. Standing: *Analysing inter-relationships between migration and employment* (Geneva, ILO, 1982), vi + 51 pp. ISBN 92-2-103309-0.

G. Standing: *Conceptualising territorial mobility in low-income countries* [1] (Geneva, ILO, 1982), 50 pp. Sw. frs. 10. E, F. ISBN 92-2-102929-8.

P. Peek: *A typology of migrants: Some methodological aspects* (Geneva, ILO, 1983), 22 pp. ISBN 92-2-102884-4.

G. Standing: *Measuring population mobility in migration surveys* (Geneva, ILO, 1983), 55 pp. ISBN 92-2-103463-1.

Urbanisation, informal sector and employment: A progress report on research, advisory services and technical cooperation (Geneva, ILO, 1984), iii + 40 pp. E, F. ISBN 92-2-103767-3

- **Africa.**

O.J. Fapohunda and H. Lubell with J. Reijmerink and M.P. van Dijk: *Lagos: Urban development and employment* (Geneva, ILO, 1978), xii + 110 pp. Sw. frs. 17.50. [NGA] ISBN 92-2-101997-7.

W.R. Böhning (ed): *Black migration to South Africa - A selection of policy-oriented research.* (Geneva, ILO, 1981), x + 184 pp. Sw. frs. 20. [ZAF, SWZ, LSO] ISBN 92-2-102759-7.

Income-generating activities for refugees in the Sudan. Report of the UNHCR/ILO Interdisciplinary mission on the employment, income generation and training of refugees in the Sudan (Geneva, ILO, 1982), xiv + 88 pp. [SDN] ISBN 92-2-103095-4.

J. Gaude (Publié sous la direction de): *Phénomène migratoire et politiques associées dans le contexte africain*. Etudes de cas en Algérie, au Burundi, en République-Unie du Cameroun et en Haute-Volta (Geneva, ILO, 1982), 298 pp. Sw. frs. 30. [DZA, BDI, CMR, BFA] ISBN 92-2-202953-4.

Skill profiles of migrant workers. Findings of a pilot survey in Lesotho. Study carried out by SATEP on behalf of the Southern Africa Labour Commission (SALC) (Lusaka, SATEP, 1985), vi + 45 pp. Annex. [LSO]

- Latin America and the Caribbean

E. Arriaga: *Caracteristicas laborales y educacionales de migrantes y no migrantes en Chile*. Occasional papers No. 18 (Santiago, PREALC, Jan. 1978). [CHL]

H. Lubell and D. McCallum: *Bogotá: Urban development and employment* (Geneva, ILO, 1978), xiv + 146 pp. Sw. frs. 17.50. [COL] ISBN 92-2-101998-5.

N. Saavedra: *Migraciones internas y sector informal en Chile*. Monograph No. 19 (Santiago, PREALC, July 1981). [CHL]

- Asia

Tradition and dynamism among Afghan refugees. Report of an ILO mission to Pakistan (November 1982) on income-generating activities for Afghan refugees (Geneva, ILO/UNHCR, 1983), xvi + 174 pp. Sw. frs. 20. [AFG] ISBN 92-2-103517-4.

Impact of return migration on domestic employment in Pakistan: A preliminary analysis. A report for the Ministry of Labour, Manpower and Overseas Pakistanis, Government of Pakistan (Bangkok, ARTEP, 1984), 113 pp.* [PAK]

- OECD Countries

U. Hiemenz and K.W. Schatz: *Trade in place of migration*. An employment-oriented study with special reference to the Federal Republic of Germany, Spain and Turkey (Geneva, ILO, 1979), x + 118 pp. Sw. frs. 17.50. E, S. [DEU, ESP, TUR] ISBN 92-2-101865-2.

- Middle East

J.S. Birks and C.A. Sinclair: *International migration and development in the Arab region*. (Geneva, ILO, 1980), xii + 176 pp.* Sw. frs. 25. [TUN, SDN, EGY, LBY, KWT, QAT, BHR, ARE, SAU, JOR, SYR, OMN, YEM] ISBN 92-2-102251-X.

Articles in the International Labour Review

- General

H. Lubell: "Urban development and employment: The Third World metropolis", Vol. 117, No. 6, Nov.-Dec. 1978.

P. Peek and G. Standing: "Rural-urban migration and government policies in low-income countries", Vol. 118, No. 6, Nov.-Dec. 1979.

R.P. Shaw: "Bending the urban flow: A construction-migration strategy", Vol. 119, No. 4, July-Aug. 1980.

S.O. Asiama: "The rich slum dweller: A problem of unequal access", Vol. 124, No. 3, May-June 1985.

- Latin America and the Caribbean

P. Peek: "Agrarian change and labour migration in the Sierra of Ecuador", Vol. 119, No. 5, Sep.-Oct. 1980, pp. 609-621. [ECU]

- Asia

A.S. Oberai and H.K.M. Singh: "Migration, remittances and rural development: Findings of a case study in the Indian Punjab", Vol. 119, No. 2 Mar.-Apr. 1980. [IND]

A.S. Oberai: "State policies and internal migration in Asia", Vol. 120, No. 2, Mar.-Apr. 1981.

A. Stretton: "Circular migration, segmented labour markets and efficiency: The building industry in Manila and Port Moresby", Vol. 122, No. 5, Sep.-Oct. 1983. [PHL, PNG]

A.S. Oberai and H.K.M. Singh: "Migration, employment and the urban labour market: A study in the India Punjab", Vol. 123, No. 4, July-Aug. 1984. [IND]

- OECD Countries

D. Maillat, C. Jeanrenaud and J.-Ph. Widmer: "Reactions of Swiss employers to the immigration freeze", Vol. 117, No. 6, Nov.-Dec. 1978. [CHE]

W.R. Böhning: "International migration in Western Europe: Reflections on the past five years", Vol. 118, No. 4, July-Aug. 1979.

W.R. Böhning: "Legal and illegal migration to the United States", Vol. 119, No. 2, Mar.-Apr. 1980. [USA]

- Middle East

R.P. Shaw: "Migration and employment in the Arab world: Construction as a key policy variable", Vol. 118, No. 5, Sep.-Oct. 1979.

Working Papers

- General

W.R. Böhning: *Elements of a theory of international migration and compensation*, Nov. 1978 (WEP 2-26/WP.34). M.

H. Entzinger: *Return migration from West European to Mediterranean countries*, Mar. 1978 (WEP 2-26/WP.23). M.

K.H. Höpfner and M. Huber: *Regulating international migration in the interest of the developing countries: With particular reference to Mediterranean countries*, Feb. 1978 (WEP 2-26/WP.21). M.

G.B. Rodgers and R. Anker: *Urban employment in the 1980s: The cases of Kenya and the Philippines*, May 1978 (WEP 2-21/WP.63). [PHL, KEN]

W.R. Böhning: *Migration, the idea of compensation, and the international economic order,*[2] Dec. 1979 (WEP 2-26/WP.45). M.

W.R. Böhning: *Regularising indocumentados*, Apr. 1979 (WEP 2-26/WP.36). M.

P.A. Cornelisse, J. Gaude and P. Antolinez: *A simple migration model with market intervention*, Sep. 1979 (WEP 10-6/WP.27). M.

G. Standing: *Migration and modes of exploitation: The social origins of immobility and mobility*, June 1979 (WEP 2-21/WP.72).

R.E. Bilsborrow: *Surveys of internal migration in low-income countries: The need for and content of community-level variables,* [1] Apr. 1981 (WEP 2-21/WP.104) M. ISBN 92-2-102738-4.

A.S. Oberai: *Demographic and social information in migration surveys: Analytical significance and guidelines for data collection,* [1] Jan. 1981 (WEP 2-21/WP.99) M. E, F. ISBN 92-2-102638-8.

A.S. Oberai: *Migration, production and technological change: Analytical issues and guidelines for data collection and analysis,* [1] June 1981 (WEP 2-21/WP.107) M. ISBN 92-2-102830-5.

P. Peek: *A typology of migrants: Some methodological aspects*, Sep. 1981 (WEP 10-6/WP.50). M. ISBN 92-2-102884-4.

G.B. Rodgers *Migration and income distribution*, July 1981 (WEP 2-21/WP.108). M. ISBN 92-2-102844-5.

G. Standing: *Conceptualising territorial mobility in low-income countries,* [1] Oct. 1981 (WEP 2-21/WP.112). M. ISBN 92-2-102929-8.

G. Standing: *Income transfers and remittances: A module for migration surveys,* [1] Apr. 1981 (WEP 2-21/WP.105). M. ISBN 92-2-102755-4.

G. Standing: *Migrants and the labour process: A module for migration surveys,* [1] Feb. 1981 (WEP 2-21/WP.100) M. ISBN 92-2-102640-X.

G. Standing: *Circulation and proletarianisation*, Sep. 1982 (WEP 2-21/WP.119). ISBN 92-2-103248-5.

- Africa

A. Benachenhou: *Politiques rurales et migrations en Algérie,* [3] June 1978 (WEP 10-6/WP.18). *M. [DZA]

J.S. Birks and C.A. Sinclair: *Human capital on the Nile: Development and emigration in the Arab Republic of Egypt and the Democratic Republic of Sudan*, May 1978 (WEP 2-26/WP.27). M. [EGY, SDN]

D.G. Clarke: *International labour supply trends and economic structure in Southern Rhodesia/Zimbabwe in the 1970s*, Jan. 1978 (WEP 2-26/WP.20). M. [ZWE]

F. de Vletter: *Migrant labour in Swaziland: Characteristics, attitudes and policy implications*, Feb. 1978 (WEP 2-26/WP.22). M. [SWZ]

B.D. Rosen-Prinz and F.A. Prinz: *Migrant labour and rural homesteads: An investigation into the sociological dimensions of the migrant labour system in Swaziland,* [4] Sep. 1978 (WEP 2-26/WP.31). M. [SWZ]

W.M. Woods: *LR-12: A preliminary simulation model of the effects of declining migration to South Africa on households in Botswana*, Sep. 1978 (WEP 2-26/WP.32). M. [ZAF, BWA]

N. Bromberger: *Mining employment in South Africa, 1946-2000*, May 1979 (WEP 2-26/WP.38). M. [ZAF]

E. Molapi Sebatane: *An empirical study of the attitudes and perceptions of migrant workers: The case of Lesotho*, Sep. 1979 (WEP 2-26/WP.42). M. [LSO]

S. Rugege: *Legal aspects of labour migration from Lesotho to the South African mines*, July 1979 (WEP 2-26/WP.40). M. [LSO, ZAF]

C.W. Stahl and W.R. Böhning: *Reducing migration dependence in Southern Africa*, Apr. 1979 (WEP 2-26/WP.37).

C.W. Stahl: *Southern African migrant labour supplies in the past, the present and the future with special reference to the gold-mining industry,* [4] Aug. 1979 (WEP 2-26/WP.41). [ZAF]

S. Adler: *Swallows' children - Emigration and development in Algeria*, May 1980 (WEP 2-26/WP.46). M. [DZA]

F. de Vletter: *Migrant labour conditions in South Africa. A case study of the gold mines,* [4] Aug. 1980 (WEP 2-26/WP.49). M. [ZAF]

J. Trouvé and C. Bessat: *L'exode rural des jeunes et les politiques gouvernementales de développement: L'expérience camerounaise,* [3] Nov. 1980 (WEP 10-6/WP.38). M. [CMR]

J. Trouvé in collaboration with C. Bessat: *Les liens entre migrations rurales et politiques gouvernementales*, Jan. 1980 (WEP 10-6/WP.29). M. [BFA]

N.O. Addo: *The impact of public policies on migration and development in Ghana, with special reference to the Autsuare sugar area*, Aug. 1981 (WEP 2-21/WP.110). M. [GHA] ISBN 92-2-102859-3.

H. Bernstein: *Patterns of migration in the United Republic of Tanzania*, Mar. 1981 (WEP 2-21/WP.101). M. [TZA] ISBN 92-2-102706-6.

A. Guichaoua: *"Surpeuplement" et stratégies migratoires des paysans au Burundi,* [3] May 1981 (WEP 10-6/WP.46). M. [BDI] ISBN 92-2-202754-X.

C. Lwoga: *Seasonal labour migration in the United Republic of Tanzania: The case of Ludewa district*, Nov. 1982 (WEP 2-21/WP.121). [TZA] ISBN 92-2-103304-X.

F. de Vletter: *Labour migration to South Africa: Recent trends and prospects* (Lusaka, SATEP), May 1985. [ZAF]

C. Maldonado et G. Le Boterf: *L'apprentissage et les apprentis dans les petits métiers urbains: Le cas de l'Afrique francophone*, Jan. 1985 (WEP 2-33/Doc. 24). [MLI, TGO, MRT, CMR] ISBN 92-2-205012-6.

J.C. Woillet: *L'artisanat urbain au Mali: Choix de produits et politiques visant à la promotion du secteur non-structuré urbain du Mali*, Feb. 1985 (WEP 2-33/Doc. 20). [MLI] ISBN 92-2-205069-X.

- **Latin America and the Caribbean**

Urban services and public contracts - Access and distribution in Lima and Caracas (Santiago, PREALC), Dec. 1978 (No. 165). [PER, VEN]

P.A. Cornelisse, J. Gaude and P. Antolinez: *The Bicoa model: A socio-economic model of rural-urban migration in the Sierra of Ecuador*, July 1978 (WEP 10-6/WP.21). M. [ECU]

P. Peek: *Urban poverty, migration and land reform in Ecuador*, June 1979 (WEP 10-6/WP.24)*. M. [ECU]

G. Standing: *Semi-feudalism, migration and the state of Guyana*, Sep. 1979 (WEP 2-21/WP.73). [GUY]

Migración laboral en el área de influencia de Quito (Santiago, PREALC), Feb. 1980 (No. 180). [ECU]

E. de Labastida and J. Gaude: *A socio-economic input-output matrix adapted for an analysis of internal migration: The case of Ecuador*, Dec. 1980 (WEP 10-6/WP.42). M. [ECU]

P. Peek and P. Antolinez: *Labour migration in the Sierra of Ecuador: Causes and incidence*, Aug. 1980 (WEP 10-6/WP.36). M. [ECU]

Acceso a los servicios urbanos y a los contratos públicos en Lima y Caracas (Santiago, PREALC), Jan. 1981 (No. 197). [PER, VEN]

P. Antolinez and J. Gaude: *Landholding status, farm size and rural-urban migration: A micro-macro approach to the Sierra of Ecuador*, 1981 (WEP 10-6/WP.43). [ECU] ISBN 92-2-102626-4.

J. Balan: *Migraciones temporarias y mercado de trabajo rural en América Latina: Una revisión del problema y de la información disponible*, Sep. 1981 (WEP 10-6/WP.48). M. [ARG, BRA, MEX] ISBN 92-2-302865-5.

E.A. Lira and S. Commander: *"Mexico: Commercialisation and the growth of a migratory labour market"*, Aug. 1983, (WEP 10-6/WP.56). M. [MEX] ISBN 92-2-103565-4.

J. Laite: *Circulatory migration and social differentiation in the Andes*, Apr. 1983 (WEP 2-21/WP.131). M. [PER] ISBN 92-2-103464-X.

S.E. Findley: *Colonist constraints, strategies and mobility: Recent trends in Latin American frontier zones*, Nov. 1984 (WEP 2-21/WP.145). ISBN 92-2-103972-2.

Las migraciones a Lima metropolitana, crisis económica y cambios en la inserción laboral de los migrantes (Santiago, PREALC), Aug. 1987 (No. 304). [PER]

Migraciones internas y mercado de trabajo en San José, Costa Rica (Santiago, PREALC), June 1987 (No. 300). [CRI]

- Asia

J.P. Perez-Sainz: *Transmigration and accumulation in Indonesia*, Sep. 1979 (WEP 2-21/WP.74). [IDN]

A.S. Oberai and H.K.M. Singh: *Migration, urbanisation and fertility: The case of the Indian Punjab*, Sep. 1980 (WEP 2-21/WP.95). [IND]

A.S. Oberai: *An overview of state policies and internal migration in Asia*, May 1980 (WEP 2-21/WP.88). M.

A.S. Oberai and H.K.M. Singh: *Migration, unemployment and the urban labour market: A case study of Ludhiana in the Indian Punjab*, Dec. 1981 (WEP 2-21/WP.113). M. [IND] ISBN 92-2-102966-2.

A.S. Oberai and H.K.M. Singh: *Urban in-migration and remittances: A case study of Ludhiana in the Indian Punjab*, Jan. 1981 (WEP 2-21/WP.97). M. [IND] ISBN 92-2-102614-0.

H.W. Arndt: *Transmigration in Indonesia*, Nov. 1984 (WEP 2-21/WP.146). [IDN] ISBN 92-2-103973-0.

E.M. Pernia: *Migration, development and employment in East and Southeast Asia: Patterns and implications*, Oct. 1985 (WEP 2-21/WP. 151). M. [TWN, KOR, MYS, PHL, THA, IDN] ISBN 92-2-105314-8.

Farooq-i-Azam: *Re-integration of return migrants in Asia: A review and proposals* (New Delhi, ARTEP), Dec. 1987. [LKA, THA, PHL, PAK] ISBN 92-2-106103-5

S. Mukhopadhyay: *Intra-rural labour circulation in India: An analysis* (New Delhi, ARTEP), July 1987. [IND] ISBN 92-2-106035-7.

A. Saith: *Macro-economic issues in international labour migration: A review* (New Delhi, ARTEP), May 1987. ISBN 92-2-105775-5.

- OECD Countries

C. Bock and F. Tiedt: *Biefragung Jugoslawischer Haushalte in der Bundesrepublik Deutschland*, Sep. 1978 (WEP 2-26/WP.33(G)). M. [DEU, YUG]

G. Tapinos et al: *Possibilités de transfert d'emplois vers les pays d'émigration en tant qu'alternative aux migrations internationales des travailleurs: Le cas français (I: éléments introductifs)*, Mar. 1978 (WEP 2-26/WP.24). M. [FRA]

G. Tapinos et al: *Possibilités de transfert d'emplois vers les pays d'émigration en tant qu'alternative aux migrations internationales des travailleurs: Le cas français (II: études sectorielles)*, Apr. 1978 (WEP 2-26/WP.25). M. [FRA]

G. Tapinos et al: *Possibilités de transfert d'emplois vers les pays d'émigration en tant qu'alternative aux migrations internationales des travailleurs: Le cas français (III: les pays de départ et synthèse)*, May 1978 (WEP 2-26/WP.26). M. [FRA]

M. Werth and N. Yalcintas: *Migration and reintegration: Transferability of the Turkish model of return migration and self-help organisations to other Mediterranean labour-exporting countries*, June 1978 (WEP 2-26/WP.29). M. [TUR]

M.J. Miller and D.J. Yeres: *A massive temporary worker programme for the US: Solution or mirage?*, Nov. 1979 (WEP 2-26/WP.44). M. [USA]

D.S. North: *The Canadian experience with amnesty for aliens: What the United States can learn*, Oct. 1979 (WEP 2-26/WP.43). M. [CAN, USA]

W.R. Böhning: *Guest worker employment, with special reference to the Federal Republic of Germany, France and Switzerland - Lessons for the United States?*, [2] June 1980 (WEP 2-26/WP.47). M. [DEU, FRA, CHE]

S. Adler: *A Turkish conundrum: Emigration, politics and development, 1961-1980*, Aug. 1981 (WEP 2-26/WP.52). [TUR] ISBN 92-2-102862-3.

I. Musillo: *Retour et emploi des migrants dans le mezzogiorno: Enquête sur un échantillon de migrants italiens*, Mar. 1981 (WEP 2-26/WP.51). [ITA] ISBN 92-2-202718-3.

- **Middle East**

J.S. Birks and C.A. Sinclair: *Nature and process of labour importing: The Arabian Gulf States of Kuwait, Bahrain, Qatar and the United Arab Emirates*, Aug. 1978 (WEP 2-26/WP.30). M. [BHR, KWT, QAT, ARE]

J.S. Birks and C.A. Sinclair: *The Sultanate of Oman: Economic development, the domestic labour market and international migration*, June 1978 (WEP 2-26/WP.28). M. [OMN]

J.S. Birks and C.A. Sinclair: *The Kingdom of Saudi Arabia and the Libyan Arab Jamahiriya: The key countries of employment*, May 1979 (WEP 2-26/WP.39). M. [SAU, LBY]

H.T. Azzam: *Labour mobility and human resources in the Arab region: Problems and prospects* (Beirut, LPME), 1980 (WP.2), 31 pp. ISBN 92-2-102502-0.

H. Chekir and J.P. Garson: *Perspectives d'émigration maghrebine vers les pays du Golf*, July 1980 (WEP 2-26/WP.48). M. [BHR, KWT, SAU, FRA, TUN, DZA, LBY]

N. Fergany: *The affluent years are over - Emigration and development in the Yemen Arab Republic*, Sep. 1980 (WEP 2-26/WP.50). M. [YEM]

J.N. Sinha and M.J. Murad: *Population redistribution, employment and development in Syria* (Beirut, LPME), 1980 (WP.6), 71 pp. [SYR] ISBN 92-2-102513-6.

N.F. Khoury: *Interrelationship between urbanisation and socio-economic changes in Syria* (Beirut, LPME), Jan. 1982 (WP. 7). [SYR]

ILO works published by commercial and non-profit-making publishers

- General

A.S. Oberai (ed.): *State policies and internal migration*. Studies in market and planned economies (London, Croom Helm; New York, St. Martin's Press, 1983), 347 pp. [MYS, LKA, NPL, POL, IND, IDN] ISBN 0-7099-1933-6.

R.E. Bilsborrow, A.S. Oberai and G. Standing: *Migration surveys in low-income countries: Guidelines for survey and questionnaire design* (London, Croom Helm, 1984), 552 pp. ISBN 0-7099-3266-9.

G. Standing (ed.): *Labour circulation and the labour process* (London, Croom Helm, 1985), xvi + 416 pp. [IDN, TZA, NGA, KEN, IND, BRA, MEX] ISBN 0-7099-3342-8.

- Latin America and the Caribbean

M.G. Castro et al.: *Migration in Brazil: Approaches to analysis and policy design* (Liège, Ordina Editions, 1978), xiii + 200 pp. [BRA]

P. Peek and G. Standing (eds.): *State policies and migration*. Studies in Latin America and the Caribbean (London, Croom Helm, 1982), 403 pp. [CHL, PER, MEX, COL, GUY, CUB, ECU, BRA] ISBN 0-7099-2078-8.

- Asia

A.S. Oberai and H.K.M. Singh: *Causes and consequences of internal migration: A study in the Indian Punjab* (New Delhi, Oxford University Press, 1983), xxiii + 434 pp. [IND] ISBN 19-561632-4.

Related books and articles

- General

W.R. Böhning: "International migration and the Western world: Past, present, future", in *International Migration* (New York), Vol. XVI, No. 1, 1978, pp. 11-22.

D. Maillat and J.-Ph. Widmer: "Transferts d'emplois et déséquilibres régionaux", in P. Caroni, B. Dafflon and G. Enderle (eds.): *Nur Oekonomie ist keine Oekonomie* (Berne, Haupt Verlag, 1978), pp. 287-303.

G. Standing: "Aspiration wages, migration and urban unemployment", in *Journal of Development Studies* (London), Vol. 14, No. 2, Jan. 1978.

S.V. Sethuraman: "Des emplois urbains dans le tiers monde", in *Projet* (Paris), July-Aug. 1978.

W.R. Böhning: "Faits et chiffres sur les migrations internationales", in *Population* (Paris), Vol. 34, No. 6, Nov.-Dec. 1979, pp. 1130-1137.

W.R. Böhning: "L'emigrazione nel futuro ordine economico internazionale" in *Affari Sociali Internazionali* (Milano), Vol. VII, No. 1, 1979, pp. 65-76.

G. Standing: "Migration and modes of exploitation: Social origins of immobility and mobility", in *Journal of Peasant Studies* (London), Vol. 8, No. 2, Jan. 1981.

R.J. Szal: "Le problème des réfugiés: Une menace pour la paix internationale" in *Libertas* (Lausanne), June 1981.

G.B. Rodgers: "The impact of rural-urban migration on income distribution", in *Canadian Journal of Development Studies* (Ottawa), Vol. IV, No. 2, 1983.

G. Standing: *Population mobility and productive relations. Demographic links and policy evolution*. World Bank Staff Working Papers No. 695, Population and Development series No. 20 (Washington, DC, The World Bank, 1984).

- Africa

J.S. Birks and C.A. Sinclair: "Egypt: A frustrated labour exporter?", in *Middle East Journal* (Washington, DC), Vol. 33, 1979, pp. 288-303. [EGY]

W.J. House and H. Rempel: "The determinants of interregional migration in Kenya", in *World Development* (Oxford), Vol. 8, No. 1, Jan. 1980. [KEN]

- Latin America and the Caribbean

P. Peek: *Urban poverty, migration and land reform in Ecuador*, Occasional Papers No. 79 (The Hague, ISS, Mar. 1980), 28 pp. [ECU]

J. Gaude: *The temporary migration phenomenon in the Sierra of Ecuador* (Rotterdam, Centre for Development Planning, Erasmus University, 1981). [ECU]

- Asia

R. Wéry: "Internal migration in the Philippines during the 1960s", in *Population Bulletin of the United Nations* (New York), No. 12, 1979. [PHL]

A.S. Oberai and H.K.M. Singh: "Migration flows in Punjab's green revolution belt", in *Economic and Political Weekly* (Bombay), Vol. XV, No. 13, Mar. 1980. [IND]

- OECD Countries

D. Maillat and J.-Ph. Widmer: "Transferts d'emplois vers les pays qui disposent d'un surplus de main-d'oeuvre: Le cas de la Suisse", in *Studi Emigrazione/Etudes Migration* (Rome), Vol. XV, Sep. 1978, pp. 361-381. [CHE]

D. Maillat, C. Jeanrenaud and J.-Ph. Widmer: "Les entrepreneurs suisses face à l'arrêt de l'immigration", in *Hommes et Migration - Documents* (Paris), Vol. 30, No. 972, 15 June 1979, pp. 9-22. [CHE]

- Middle East

W.R. Böhning: "Perspectives of Arab policies on international migration", in Arab Planning Institute (ed): *Seminar on Population, Employment and Migration in the Arab Gulf States*, Kuwait, 16-18 December 1978, pp. 494-504.

J.S. Birks and C.A. Sinclair: "International labour migration in the Arab Middle East", in *Third World Quarterly* (London), Vol. 1, No. 2, Apr. 1979, pp. 87-99.

J.S. Birks and C.A. Sinclair: "Some aspects of the labour market in the Middle East with special reference to the Gulf States", in *Journal of Developing Areas* (Macomb, IL 61455), Vol. 13, 1979, pp. 301-318.

J.S. Birks and C.A. Sinclair: "The international migration project: An inquiry into the Middle East labour market", in *International Migration Review* (New York), Vol. XIII, No. 1, Spring 1979, pp. 122-135.

J.S. Birks and C.A. Sinclair: "The Libyan Arab Jamahiriya: Labour migration sustains dualistic development", in *Maghreb Review* (Paris), Vol. 4, No. 3, 1979, pp. 95-102. [LBY]

Notes:

1 Published in R.E. Bilsborrow, A.S. Oberai and G. Standing: Migration surveys in low-income countries. Guidelines for survey and questionnaire design (London, Croom Helm, 1984).

2 Also published in W.R. Böhning, Studies in international labour migration (London, Macmillan, 1984).

3 Also published in J. Gaude (ed.): Phenomène migratoire et politiques associées dans le contexte africain (Geneva, ILO, 1982).

4 Also published in W.R. Böhning (ed.): Black migration to South Africa. A selection of policy-oriented research (Geneva, ILO, 1981).

Population and employment

ILO publications

Books and reports

- General

The educational activities of the ILO population and labour policies programme (Geneva, ILO, 1978), 54 pp. E, F. ISBN 92-2-101985-3.

G. Standing and G. Sheehan (eds.): *Labour force participation in low-income countries* (Geneva, ILO, 1978), 342 pp.* Sw. frs. 22.50 [COL, CHL, CRI, ECU, SDN, SLV, YUG, LKA, SGP, PNG, THA, PHL, VEN, MEX, GHA, NGA] ISBN 92-2-101812-1.

G. Standing: *Labour force participation and development* (Geneva, ILO, 1978; 2nd edition, 1981), 266 pp. Sw. frs. 30. ISBN 92-2-102763-5.

Population, human resources and development planning. The ILO contribution (Geneva, ILO, 1983; 2nd impression, 1984), vi + 55 pp. F, S. ISBN 92-2-103888-2

Population, development, family welfare. The ILO's contribution (Geneva, ILO, 1984), 56 pp. ISBN 92-2-103874-2.

Report of the informal inter-agency expert group meeting on methodologies for integrated population and development planning, Geneva, 21-24 May 1984 (Geneva, ILO, 1984), 42 pp.

G.B. Rodgers *Poverty and population. Approaches and evidence* (Geneva, ILO, 1984), 213 pp. Sw. frs. 27.50. ISBN 92-2-103803-3.

G.M. Farooq: *Population and employment in developing countries*. Background papers for training in population, human resources and development planning, paper No. 1 (Geneva, ILO, 1985), 65 pp. + annex. Sw. frs. 15. E,F,S. ISBN 92-2-100515-1.

G. Greene: *Planning for population, labour force and service demand: A microcomputer-based training module*. Background papers for training in population, human resources and development planning, paper No. 3 (Geneva, ILO, 1986), v + 100 pp. Sw. frs. 15. E,F,S. ISBN 92-2-105622-8.

J.M. Sehgal: *An introduction to techniques of population and labour force projections*. Background papers for training in population, human resources and development planning, paper No. 4 (Geneva, ILO, 1986), vi + 78 pp. Sw. frs. 15. E,F. ISBN 92-2-105623-6.

A. Uthoff and E.M. Pernia: *An introduction to human resource planning in developing countries*. Background papers for training in population, human resources and development planning, paper No. 2 (Geneva, ILO, 1986), vii + 67 pp. Sw. frs. 15. E,F,S. ISBN 92-2-105390-3.

Population and labour research news, 10. A report on research and related policy activities in the ILO's Population and Labour Policies Programme, mainly with financial support from the United Nations Fund for Population Activities, February 1987 (Geneva, ILO, 1987), 36 pp.

Population, human resources and development planning. The ILO contribution (Geneva, ILO, 1987), vi + 74 pp. ISBN 92-2-105869-7.

A.S. Oberai: *Migration, urbanisation and development.* Background papers for training in population, human resources and development planning, paper No. 5 (Geneva, ILO, 1987), vi + 108. Sw. frs. 15. ISBN 92-2-106129-9.

- Africa

Inquérito ás famílias sobre emprego e desemprego - Criaçao de um sistema de Estatística de emprego (Anexo: Tratamento informático) (Geneva, ILO, 1978) [CPV]

- Latin America and the Caribbean

A. Uthoff: *Fecundidad y desarrollo económico y social en Chile: 1952-1970.* Occasional papers No. 22 (Santiago, PREALC, May 1978). [CHL]

S.L. de Bragança, J.B. Burle de Figueiredo and M.H. da Cunha Rato: *The simulation of economic and demographic development in Brazil.* A progress report on activities of the Brazilian Institute of Geography and Statistics, Rio de Janeiro, undertaken in collaboration with the ILO, (Geneva, ILO, 1980), iv + 102pp. Portuguese, E. [BRA] ISBN 92-2-102369-9.

- Asia

C. Mukherjee and A.V. Jose: *Report of a survey of rural households in the Hat Xai Fong district in Vientiane province of the Laos People's Democratic Republic* (Bangkok, ARTEP, 1982), viii + 48 pp. Sw. frs. 5.50. [LAO] ISBN 92-2-103279-5.

- East European Countries

M. Rasevic, T. Mulina and M. Macura: *The determinants of labour force participation in Yugoslavia* (Geneva, ILO 1978), v + 229 pp.* Sw.frs 25. [YUG] ISBN 92-2-101900-4.

Articles in the International Labour Review

- General

R. Anker and G.M. Farooq: "Population and socio-economic development: The new perspective", Vol. 117,. No. 2, Mar.-Apr. 1978.

G.M. Farooq: "Population, human resources and development planning: Towards an integrated approach", Vol. 120. No. 3, May-June 1981.

G.B. Rodgers: "Population growth, inequality and poverty", Vol. 122, No. 4, July-Aug. 1983.

A.S. Oberai: "Land settlement policies and population redistribution in developing countries: Performance, problems and prospects", Vol. 125, No. 2, Mar.-Apr. 1986.

- Latin America and the Caribbean

J.L. Petruccelli, M.H. Rato and S.L. Bragança: "The socio-economic consequences of a reduction in fertility. Application of the ILO-IBGE national model (BACHUE-Brazil)", Vol. 119, No. 5, Sep.-Oct. 1980. [BRA]

- East European Countries

B.N. Khomelyansky: "Stabilising the USSR's rural population through development of the social infrastructure ", Vol. 121, No. 1, Jan.-Feb. 1982, pp. 89-100. [SUN]

Working Papers

- General

S. Moreland: *A demographic-economic model for developing countries: BACHUE-International*, Dec. 1978 (WEP 2-21/WP.70). M.

T.P. Schultz: *Interpretation of relations among mortality, economics of the household and the health environment.* Paper presented to joint UN/WHO meeting on Socio-Economic Determinants and Consequences of Mortality, Mexico City, 19-25 June 1979 (WEP 2-21/WP.78). M.

R. Blandy: *Soft-science: On thinking about population*, Aug. 1980 (WEP 2-21/WP.92). M.

R. Wéry and G.B. Rodgers: *Endogenising demographic variables in demo-economic models: The BACHUE experience*, Apr. 1980 (WEP 2-21/WP.86).

R. Wéry: *BACHUE modules: Population, household income and labour market*, Jan. 1980 (WEP 2-21/WP.84).

I. Adelman and J.M. Hihn: *The political economy of investment in human capital*, Mar. 1981 (WEP 2-21/WP.103). M. ISBN 92-2-102734-1.

G.B. Rodgers: *Population growth, poverty and inequality in an international perspective*, Dec. 1982 (WEP 2-21/WP.127). ISBN 92-2-103346-5.

G.B. Rodgers: *Population growth, poverty and inequality in an international perspective: Mark II*, June 1983 (WEP 2-21/WP.135). M. ISBN 92-2-103501-8.

- Africa

W.J. House: *The state of human resources, conditions of employment and determinants of incomes and poverty in Southern Sudan: Evidence from the urban Juba infomal economy*, May 1985 (WEP 2-21/WP. 149). [SDN] ISBN 92-2-105144-7.

W.J. House: *Population, poverty and deprivation in Southern Sudan: A review*, Nov. 1986 (WEP 2-21/WP.154). [SDN] ISBN 92-2-105814-X.

- Latin America and the Caribbean

Dinámica poblacional y empleo en Guatemala: Una síntesis (Santiago, PREALC), Aug. 1980 (No. 204).* [GTM]

M.H. da Cunha Rato and S.L. de Bragança: *The labour market of BACHUE Brazil*, Sep. 1980 (WEP 2-21/WP.93). M. [BRA] ISBN 92-2-102509-8.

Household behaviour and economic crisis. Costa Rica 1979-1982 (Santiago, PREALC), Aug. 1985 (No. 270). [CRI]

Población y fuerza de trabajo en América Latina, 1950-1980 (Santiago, PREALC), Mar. 1985 (No. 259).

- Asia

G.B. Rodgers: *An analysis of education, employment and income distribution using an economic-demographic model of the Philippines*, June 1978 (WEP 2-21/WP.65). [PHL]

A. Elek: *Feasibility study for the construction of an economic-demographic model for Indonesia*, Jan. 1980 (WEP 2-21/WP.82). [IDN]

P.H. Prasad, G.B. Rodgers, S. Gupta, A.N. Sharma and B. Sharma: *The pattern of poverty in Bihar*, Sep. 1986 (WEP 2-21/WP.152). [IND] ISBN 92-2-105693-73.

G.B. Rodgers, S. Gupta, A.N. Sharma and B. Sharma: *Demography and poverty at the micro-level in Bihar*, Oct. 1986 (WEP 2-21/WP.153). [IND] ISBN 92-2-105749-6.

M.E. Khan, R. Anker, S.K. Ghosh and S. Bairathi: *Inequalities between men and women in nutrition and family welfare services: An in-depth enquiry in an Indian village*, June 1987 (WEP 2-21/WP.158). [IND] ISBN 92-2-106134-5.

- OECD Countries

G. Blardone, M.Ch. Leroy and G. Parisot: *Population, progrès technique et social, développement économique et emploi - Modèle démographique et socio-économique ISSA 10 - ISSA 11. Application à une région rurale française*, June 1978 (WEP 2-21/WP.66). [FRA]

S.S. Lieberman: *An analysis of aggregate demographic patterns in rural Turkey*, June 1978 (WEP 2-21/WP.67). M. [TUR]

C. Bock and F. Tiedt: *Survey of Yugoslav households in the Federal Republic of Germany*, June 1979 (WEP 2-26/WP.33(E)). M. [YUG, DEU]

- East European Countries

B. Popovic, M. Macura, R. Wéry and P. Cornu: *Predicting long-term changes in Yugoslav personal consumption with a comprehensive regionalised economic demographic model*, Jan. 1984 (WEP 2-21/WP.142). [YUG] ISBN 92-2-103697-9.

- Middle East

H.T. Azzam and R.P. Shaw: *Population, labour force and rural employment in the five least developed Arab countries* (Beirut, LPME), 1980 (WP. 4), 66 pp. [SDN, SOM, YMD, MRT] ISBN 92-2-102504-7.

H.T. Azzam and N. Khoury: *Population, employment and development in the Arab region: Scope and prospects* (Beirut, LPME) 1981, (WP. 11), 39 pp., Appendices. ISBN 92-2-102585-3.

ILO works published by commercial and non-profit-making publishers

- General

R.S. Moreland: *Population, development and income distribution - A modelling approach. BACHUE-International* (Aldershot, Hampshire, Gower and New York, St. Martin's Press, 1984), x + 197 pp. ISBN 0-566-00701-0.

- Africa

R. Anker and J.C. Knowles: *Population growth, employment and economic-demographic interactions in Kenya: BACHUE-Kenya* (Aldershot, Hampshire, Gower, 1983), xix + 733. [KEN] ISBN 0-566-00258-2.

- Asia

G.B. Rodgers, M.J.D. Hopkins and R. Wéry: *Population, employment and inequality. BACHUE-Philippines*. An application of economic-demographic modelling to development planning. (Westmead, Farnborough, Saxon House, 1978), xiii + 434 pp. [PHL] ISBN 0-566-00204-3.

Related books and articles

- **General**

G.B. Rodgers and G. Standing: "Population and development: The search for selective interventions", in *Land Economics* (Madison), Vol. 54, No. 2, May 1978.

R. Wéry: "Les modèles démo-économiques BACHUE: Quelques traits de leur développement", in *Approche systématique en sciences de la population*. Chaire Quetelet, Université catholique de Louvain (Liège, Ordina, 1978).

G.B. Rodgers: "Income and inequality as determinants of mortality: An international cross-section analysis", in *Population Studies* (London), Vol. 33, No. 2, July 1979.

R.S. Moreland: "Modelling labour markets in developing countries: The BACHUE approach", in *Perspectives de population, d'emploi et de croissance urbaine*, Chaire Quetelet, Université catholique de Louvain (Liège, Ordina, 1980).

R. Wéry and G.B. Rodgers: "Endogenising demographic variables in demo-economic models: The BACHUE experience" in *Pakistan Development Review* (Karachi), Vol. XIX, No. 3, Autumn 1980.

G.B. Rodgers: "Population growth, inequality and poverty", in United Nations, Department of International Economic and Social Affairs: *Population, Resources, Environment and Development*, Proceedings of the Expert Group on Population, Resources, Environment and Development, Geneva, 25-29 April 1983 (New York, 1984).

G.B. Rodgers: "Demographic components of poverty", in *Journal of Social and Economic Studies* (New Delhi, Sage Publications) (N.S.) 1, 2 (1984).

G. Standing: *Population mobility and productive relations. Demographic links and policy evolution*, World Bank Staff Working Papers No. 695. Population and Development series No. 20 (Washington, DC, The World Bank, 1984).

- **Africa**

R. Anker and J.C. Knowles: "An empirical analysis of mortality differentials in Kenya at the macro and micro levels", in *Economic Development and Cultural Change* (Chicago), Vol. 29, No. 1, Oct. 1980. [KEN]

- **Latin America and the Caribbean**

Fundaçao Instituto Brasileiro de Geografia e Estatistica: *Atividade de simulaçao na area economico-demografica no IBGE* (Rio de Janeiro, Superintendencia de Estudos geograficos e socio-economicos, 1979), 87 pp. [BRA]

- **Asia**

R. Wéry, G.B. Rodgers and M.J.D. Hopkins: "Population, employment and poverty in the Philippines", in *World Development* (Oxford), Vol. 6, No. 4, Apr. 1978. [PHL]

G.B. Rodgers: "A cluster analysis of Bihar districts according to indicators of agricultural development and demographic characteristics" in *Journal of Social and Economic Studies* (Patna, Bihar), Vol. IX, No.1, 1981, pp. 73-84. [IND]

G.B. Rodgers: "An analysis of education, employment, and income distribution using an economic-demographic model of the Philippines" in *Research in Human Capital and Development* (Greenwich, Jai Press), 1981, Vol. 2, pp. 143-180. [PHL]

- OECD Countries

R. Minami and A. Ono: "Modelling dualistic development in Japan". Reprinted from *Hitotsubashi Journal of Economics* (Kunitachi, Tokyo), Vol. 18, No. 2, Feb. 1978, pp.18-32. [JPN]

Technology and employment

ILO publications

Books and reports

- **General**

A.S. Bhalla (ed.): *Technology and employment in industry. A case study approach*. A collection of case studies (Geneva, ILO, 1975; 3rd revised and enlarged edition, 1985), xv + 324 pp. Sw. frs. 37.50. E, S. [KEN, TZA, THA, KOR, IND, MYS, COL, MEX] ISBN 92-2-103970-6.

Appropriate technology for employment creation in the food processing and drink industries of developing countries - Industrial Committee Report III (Geneva, ILO, 1978). E, F. ISBN 92-2-101880-6.

The employment implications of technological choice and of changes in international trade in the leather and footwear industry - Industrial Committee Report III (Geneva, ILO, 1979). E, F. ISBN 92-2-102197-1.

J. Rada: *The impact of micro-electronics* - A tentative appraisal of information technology. (Geneva, ILO, 1980; 3rd impression, 1982), viii + 110 pp. Sw. frs. 17.50, E*, F. ISBN 92-2-102378-8.

Guide to tools and equipment for labour-based road construction (Geneva, ILO, 1981), 544 pp. Sw. frs. 60. ISBN 92-2-102539-X.

Tanning of hides and skins. Technical memorandum No. 1 prepared under the joint auspices of the ILO and UNIDO (Geneva, ILO, 1981; 2nd impression, 1985; UNIDO edition, 1982), xii + 230 pp. Sw. frs. 27.50. ISBN 92-2-102904-2.

Technological developments and their implications for employment in the printing and allied trades, with particular reference to developing countries - Industrial Committee Report III (Geneva, ILO, 1981). E,F,S,G,R. ISBN 92-2-102693-0.

J. de Veen, J. Boardman and J. Capt: *Productivity and durability of traditional and improved hand tools for civil construction* (Geneva, ILO/FAO, 1981), x + 118 pp.

G.A. Edmonds and J. de Veen: *The application of appropriate technology in road construction and maintenance. A learning methodology* (Geneva, ILO, 1981), v + 34 pp.

L.S. Karlsson and J. de Veen: *Guide to the training of supervisors for labour-based road construction and maintenance - Instructors manual* (Geneva, ILO, 1981). Sw. frs. 120. ISBN 92-2-102887-9.

L.S. Karlsson and J. de Veen: *Guide to the training of supervisors for labour-based road construction and maintenance - Trainees' manual* (Geneva, ILO, 1981). Sw.frs 120. ISBN 92-2-102829-1.

Small-scale manufacture of footwear. Technical memorandum No. 2 prepared under the joint auspices of the ILO and UNIDO (Geneva, ILO, 1982), xvi + 208 pp. Sw. frs. 20. ISBN 92-2-103079-2.

Small-scale processing of fish. Technical memorandum No. 3 prepared under the joint auspices of the ILO, the Food and Agriculture Organisation and the United Nations

Environment Programme (Geneva, ILO, 1982; 2nd impression, 1985), xii + 122 pp. Sw. frs. 15. ISBN 92-2-103205-1.

Technology, employment and social implications of alternative energy policies in developing countries. A progress report on current activities (Geneva, ILO, 1982), vi + 32 pp.

Small-scale oil extraction from groundnuts and copra. Technical memorandum No. 5 prepared under the joint auspices of the ILO and UNIDO (Geneva, ILO, 1983), xi + 112 pp. Sw. frs. 15. ISBN 92-2-103503-4.

Small-scale weaving. Technical memorandum No. 4 prepared under the joint auspices of the ILO and UNIDO (Geneva, ILO, 1983; 2nd impression, 1985), viii + 130 pp. Sw. frs. 20. ISBN 92-2-103419-4.

Road construction and maintenance. Choice of technology in developing countries (Geneva, ILO, 1984), 23 pp. ISBN 92-2-103839-4.

Small-scale brickmaking. Technical memorandum No. 6 prepared under the joint auspices of the ILO and the UNIDO (Geneva, ILO, 1984), xi + 210 pp. Sw. frs. 25. ISBN 92-2-103567-0.

Small-scale maize milling. Technical memorandum No. 7 prepared under the joint auspices of the ILO and UNIDO (Geneva, ILO, 1984; 2nd impression, 1987), xii + 143 pp. Sw. frs. 17.50. ISBN 92-2-103640-5.

J.C. Woillet et M. Allal: *Répertoire des Instituts africains de technologie*, 2 vols. (Geneva, ILO, 1984), Sw. frs. 65. E,F. ISBN 92-2-203662-X.

Facing the technological challenge. A review of ILO activities on technology since the United Nations Conference on Science and Technology for Development, Vienna, 1979 (Geneva, ILO, 1985; 2nd revised ed., forthcoming, 1988), 85 pp. ISBN 92-2-105126-9.

Fish smoking. Technologies for rural women - Ghana, Technical manual No. 3 prepared under the joint auspices of the International Labour Office, the Royal Netherlands Government and the National Council on Women and Development, Ghana (Accra, ILO/NCWD, 1985), vi + 50 pp. ISBN 92-2-105018-1.

Palm oil processing. Technologies for rural women - Ghana, Technical manual No. 1 prepared under the joint auspices of the International Labour Office, the Royal Netherlands Government and the National Council on Women and Development, Ghana (Accra, ILO/NCWD, 1985), vi + 43 pp. ISBN 92-2-105016-5.

Small-scale paper-making. Technical memorandum No. 8 prepared under the joint auspices of the ILO and UNIDO (Geneva, ILO, 1985), vi + 159 pp. Sw. frs. 22.50. ISBN 92-2-103971-4.

Small-scale processing of beef. Technical memorandum No. 10, prepared under the joint auspices of the ILO and the United Nations Environment Programme (Geneva, ILO, 1985), x + 121 pp. Sw. frs. 20. ISBN 92-2-105050-5.

Small-scale processing of pork. Technical memorandum No. 9, prepared under the joint auspices of the ILO and the United Nations Environment Programme (Geneva, ILO, 1985), x + 129 pp. Sw. frs. 20. ISBN 92-2-100542-9.

Soap manufacturing. Technologies for rural women - Ghana, Technical manual No. 2 prepared under the joint auspices of the International Labour Office, the Royal Netherlands Government and the National Council on Women and Development, Ghana (Accra, ILO/NCWD, 1985), vi + 36 pp. ISBN 92-2-105017-3.

Le stockage du grain. Dossier technique No. 11, publié conjointement par le BIT et l'Organisation des Nations Unies pour le développement industriel (Geneva, ILO, 1986), xi + 121 pp. Sw. frs. 20. ISBN 92-2-205415-6.

Solar drying: Practical methods of food preservation (Geneva, ILO, 1986), vii + 127 pp. Sw. frs. 20. ISBN 92-2-105357-1.

Technologie du travail de la corne. Mis au point par le BIT avec le concours de M. Chartier, expert du BIT, M. Randriamihajamanana, artisan cornetier malgache et M. Ramanana, dessinateur (Geneva, ILO, 1986), viii + 103 pp. Sw. frs. 15. ISBN 92-2-205358-3.

Coconut oil processing. Technologies for rural women - Ghana, Technical manual No. 5 prepared under the joint auspices of the International Labour Office, the Royal Netherlands Government and the National Council on Women and Development, Ghana (Accra, ILO/NCWD, 1987), vi. + 33 pp. ISBN 92-2-205020-3.

Gari processing. Technologies for rural women - Ghana, Technical manual No. 4 prepared under the joint auspices of the International Labour Office, the Royal Netherlands Government and the National Council on Women and Development, Ghana (Accra, ILO/NCWD, 1987), vi + 32 pp. ISBN 92-2-105019-X.

Précis de dessin technique à l'usage des formateurs d'artisans. Mis au point par J.N. Chartier, expert du BIT (Geneva, ILO, 1987), ix + 84 pp. Sw. frs. 15. ISBN 92-2-205686-8.

Small-scale manufacture of stabilised soil blocks. Technical memorandum No. 12 prepared under the joint auspices of the ILO and UNIDO (Geneva, ILO, 1987), xiv + 181 pp. Sw. frs. 20. ISBN 92-2-105838-7.

R. Kaplinsky: *Micro-electronics and employment revisited: A review* (Geneva, ILO, 1987), xiv + 181 pp. Sw. frs. 30. [JPN, USA, GBR, FRA, SGP] ISBN 92-2-105611-2

- Africa.

R. Ferchiou and F. Lakhoua: *Technologie et emploi dans le secteur de la construction en Tunisie* (Geneva, ILO, 1979), vi + 70 pp. Sw. frs. 10. [TUN] ISBN 92-2-202179-7.

Adaptation des technologies artisanale et traditionnelle en Côte-d'Ivoire (Addis Ababa, JASPA, 1980).* [CIV]

Appropriate technology. Scope for co-operation among the countries of the West African Economic Community. Report of a study tour undertaken in Dakar, Nouakchott, Abidjan, Bamako, Niamey and Ouagadougou prepared by J.C. Woillet (Geneva, ILO, 1980; 2nd impression, 1982), iv + 126 pp. Sw. frs. 15. E, F. [SEN, MRT, MLI, CIV, NER, BFA] ISBN 92-2-102359-1.

Appropriate technologies in cereal milling and fruit processing industries. A comparative sub-regional study of four East African countries - Kenya, Somalia, the United Republic of Tanzania and Zambia (Addis Ababa, JASPA, 1981). [KEN, SOM, TZA, ZMB]

Appropriate technologies in cereal milling and fruit processing industries. A comparative sub-regional study of four West African countries - The Gambia, Ghana, Liberia and Sierra Leone (Addis Ababa, JASPA, 1981). [GMB, GHA, LBR, SLE]

Report of the ILO/DANIDA African regional seminar on the application of appropriate technology in road construction, Addis Ababa, 10-20 March 1980 (Geneva, ILO, May 1981).

African regional meetings of senior engineers on road maintenance. Gaborone, 11-19 March 1982. SIDA/ILO in collaboration with the Ministry of Works and Communications, Botswana. Summary of proceedings (Geneva, ILO, 1982), iv + 68 pp. [BWA, CMR, TZA, ZMB, ZWE, ETH, GMB, GHA, LSO, MWI, SWZ]

Appropriate technologies in cereal milling and fruit processing industries. Report of a JASPA seminar held in Addis Ababa from 30 November to 4 December 1981 to consider comparative studies in eight English-speaking African countries (Addis Ababa, JASPA, 1982), vi + 50 pp. [GMB, GHA, KEN, LBR, SLE, SOM, TZA, ZMB]

Technologies appropriées dans les industries de transformation alimentaire et de conservation de fruits au Bénin. Rapport soumis au Governement du Bénin par une mission technique du PECTA (Addis Ababa, JASPA, 1982), ii + 132 pp. [BEN]

Technologies appropriées dans les industries de transformation alimentaire et de conservation de fruits au Burundi. Rapport soumis au Gouvernement du Burundi par une mission technique du PECTA (Addis Ababa, JASPA, 1982), vi + 134 pp. [BDI]

Technologies appropriées dans les industries de transformation alimentaire et de conservation de fruits dans quatre pays de la CEAO: Haute-Volta, Mali, Niger, Sénégal (Addis Ababa, JASPA, 1982), ii + 180 pp. [BFA, MLI, NER, SEN]

Technologies appropriées dans les industries de transformation alimentaire et de conservation des fruits au Gabon. Rapport soumis au Gouvernement du Gabon par une mission technique du PECTA (Addis Ababa, JASPA, 1982), 106 p. [GAB]

Technologies appropriées dans les industries de transformation alimentaire et de conservation des fruits au Zaire. Rapport soumis au Gouvernement du Zaire par une mission technique comparative du PECTA (Addis Ababa, JASPA, 1982), 160 pp. [ZAR]

Technologies appropriées dans les industries de transformation alimentaire et de conservation des fruits en Afrique noire francophone. Rapport de synthèse. Rapport soumis aux Gouvernements du Bénin, Gabon, Haute-Volta, Mali, Niger, Sénégal et Zaïre (Addis Ababa, JASPA, 1982), x + 300 pp. [BEN, GAB, BFA, MLI, NER, SEN, ZAR]

G.A. Edmonds and J. de Veen: *Road maintenance: Options for improvement* (Geneva, ILO, 1982), vi + 62 pp. E,F. [KEN] ISBN 92-2-103275-2.

Appropriate farm equipment technology for the small-scale traditional sector. Synthesis report. Regional project on farm tool and equipment technology, basic needs and employment No. ILO/FIN/78/RAF/2 (Addis Ababa, ILO, JASPA, Government of Finland, 1983), xvi + 280 pp. [TZA, ZMB, BWA, KEN, SDN] ISBN 92-2-103613-8.

Appropriate farm equipment technology for the small-scale traditional sector: The case of Botswana (Country profile 1). Regional project on farm tool and equipment technology, basic needs and employment No. ILO/FIN/78/RAF/2 (Addis Ababa, ILO, JASPA, Government of Finland, 1983), 102 pp. [BWA] ISBN 92-2-103608-1.

Appropriate farm equipment technology for the small-scale traditional sector: The case of Kenya (Country profile 2). Regional project on farm tool and equipment technology, basic needs and employment No. ILO/FIN/78/RAF/2 (Addis Ababa, ILO, JASPA, Government of Finland, 1983), 74 pp. [KEN] ISBN 92-2-103612-X.

Appropriate farm equipment technology for the small-scale traditional sector: The case of Sudan (Country profile 4). Regional project on farm tool and equipment technology, basic needs and employment No. ILO/FIN/78/RAF/2 (Addis Ababa, ILO, JASPA, Government of Finland, 1983), 64 pp. [SDN] ISBN 92-2-103609-X.

Appropriate farm equipment technology for the small-scale traditional sector: The case of the United Republic of Tanzania (Country profile 3). Regional project on farm tool and equipment technology, basic needs and employment No. ILO/FIN/78/RAF/2 (Addis Ababa, ILO, JASPA, Government of Finland, 1983), 124 pp. [TZA] ISBN 92-2-103610-3.

Appropriate farm equipment technology for the small-scale traditional sector: The case of Zambia (Country profile 5). Regional project on farm tool and equipment technology, basic needs and employment, No. ILO/FIN/78/RAF/2 (Addis Ababa, ILO, JASPA, Government of Finland, 1983), 106 pp. [ZMB] ISBN 92-2-103611-1.

Tools and equipment manual for labour intense farming. A sub-regional manual for Botswana, Kenya, Sudan, the United Republic of Tanzania and Zambia (Addis

Ababa, ILO, JASPA, Government of Finland, 1983), 112 pp. [BWA, KEN, SDN, TZA, ZMB] ISBN 92-2-103617-0.

- Latin America and the Caribbean

V.E. Tokman: *Tecnología para el sector informal urbano*. Occasional papers No. 19 (Santiago, PREALC, Jan. 1978). [CHL]

A. Gutiérrez: *Demanda de ingenieros y tecnólogos en el litoral ecuatoriano 1980-1990*. Occasional papers No. 32 (Santiago, PREALC, June 1980). [ECU]

A. Gutiérrez: *Requerimientos de ingenieros y tecnólogos en la costa ecuatoriana*. Occasional papers No. 34 (Santiago, PREALC, Nov. 1980). [ECU]

V.E. Tokman: *Employment and technological change in capital goods production in Latin America*. Monograph No. 23 (Santiago, PREALC, Sep. 1981).

A. Pereira: *Ethanol, employment and development: Lessons from Brazil* (Geneva, ILO, 1986), xiv + 195 pp. Sw. frs. 25. [BRA] ISBN 92-2-105380-6.

- Asia

D. Lal, assisted by A. Heap, H. Boissen, B. Nilsson and L.S. Karlsson: *Men or machines*. A study of labour-capital substitution in road construction in the Philippines (Geneva, ILO, 1978), xi + 164 pp. Sw. frs. 25. [PHL] ISBN 92-2-101720-6.

Report of the ILO Tripartite Symposium on choice of technology and employment generation in Asia (with particular reference to manufacturing industries). 18-27 June 1979 - Asian Institute of Technology, Bangkok (Geneva, ILO, 1980), iv + 406 pp. [MYS, CHN, BGD, LKA] ISBN 92-2-102317-6.

Field handbook on the choice of appropriate technology in Philippine forestry (Manila, ILO and the Philippine Bureau of Forest Department, 1981) [PHL]

Implementation of appropriate technology in Philippine forestry. Report of the joint Philippines Bureau of Forest Development/ILO/Government of Finland Project (Manila, Philippine Bureau of Forest Development/Government of Finland Project/ILO, 1982), xxx + 246 pp. [PHL]

D.J.C. Forsyth: *Assessment of national technology policy in Fiji* (Geneva, ILO, 1985) [FJI]

A.G. Fluitman: *Technology policy and employment creation in Indonesia: A preliminary assessment* (Geneva, ILO, 1986) [IDN] ISBN 92-2-105689-9.

M.S. Kumar (ed.): *Energy pricing policies in developing countries*. Theory and empirical evidence (New Delhi, ESCAP/ARTEP, 1987), 314 pp. US$ 8. [IND, NPL, THA, PHL, LKA] ISBN 92-2-106036-5.

- OECD Countries

D. Werneke: *Microelectronics and office jobs. The impact of the chip on women's employment* (Geneva, ILO, 1983; 3rd impression, 1985), 102 pp., Sw. frs. 17,50. [GBR, FRA, AUS] ISBN 92-2-103278-7.

Articles in the International Labour Review

- General

C.G. Baron: "Appropriate technology comes of age: A review of some recent literature and aid policy statement", Vol. 117, No. 5, Sep.-Oct. 1978.

G.A. Edmonds: "The construction industry in developing countries", Vol. 118, No. 3, May-June 1979.

C.G. Baron: "Energy policy and social progress in developing countries", Vol. 119, No. 5, Sep.-Oct. 1980.

S. Watanabe: "Institutional factors, government policies and appropriate technologies", Vol. 119, No. 2, Mar.-Apr. 1980.

F. Stewart: "Macro-policies for appropriate technology: An introductory classification", Vol. 122, No. 3, May-June 1983.

Y. Sabolo: "Trade between developing countries, technology transfers and employment", Vol. 122, No. 5, Sep.-Oct. 1983.

S. Watanabe: "Employment and income implications of the "bio-revolution": A speculative note", Vol. 124, No. 3, May-June 1985.

S. Watanabe: "Labour-saving versus work-amplifying effects of micro-electronics", Vol. 125, No. 3, May-June 1986.

- Africa

S. Watanabe: "Technological capability and industrialisation. Effects of aid and sanctions in the United Republic of Tanzania and Zimbabwe", Vol. 126, No. 5, Sep.-Oct. 1987. [TZA, ZWE]

- Latin America and the Caribbean

A. Pereira: "Employment implications of ethanol production in Brazil", Vol. 122, No. 1, Jan.-Feb. 1983. [BRA]

- Asia

I. Ahmed and J.G. Laarman: "Technologies for basic needs: The case of Philippine forestry", Vol. 117, No. 4, July-Aug. 1978. [PHL]

Other Articles

- General

A.S. Bhalla: "Third World's technological dilemma", in *Labour and Society* (Geneva, IILS), Vol. 9, No. 4, Oct.-Dec. 1984.

- Asia

I. Ahmed: "Technologies for improved working conditions and environment in Philippine forestry", in *Technology to improve working conditions in Asia* (Geneva, ILO, 1979). [PHL]

Working Papers

- General

A.S. Bhalla: *Technologies appropriate for a basic needs strategy*, Aug. 1978 (WEP 2-22/WP.36).

J.D.G.E. Howe and I. Barwell: *Equipment for labour-based road construction*, Nov. 1978 (WEP 2-22/WP.40). M.

M.I. Hussain: *Scope for application and upgrading of indigenous technology: The case of irrigation works*, Nov. 1978 (WEP 2-22/WP.41).

A.K.N. Reddy: *National appropriate technology groups and institutions - A preliminary assessment*, Sep. 1978 (WEP 2-22/WP.37).

H.J. Burton: *On the production of appropriate technology*, June 1979 (WEP 2-22/WP.49). M.

A. Herrera: *The generation and dissemination of appropriate technologies in developing countries: A methodological approach*, Oct. 1979 (WEP 2-22/WP.51). M. [MEX]

G. Lamb: *Organising for technology appropriation: An approach to appropriate technology implementation*, Dec. 1979 (WEP 2-22/WP.53). M.

A.K. Biswas: *Labour-based technology for large irrigation works: Problems and prospects*, Aug. 1980 (WEP 2-22/WP.63). M.

C.G. Baron: *Energy policy and the social objectives of development*, Oct. 1980 (WEP 2-22/WP.72). M.

D.R. Birch and J.R. Rydzewski: *Energy options for low-lift irrigation pumps in developing countries: The case of Bangladesh and Egypt*, Apr. 1980 (WEP 2-22/WP.57). M. [BGD, EGY]

G.A. Edmonds: *Institutional aspects of the construction industry in developing countries*, Oct. 1980 (WEP 2-22/WP.70). M.

D.J.C. Forsyth: *Market structure, industrial organisation and technology*, Oct. 1980 (WEP 2-22/WP.71). M.

J. James: *Product choice and poverty: A study of the inefficiency of low-income consumption and the distributional impact of product changes*, May 1980 (WEP 2-22/WP.59). M.

A. Kuyvenhoven: *Technology, employment and basic needs in leather industries in developing countries*, Aug. 1980 (WEP 2-22/WP.65). M.

G.A. Aryee: *Income redistribution, technology and employment in the footwear industry*,[3] Jan. 1981 (WEP 2-22/WP.78 - WEP 2-23/WP.96). [GHA] ISBN 92-2-102609-4.

F. Fluitman and J. White: *External development finance and choice of technology*,[1] July 1981 (WEP 2-22/WP.81). M. ISBN 92-2-102842-9.

R.C. Sinha, S.P. Sinha, G.P. Mishra and G. Pingle: *Implications of a basic needs strategy for the edible-oil industry*, July 1981 (WEP 2-22/WP.84 - WEP 2-23/WP.102). ISBN 92-2-102847-X.

R. Winsbury: *New technologies in newspaper production in developing countries and their labour and social implications*, Sep. 1981 (WEP 2-22/WP.85). ISBN 92-2-102863-1.

S. Drewer: *Institutional constraints to the choice of appropriate construction technology*, Dec. 1982 (WEP 2-22/WP.104). M. [MUS] ISBN 92-2-103311-2.

J.L. Enos: *Market structure, industrial organisation and technology: Concepts, methodology and evidence*,[1] Feb. 1982 (WEP 2-22/WP.93). ISBN 92-2-103097-0.

J. James: *Public enterprise, technology and employment in developing countries*, Dec. 1982 (WEP 2-22/WP.107). ISBN 92-2-103331-7.

A.S. Bhalla and J. James: *An approach towards integration of emerging and traditional technologies*, Feb. 1983 (WEP 2-22/WP.112) ISBN 92-2-103398-8.

J. James: *The role of appropriate technology in a redistributive development strategy*,[1] May 1983 (WEP 2-22/WP.118). ISBN 92-2-103481-X.

B. Levy: *Public enterprises and the transfer of technology in the ammonia industry*, July 1983 (WEP 2-22/WP.121). M. ISBN 92-2-103537-9.

A. Mackillop: *Technology, employment and development implications of new and renewable sources of energy*, Mar. 1983 (WEP 2-22/WP.114). ISBN 92-2-103411-9.

K.K. Prasad: *Woodburning stoves: Their technology, economics and deployment*, Mar. 1983 (WEP 2-22/WP.115). M. ISBN 92-2-103415-1

K. Hoffman and H. Rush: *Microelectronics and the technological transformation of the clothing industry*, Dec. 1984 (WEP 2-22/WP.138). ISBN 92-2-100517-8.

D. Kaneko and E. Kurihara: *Technology adaptation in mineral processing. A review of alternative iron and steelmaking technologies*, Jan. 1984 (WEP 2-22/WP.127). ISBN 92-2-103743-6.

J. James: *The employment and income distributional impact of microelectronics: A prospective analysis for the Third World*. Sep. 1985 (WEP 2-22/WP. 153). M. ISBN 92-2-105286-9.

D.V. Smith: *Photovoltaïcs: Socio-economic impact and policy implications*, July 1985 (WEP 2-22/WP. 151). M. ISBN 92-2-105260-5.

M. Fransman: *A new approach to the study of technological capability in less developed countries*, June 1986 (WEP 2-22/WP.166). ISBN 92-2-105626-0.

C. Hurst: *Managing the commercialisation of solar energy technologies: A review of past experiences in developing countries, and an analysis of future policy implications*, Feb. 1986 (WEP 2-22/WP.160). ISBN 92-2-105456-X.

J.F. Rada: *Information technology and services*, Mar. 1986 (WEP 2-22/WP.163). ISBN 92-2-105500-0.

N. Rosenberg: *On technology blending*, Jan. 1986 (WEP 2-22/WP. 159). ISBN 92-2-105554-X.

A.K. Bagchi: *The differential impact of new technologies on developing countries: A framework of analysis*, June 1987 (WEP 2-22/WP.176). ISBN 92-2-106138-8.

- Africa

A.N. Hakam: *Technology diffusion from the formal to the informal sector: The case of auto repair industry in Ghana*,[2] July 1978 (WEP 2-22/WP.35). [GHA]

M.H. Amer: *Technology for construction and maintenance of irrigation and drainage works in Egypt: A preliminary assessment*, Sep. 1980 (WEP 2-22/WP.68). M. [EGY]

B. Balkenhol: *Technology policy and development financing: Observations on some institutional constraints in Africa*, Oct. 1980 (WEP 2-22/WP.75). M.

Y. Bresson: *Politique économique et revenus en Côte-d'Ivoire*, Nov. 1980 (WEP 2-23/WP.95). M. [CIV]

H. El Karanshawy Mohamed Sakr: *Technological linkages in the Egyptian cotton weaving industry*,[2] Apr. 1980 (WEP 2-22/WP.58). M. [EGY]

W.J. House: *Technological choice, employment generation, income distribution and consumer demand: The case of furniture making in Kenya*,[3] May 1980 (WEP 2-22/WP.60). M. [KEN]

G. Ofori: *The construction industry in Ghana*, Oct. 1980 (WEP 2-22/WP.73). M. [GHA]

E. Chuta: *Choice of appropriate technique in the African bread industry with special reference to Sierra Leone*, Jan. 1981 (WEP 2-22/WP.77). [SLE] ISBN 92-2-102615-9.

A.A. Aboagye: *Technology and employment in the capital goods industry in Ghana*, Feb. 1982 (WEP 2-22/WP.91). [GHA] ISBN 92-2-103043-1.

R. Edwards, D. Pearce and J. Sladen: *The effect of oil price increases on the economy of Sudan with special reference to employment and income distribution*, Sep. 1983 (WEP 2-22/WP.123). M. [SDN] ISBN 92-2-103597-2.

D.J.C. Forsyth: *Market structure, industrial organisation and technological development: The case of Egyptian industries,*[1] Mar. 1983 (WEP 2-22/WP.116). M. [EGY] ISBN 92-2-103462-3.

J. James: *Bureaucratic, engineering and economic men: Decision-making for technology in the United Republic of Tanzania's state-owned enterprises,* Oct. 1983 (WEP 2-22/WP.125). [TZA] ISBN 92-2-103629-4.

J. Suckling: *Energy prices, development and the policy response in a small siege economy: Zimbabwe 1964-1981,* May 1983 (WEP 2-22/WP.119). M. [ZWE] ISBN 92-2-103493-3.

J.C. Bruggink: *The socio-economic aspects of introducing solar flat plate collector technology in the Sahel,* June 1984 (WEP 2-22/WP.130). ISBN 92-2-103918-8.

J.W. Elliott: *Comparative advantages of using sandcrete blocks and clay bricks in the construction industry in Sierra Leone: A preliminary analysis,* May 1985 (WEP 2-22/WP.148). [SLE] ISBN 92-2-105204-4.

J. Suckling: *The impact of energy price increases on an export dependent economy: Zambia, 1970-82,* Apr. 1985 (WEP 2-22/WP. 147). M. [ZMB] ISBN 92-2-105142-0.

A. Kamya, I. Ali and F.D. Yamba: *Technology adaptation in mineral processing: The case of the copper industry in Zambia,* Feb. 1986 (WEP 2-22/WP. 161). [ZMB] ISBN 92-2-105461-6.

S.M. Wangwe: *Technology imports, technological learning and self-reliance in the United Republic of Tanzania,* Apr. 1986 (WEP 2-22/WP.165). [TZA] ISBN 92-2-105547-7.

A. Barampama: *Enquête sur le profil technologique des micro-entreprises du secteur métallique de Kigali et Butare (Rwanda),* Oct. 1987 (WEP 2-19/WP.40 and WEP 2-22/WP.179). [RWA] ISBN 92-2-206293-0.

J. Capt: *Capacité et maîtrise technologique des micro-enterprises métalliques à Bamako et à Ségou (Mali),* Oct. 1987 (WEP 2-19/WP.41 and WEP 2-22/WP.180). [MLI] ISBN 92-2-206292-2.

D.B. Ndlela: *Technology imports and indigenous technological capacity building: The Zimbabwean case,* Mar. 1987 (WEP 2-22/WP.173). [ZWE] ISBN 92-2-105957-X.

- Latin America and the Caribbean

Concentración, difusión tecnólogica restringida y empleo (Santiago, PREALC), May 1978 (No. 144).

Organización de las unidades productivas en la caña de azúcar, la modernización tecnológica, el empleo y el ingreso campesino: El caso de Panamá (Santiago, PREALC), Apr. 1978 (No. 124).* [PAN]

A. Mercado with A. Juarez and J. Aristy: *Technological linkages in the Mexican garment industry,* Jan. 1980 (WEP 2-22/WP.55). M. [MEX]

Capital goods and employment: Machines for the forestry and bakery industries in Chile (Santiago, PREALC), June 1981 (No. 203). [CHL]

Concepto de cambio técnico y diseño de una pauta básica de entrevista para un estudio sobre tecnología en la industria metalmecánica en Venezuela (Santiago, PREALC), May 1981 (No. 202). [VEN]

Energía y empleo: El impacto de PROALCOOL en Brasil (Santiago, PREALC), Sep. 1981 (No. 211). [BRA]

L.A. Suleta J., J.L. Londoño de la C., J. Dario Uribe E.: *The Colombian capital goods industry and technological development,* Sep. 1982 (WEP 2-22/WEP.100). [COL] ISBN 92-2-103261-2.

O. Davies, C. Davis and D. Morrison: *Technology adaptation and employment in the bauxite/aluminia industry of Jamaica*, May 1984 (WEP 2-22/WP.128). [JAM] ISBN 92-2-103861-0.

J.R. Tauile: *Employment effect of micro-electronic equipment in the Brazilian automobile industry*,[4] Aug. 1984 (WEP 2-22/WP.131). [BRA] ISBN 92-2-103925-0.

A.C. Correa Fleury: *The technological behaviour of state-owned enterprises in Brazil*, Feb. 1985 (WEP 2-22/WP. 140). [BRA] ISBN 92-2-105070-X.

E. Lizano and A. di Mare: *Macro-economic effects and policy implications of higher oil prices in Costa Rica*, 1985 (WEP 2-22/WP. 152). [CRI] ISBN 92-2-105307-5.

D. Otero in collaboration with M. Ramírez and A. Rincon: *The effects of oil price increases on the Colombian economy*, Apr. 1985 (WEP 2-22/WP. 146). [COL] ISBN 92-2-105139-1.

A. Pontoni: *The effects of external oil price increases and fuel price policies on the Peruvian economy*, Feb. 1985 (WEP 2-22/WP. 141). [PER] ISBN 92-2-105071-8

J. Lucángeli: *Technological behaviour of Argentine public enterprises: The case of Yacimientos petroliferos fiscales*, Apr. 1986 (WEP 2-22/WP.164). [ARG] ISBN 92-2-105537-X.

F.R. Sagasti with the collaboration of R. Berrios, C.E. Paredes and G. Garland: *Market structure and technological behaviour: A study of the edible oils industry in Peru*, Apr. 1987 (WEP 2-22/WP.174). [PER] ISBN 92-2-106045-4.

- **Asia**

S.N. Sharma: *Institutional and organisational aspects of promoting the use of water turbines in Nepal*, Oct. 1987 (WEP 2-22/WP.181). [NPL] ISBN 92-2-106578-2.

Chee Peng Lim: *Choice of manufacturing technology in the leather shoe industries in Malaysia*, Dec. 1978 (WEP 2-22/WP.42). M. [MYS]

Marga Institute, Sri Lanka: *The technological and employment implications of higher oil prices: A case study of Sri Lanka*, Jan. 1979 (WEP 2-22/WP.44). M. [LKA]

A. Ahmed: *The effects of higher oil prices on technology and employment in Pakistan*, Jan. 1979 (WEP 2-22/WP.43). M. [PAK]

A.V. Desai: *Impacts of higher oil prices on India*, Sep. 1979 (WEP 2-22/WP.50). M. [IND]

R. Islam: *Some economic implications of higher oil prices: The case of Bangladesh*, Nov. 1979 (WEP 2-22/WP.52). M. [BGD]

T.S. Papola and R.S. Mathur: *Inter-sectoral linkages in the metal engineering industry in Kanpur, India*,[2] Dec. 1979 (WEP 2-22/WP.54). M. [IND]

S. Watanabe: *Technical co-operation between large and small firms in the Filipino automobile industry*,[2] Mar. 1979 (WEP 2-22/WP.47) M. [PHL]

Fong Chan Onn: *Consumer income distribution and appropriate technology: The case of bicycle manufacturing in Malaysia*,[3] Mar. 1980 (WEP 2-22/WP.56). M. [MYS]

S. Ichimura: *Institutional factors and government policies for appropriate technologies in South-East Asia*, Sep. 1980 (WEP 2-22/WP.66). M. [CHN, IDN, THA]

A. Khai, S. Ch. Dutta and Md.A. Rahman: *Development and application of indigenous low-cost technology to minimise water losses due to seepage in irrigation canals: The case of Bangladesh*, Oct. 1980 (WEP 2-22/WP.69). M. [BGD]

A.K.A. Mubin and D.J.C. Forsyth: *Appropriate products employment and income distribution in Bangladesh: A case study of the soap industry*,[3] Oct. 1980 (WEP 2-22/WP.74 - WEP 2-23/WP.94). M. [BGD]

R.I. Rahman: *New technology in Bangladesh agriculture: Adoption and its impact on rural labour market* (Bangkok, ARTEP), 1981. [BGD]

M. Thobani: *Passenger transport in Karachi: A nested logit model,*[3] Dec. 1981 (WEP 2-23/WP.109). [PAK]

Linsu Kim: *Technological innovations in Korea's capital goods industry: A micro analysis*, Feb. 1982 (WEP 2-22/WP.92). [KOR] ISBN 92-2-103046-6.

S. Ganesan: *The construction industry in Sri Lanka*, Feb. 1982 (WEP 2-22/WP.90). [LKA] ISBN 92-2-103018-0.

B.K. Joshi and R.C. Sinha: *The socio-economic implications of micro-hydro power systems in India*, Dec. 1982 (WEP 2-22/WP.105). [IND] ISBN 92-2-103318-X.

T.S. Papola and R.C. Sinha: *The impact of income redistribution on technology and employment in the metal utensils sector of India,*[3] Apr. 1982 (WEP 2-22/WP.94). [IND] ISBN 92-2-103153-5.

Wahiduddin Mahmud and Muhammed Muqtada: *Institutional factors and technological innovations: The case of HYV Rice in Bangladesh*, Oct. 1983 (WEP 2-22/WP.124). M. [BGD] ISBN 92-2-103600-6.

A.V. Desai: *Market structure and technology: Their interdependence in Indian industry*, May 1983 (WEP 2-22/WP.117). M. [IND] ISBN 92-2-103480-1

S. Ichimura in collaboration with E.L. Roberto, R.B. Suhartono, I.S. Umar, S. Wun'gaeo and P. Yamlinfung: *Institutional factors and government policies for appropriate technologies: Survey findings in Indonesia, Thailand and the Philippines*, Jan. 1983 (WEP 2-22/WP.110). [IDN, THA, PHL] ISBN 92-2-103374-0.

K. Niitsu, K. Hideshima, and Y. Wachi in collaboration with K.K. Vaidya: *The capital goods sector in Nepal: Present position and prospects*, Mar. 1983 (WEP 2-22/WP.113). [NPL] ISBN 92-2-103409-7.

Fong Chan Onn: *Energy price increases and economic development in Malaysia*, Nov. 1984 (WEP 2-22/WP.133). [MYS] ISBN 92-2-103960-9.

R. Bhatia: *Energy alternatives for irrigation pumping: An economic analysis for Northern India*, Dec. 1984 (WEP 2-22/WP.137). [IND] ISBN 92-2-100520-8.

M.R. Khoju: *Commercial application of new indigenous technologies: A case study of Nepal*, Oct. 1984 (WEP 2-22/WP.132). [NPL] ISBN 92-2-103950-1.

R.K. Koti and N.P. Merchant: *Small-scale iron and steel processing in India*, Mar. 1984 (WEP 2-22/WP. 142).* [IND] ISBN 92-2-100529-1.

A.B. Deolalikar and A.K. Sundaram: *Technology choice, adaptation, and diffusion in privately- and state-owned enterprises in India*, Dec. 1985 (WEP 2-22/WP.158). [IND] ISBN 92-2-105400-4.

C. Hurst: *Energy and irrigation in India*, Sep. 1985 (WEP 2-22/WP. 154). M. [IND] ISBN 92-2-105289-3.

S. Ishikawa: *The development of capital-goods sector: Experience of pre-PRC China*, Jan. 1985 (WEP 2-22/WP. 139). [CHN] ISBN 92-2-105026-2.

K.N.S. Nair and J.G. Krishnayya: *Energy consumption by income groups in urban areas of India*, Apr. 1985 (WEP 2-22/WP. 145). M. [IND] ISBN 92-2-105134-X.

A.K. Bagchi in collaboration with D. Banerjee: *The impact of microlectronics-based technologies: The case of India*, Sep. 1986 (WEP 2-22/WP.169). [IND] ISBN 92-2-105742-9.

H.K. Pyo: *The impact of microelectronics on employment and indigenous technological capacity in the Republic of Korea*, Dec. 1986 (WEP 2-22/WP.172). [KOR] ISBN 92-2-105837-9.

M. Santikarn Kaosa-ard: *Technological acquisition in the Thai rice milling and related capital good industries*, Mar. 1986 (WEP 2-22/WP.162). [THA] ISBN 92-2-105488-8.

R. Bhatia: *Diffusion of renewable energy technologies in India: A case study of biogas dual-fuel engines*, Oct. 1987 (WEP 2-22/WP. 178) [IND] ISBN 92-2-106279-1.

R. Bhatia: *Institutional aspects of promoting renewable energy technologies in India*, Oct. 1987 (WEP 2-22/WP.177). [IND] ISBN 92-2-106278-3.

- OECD Countries

S. Watanabe: *Technological linkages between formal and informal sectors of manufacturing industries,*[2] Mar. 1978 (WEP 2-22/WP.34).

B. Haywood: *Technical change and employment in the British printing industry*, Sep. 1982 (WEP 2-22/WP.99). [GBR] ISBN 92-2-103316-3.

R.J. Rahn: *Chipping away at labour: Microelectronics and employment in Canada*, Technical report, Feb. 1982 (WEP 2-32/WP.37). [CAN] ISBN 92-2-103112-8.

S. Watanabe: *Invention and the patent system in the Third World: Some policy issues,*[1] July 1982 (WEP 2-22/WP.97). [JPN] ISBN 92-2-103207-8.

S. Watanabe: *Market structure, industrial organisation and technological development: The case of the Japanese electronics-based NC-machine tool industry*, Feb. 1983 (WEP 2-22/WP.111). M. [JPN] ISBN 92-2-103387-2.

F. Silva, P. Ferri and A. Enrietti: *Employment impact of micro-electronic "new technologies" on the Italian automobile industry,*[4] Dec. 1984 (WEP 2-22/WP.136). [ITA] ISBN 92-2-100529-1.

S. Watanabe: *Micro-electronics and employment in the Japanese automobile industry,*[4] May 1984 (WEP 2-22/WP.129). [JPN] ISBN 92-2-103868-8.

B.T. Allen: *Micro-electronics, employment and labour in the North American automobile industry,*[4] Apr. 1985 (WEP 2-22/WP. 144). [CAN, USA] ISBN 92-2-105116-1.

L. Hirschhorn and A.F. Westin: *The employment effects of micro-electronics in the office and service sector in the United States*, June 1986 (WEP 2-22/WP.167). [USA] ISBN 92-2-105627-9.

J.G. Maton: *From restructuring to new technologies: Policies of a small European country (Belgium)*, Sep. 1986 (WEP 2-22/WP.170). [BEL] ISBN 92-2-105751-8.

J. Swann: *The employment effects of microelectronics in the UK service sector*, July 1986 (WEP 2-22/WP. 168). [GBR] ISBN 92-2-105674-0.

J. Hill: *Implications of microelectronic technologies for labour and employment in the banking and retail industries in Australia*, May 1987 (WEP 2-22/WP.175). [AUS] ISBN 92-2-106046-2.

Y. Kuwahara: *The impact of microelectronics on employment in Japanese offices and service industries*, 1987 (WEP 2-22/WP.182). [JPN] ISBN 92-2-106309-7.

ILO works published by commercial and non-profit-making publishers

- General

C.G. Baron (ed.): *Technology, employment and basic needs in food processing in developing countries* (Oxford, Pergamon Press, 1980), ix + 371 pp. [KEN] ISBN 0-08-025228-1.

G.K. Boon: *Technology and employment in footwear manufacturing* (Alphen aan den Rijn, Sijthoff and Noordhoff, 1980), xii + 218 pp. [MEX, ESP] ISBN 90-286-0170-8.

G.A. Edmonds and J.D.G.E. Howe (eds.): *Roads and resources: Appropriate technology in road construction in developing countries* (London, Intermediate Technology Publications, 1980), 200 pp. [MEX, AFG, IND, IRN] ISBN 0-903031-69-8.

S. Watanabe (ed.): *Technology, marketing and industrialisation: Linkages between large and small enterprises* (New Delhi, Macmillan India, 1983), xii + 256 pp. [JPN, GHA, EGY, CHN, PHL, IND, MEX] ISBN 33390-395-5.

A.S. Bhalla, D. James and Y. Stevens (eds.): *Blending of new and traditional technologies. Case studies* (Dublin, Tycooly International Publishing, 1984), xvi + 285 pp. [PRT, ITA, BRA, GBR, USA, COL, LKA, THA, MYS, PAK, BFA, CRI] ISBN 0-86346-055-0.

G.A. Edmonds and D.W.J. Miles: *Foundations for change. Aspects of the construction industry in developing countries* (London, Intermediate Technology Publications, 1984), viii + 143 pp. [LKA, KEN] ISBN 0-9466-88-001.

J.F. Rada: *Die Mikroelektronik und ihre Auswirkungen*. Versuche einer Bewertung der Informationstechnologie (Berlin West, Wissenschaftlicher Autoren-Verlag, 1984), 140 pp. ISBN 3-88840-212-3.

W. van Ginneken and C.G. Baron (eds.): *Appropriate products, employment and technology*. Case-studies on consumer choice and basic needs in developing countries (London, Macmillan Press, 1984), xi + 260 pp. [BGD, MYS, PAK, BRB, IND, GHA, KEN, ETH] ISBN 0-333-35302-1.

I. Barwell, G.A. Edmonds, J.D.G.E. Howe and J. de Veen: *Rural transport in developing countries* (London, Intermediate Technology Publications, 1985), 145 pp. [MYS, IND, NGA, BGD, WSM, KEN, KOR, PHL, TZA] ISBN 0-946688-80-X.

J. James and S. Watanabe (eds.): *Technology, institutions and government policies* (London, Macmillan, 1985), x + 265 pp. [EGY] ISBN 0-333-38562-4.

A. Pereira, A. Ulph and W. Tims: *Socio-economic and policy implications of energy price increases* (Aldershot, Hampshire, Gower, 1987), xxiv + 317 pp. ISBN 0-566-05520-1.

D. Werneke: *La microelectrónica y los puestos de trabajo en oficinas*. La importancia del circuito integrado en el empleo feminino (Madrid, Centro de Publicaciones, Ministerio de Trabajo y Seguridad Social, 1987), 119 pp. ISBN 84-734-377-1.

S. Watanabe (ed.): *Microelectronics, automation and employment in the automobile industry* (Chichester, United Kingdom, John Wiley and Sons, 1987), xix + 203 pp. [JPN, USA, FRA, ITA, BRA] ISBN 0-471-91484-3.

- Asia

J.G. Laarman, K. Virtanen and M. Jurvelius: *Choice of technology in forestry - A Philippine case study* - foreword by B. Ople, Minister for Labour, Republic of the Philippines (Quezon City, New Day Publishers, 1981), 115 pp. [PHL]

Related books and articles

- General

G.A. Edmonds: "Manpower - horsepower - making the best of both worlds", in *New Civil Engineer* (London), 6 Apr. 1978.

M.I. Hussain: "Water development and appropriate technology: A discussion of planning and implementation issues", in *Water Pollution Control in Developing Countries* (Bangkok), Vol. II, AIT, 1978.

W.P. Strassman: *Building technology and employment in the housing sector of developing countries* (East Lansing, Michigan State University, 1978), 277 pp.

A.S. Bhalla (ed.): *Towards global action for appropriate technology*. (Oxford, Pergamon Press, 1979), x + 220 pp.

Appropriate technology: An overview in K.-H. Standke and M.A. Krishna (eds.): *Science, technology and society: Needs, challenges and limitations* - Proceedings of the International Symposium, Vienna, Austria, 13-17 Aug. 1979. (Oxford, Pergamon Press, 1980).

A.S. Bhalla and J. James: "New technology revolution: Myth or reality for developing countries?", in *Greek Economic Review* (Athens), Dec. 1984.

A.S. Bhalla and D. James: "Towards new technological frontiers", in *Productivity* (New Delhi), Vol. XXV, No. 3, Oct.-Dec. 1984.

- Africa

W.J. House: "Redistribution, consumer demand and employment in Kenyan furniture making", in *Journal of Development Studies* (London), Vol. 17, No. 4, July 1981. [KEN]

- Asia

S. Watanabe (ed.): *International subcontracting: A tool of technology transfer* (Tokyo, Asian Productivity Organisation (APO), 1978), x + 132 pp. [PHL, IND, KOR, PAK, HKG, SGP]

Notes:

1 Published in J. James and S. Watanabe (eds.): Technology, institutions and government policies (London, Macmillan, 1985).

2 A revised version appears in S. Watanabe (ed.): Technology, marketing and industrialisation: Linkages between large and small enterprises (New Delhi, Macmillan India, 1983).

3 Published in W. van Ginneken and C. Baron (eds.): Appropriate products, employment and technology. Case studies on consumer choice and basic needs in developing countries (London, Macmillan, 1984).

4 Reproduced in S. Watanabe (ed.): Microelectronics, automation and employment in the automobile industry (Chicester, United Kingdom, John Wiley and Sons, 1987).

Special employment programmes and vulnerable groups

ILO publications

Books and reports

- **General**

P. Garnier and L. Guérin: *Guide à l'usage du formateur*. Perfectionnement des chefs de chantier à la conduite des travaux à haute intensité de main-d'oeuvre (Geneva, ILO, 1981), 55 pp. F, E. ISBN 92-2-202958-5.

P. Garnier and L. Guérin: *Guide pratique du chef de chantier*. Principes élémentaires de conduite des travaux à haute intensité de main-d'oeuvre (Geneva, ILO, 1981), 107 pp. F, E. ISBN 92-2-202958-5.

P. Garnier and L. Guérin: *Supports pédagogiques à l'usage du formateur* (Geneva, ILO, 1981), 95 pp. ISBN 92-2-202958-5.

P. Garnier: *Introduction aux programmes spéciaux de travaux publics* - Planification, organisation et exécution de programmes spéciaux de travaux publics (Geneva, ILO, 1981), vi + 194 pp. F, E. ISBN 92-2-202885-6.

G.B. Rodgers and G. Standing (eds.): *Child work, poverty and underdevelopment* (Geneva, ILO, 1981), xii + 310 pp. Sw. frs. 25. E,S. ISBN 92-2-102813-5.

L. Guérin: *Données types sur les besoins de main-d'oeuvre dans les programmes spéciaux de travaux publics* (Geneva, UNDP/ILO, 1984), x + 204 pp. Annexes. Sw. frs. 20. ISBN 92-2-203711-1.

L. Guérin: *Training element and technical guide for SPWP workers: Anti-erosion ditches* (Geneva, UNDP/ILO, 1984), 2 vol. E, F.

B. Leblond and L. Guérin: *Travaux de conservation des sols - l'étude des projets et leur réalisation par des techniques à haute intensité de main-d'oeuvre* (Geneva, UNDP/ILO, 2nd revised ed., 1984), vii + 223 pp. Sw. frs. 20. F, E. ISBN 92-2-203395-7.

L. Guérin (publié sous la direction de): *Principes directeurs pour l'emploi de la terre crue*. Construction à faible coût dans les programmes spéciaux de travaux publics (Geneva, ILO, 1985), xi + 274 pp. Sw. frs. 30. [SOM] ISBN 92-2-200537-6.

Community water supply. A manual for user education. A community participation training element for SPWP user beneficiaries (Geneva, ILO, 1987), 89 pp. Sw. frs. 10. E,F. ISBN 92-2-105943-X.

- **Africa**

School leavers, unemployment and manpower development in Liberia. Report submitted to the Government of Liberia by a JASPA technical assistance mission (Addis Ababa, JASPA, 1980), ii + 44 pp. [LBR]

Paper qualification syndrome and the unemployment of school leavers. A comparative subregional study of four East African countries - Kenya, Somalia, the United Republic of Tanzania and Zambia (Addis Ababa, JASPA, 1981). [KEN, SOM, TZA, ZMB]

Paper qualification syndrome and the unemployment of school leavers. A comparative sub-regional study of four West African countries - The Gambia, Ghana, Liberia and Sierra Leone (Addis Ababa, JASPA, 1981). [GMB, GHA, LBR, SLE]

M. Knowles: *Manual on low-cost building construction (A Somalia case study)* (Geneva, ILO, 1981), 56 pp. [SOM]

L'éducation et l'emploi au Gabon. Perspectives à moyen terme (Addis Ababa, JASPA, 1982), xv + 146 pp. [GAB]

Le syndrome du diplôme et le chômage des diplomés: 1. Le cas du Bénin 2. Le cas de la Côte d'Ivoire 3. Le cas du Sénégal 4. Le cas du Togo 5. Réflexions de synthèse. Rapport d'une mission technique du PECTA (Addis Ababa, JASPA, 1982), 5 vols. [BEN, CIV, SEN, TGO]

Paper qualification syndrome (PQS) and unemployment of school leavers. A comparative sub-regional study (Addis Ababa, JASPA, 1982), xii + 228 pp. Sw. frs. 16. [KEN, SOM, TZA, ZMB, GMB, GHA, LBR, SLE] ISBN 92-2-102970-0.

Développement rural et emploi des jeunes aux Comores. Rapport soumis au Gouvernement de Comores par une mission d'assistance technique du PECTA (Addis Ababa, JASPA, 1985), ix + 156 pp. Sw. frs. 14. [COM] ISBN 92-2-205104-1.

Le syndrome du diplome et le chômage des diplomés en Afrique francophone au Sud du Sahara. Réflexions de synthèse (Addis Ababa, JASPA, 1985), ii + 27 pp. [CMR, COG, BFA, ZAR]

Le syndrome du diplome et le chômage des jeunes diplomés. Le cas de la République Populaire du Congo (Addis Ababa, JASPA, 1985), ii + 90 pp. [COG] ISBN 92-2-205053-3.

Le syndrome du diplome et le chômage des jeunes diplomés. Le cas du Burkina-Faso (Addis Ababa, JASPA, 1985), ii + 50 pp. [BFA] ISBN 92-2-205051-7.

Le syndrome du diplome et le chômage des jeunes diplomés. Le cas du Cameroun (Addis Ababa, JASPA, 1985), iii + 95 pp. [CMR] ISBN 92-2-205052-5.

Le syndrome du diplome et le chômage des jeunes diplomés. Le cas du Zaïre (Addis Ababa, JASPA, 1985), ii + 62 pp. [ZAR] ISBN 92-2-205054-1.

Les programmes spéciaux d'emploi et de formation de la jeunesse au Burkina Faso (Addis Ababa, JASPA, 1985), ii + 78 pp. [BFA] ISBN 92-2-205164-5.

Les programmes spéciaux d'emploi et de formation de la jeunesse en République de Côte d'Ivoire (Addis Ababa, JASPA, 1985), i + 69 pp. [CIV] ISBN 92-2-205187-4.

Les programmes spéciaux d'emploi et de formation de la jeunesse en République du Mali (Addis Ababa, JASPA, 1985), 41 pp. [MLI] ISBN 92-2-205189-0.

Les programmes spéciaux d'emploi et de formation de la jeunesse en République islamique de Mauritanie (Addis Ababa, JASPA, 1985), i + 48 pp. [MRT] ISBN 92-2-205188-2.

Les programmes spéciaux d'emploi et de formation de la jeunesse en République populaire du Bénin (Addis Ababa, JASPA, 1985), iii + 55 pp. [BEN] ISBN 92-2-205163-7.

Les programmes spéciaux d'emploi et de formation de la jeunesse. Rapport de synthèse (Addis Ababa, JASPA, 1985), ii + 54 pp. ISBN 92-2-205191-2.

Youth employment and youth employment programmes in Africa. A comparative sub-regional study. The case of Nigeria (Addis Ababa, JASPA, 1986), v + 67 pp. [NGA] ISBN 92-2-105817-4.

Youth employment and youth employment programmes in Africa. A comparative sub-regional study: The case of Botswana (Addis Ababa, JASPA, 1986), ix + 131 pp. [BWA] ISBN 92-2-105527-2.

Youth employment and youth employment programmes in Africa. A comparative sub-regional study: The case of Ethiopia (Addis Ababa, JASPA, 1986), ix + 110 pp. [ETH] ISBN 92-2-105524-8.

Youth employment and youth employment programmes in Africa. A comparative sub-regional study: The case of Kenya (Addis Ababa, JASPA, 1986), ix + 142 pp. [KEN] ISBN 92-2-105525-6.

Youth employment and youth employment programmes in Africa. A comparative sub-regional study: The case of Malawi (Addis Ababa, JASPA, 1986), iii + 89 pp. [MWI] ISBN 92-2-105528-0.

Youth employment and youth employment programmes in Africa. A comparative sub-regional study: The case of Mauritius (Addis Ababa, JASPA, 1986), vi + 123 pp. [MUS] ISBN 92-2-105529-9.

Youth employment and youth employment programmes in Africa. A comparative sub-regional study: The case of Somalia (Addis Ababa, JASPA, 1986), iv + 92 pp. [SOM] ISBN 92-2-105523-X.

Youth employment and youth employment programmes in Africa. A comparative sub-regional study: The case of Zambia (Addis Ababa, JASPA, 1986), iv + 130 pp. [ZMB] ISBN 92-2-105526-4.

Youth employment and youth employment programmes in Anglophone African countries. A comparative sub-regional study. Synthesis report (Addis Ababa, JASPA, 1986), iii + 71 pp. [ZMB, MWI, KEN, ETH, BWA, MUS, SOM] ISBN 92-2-105530-2.

Emplois des jeunes et activités rurales en République islamique du Mauritanie. Rapport d'une mission sectorielle d'emploi soumis au Gouvernement de la République de Mauritanie par l'OIT/PECTA (Addis Ababa, JASPA, 1987), xvii + 93 pp. [MRT] ISBN 92-2-205972-7.

Youth employment promotion in African countries. Report on a regional workshop held on 24-28 November 1986, Buea, Cameroun (Addis Ababa, JASPA, 1987), ii + 288 pp.

A. Guichaoua: *Les paysans et l'investissement-travail au Burundi et au Rwanda* (Geneva, ILO, 1987), xx + 196 pp. Sw. frs. 25. [BDI, RWA] ISBN 92-2-206145-4.

Articles in the International Labour Review

- General

E. Costa and N. Phan-Thuy: "Employment promotion through fuller utilisation of industrial capacity", Vol. 119, No. 3, May-June 1980.

B. Balkenhol: "Direct job creation in industrialised countries", Vol. 120, No. 4, July-Aug. 1981.

S. Guha: "Income redistribution through labour-intensive rural public works: Some policy issues", Vol. 120, No. 1, Jan.-Feb. 1981.

G.B. Rodgers and G. Standing: "Economic roles of children in low-income countries", Vol. 120, No. 1, Jan.-Feb. 1981.

J. Gaude, N. Phan-Thuy and C. Van Kempen: "Evaluation of special public works programmes: Some policy conclusions", Vol. 123, No. 2, Mar.-Apr. 1984.

N. Phan-Thuy: "Employment and training schemes for rural youth: Learning from experience", Vol. 124, No. 4, July-Aug. 1985.

G. Standing: "Labour flexibility and older worker marginalisation: The need for a new strategy", Vol. 125, No. 3, May-June 1986.

Working Papers

- **General**

Youth unemployment in industrialised market economy countries, Proceedings of an informal consultants' meeting (Geneva, 2-4 Nov. 1977), Apr. 1978 (WEP 47-1/WP.4). M.

M. Kabaj: *Utilisation of industrial capacity shift work and employment promotion in developing countries,*[1] July 1978 (WEP 2-24/WP.11). M. [IND, PAK, NGA, SDN, ARG, PER]

J. Versluis: *Education and employment: A synthesis*, June 1978 (WEP 2-18/WP.19). M.

B. Balkenhol: *Marginal employment subsidies - Issues and evidence*, Dec. 1979 (WEP 2-24/WP.15). M.

J. Hallak and J. Versluis: *Education, training and recruitment policies of employers. The case of Rwanda and Panama*, 1979 (WEP 2-18/WP.18). [RWA, PAN]

N. Phan-Thuy: *Controversies on marginal employment in premiums as an anti-inflationary job promotion measure in industrialised countries: Preliminary view*, Mar. 1979 (WEP 2-24/WP.14). M.

G.B. Rodgers and G. Standing: *The economic roles of children in low-income countries: A framework for analysis*, Oct. 1979 (WEP 2-21/WP.81). M.

B. Balkenhol: *Direct job creation schemes in industrialised countries - Issues and evidence,*[2] July 1980 (WEP 2-24/WP.17) M.

A. Morice: *The exploitation of children in the "informal sector": Some propositions for research*, May 1980 (WEP 2-21/WP.87).

J. Gaude and N. Phan-Thuy: *Flows of benefits analysis of special public works programmes: A methodological approach*, May 1982 (WEP 2-24/WP.18). ISBN 92-2-103116-0.

G. Standing: *Vulnerable groups in urban labour processes*, May 1987 (WEP 2-43/WP.13). ISBN 92-2-106041-11.

- **Africa**

N. Phan-Thuy: *Promotion de l'emploi au Maroc par la pleine utilisation de la capacité industrielle*, Mar. 1979 (WEP 2-24/WP.13). M. [MAR]

J. Trouvé and C. Bessat: *L'exode rural des jeunes et les politiques gouvernementales de développement: L'expérience camerounaise*, Nov. 1980 (WEP 10-6/WP.38). M. [CMR]

G.A. Aryee: *Youth employment prospects in the informal sector: The need and scope for apprenticeship training* (Lusaka, SATEP), Nov. 1981.

I. Carle: *The Malawi young pioneers*, Jan. 1983 (WEP 2-24/WP.21). [MWI] ISBN 92-2-103494-1

P-A. Andersson: *"Non-formal" youth training schemes in Zambia* (Lusaka, SATEP), Apr. 1987. [ZMB] ISBN 92-2-106073-X.

B. Martens in collaboration with T. van Dijk and V. van Gent and the Institute of Rural Development Planning in Dodoma: *A socio-economic impact study of the Mto Wa Mbu (Arusha) and the Mnenia (Dodoma) irrigation projects, the United Republic of Tanzania*, Jan. 1987 (WEP 2-24/WP.24). [TZA] ISBN 92-2-105885-9.

- **Latin America and the Caribbean**

Antecedentes sobre el trabajo de los menores en Chile (Santiago, PREALC), Nov. 1978 (No. 163). [CHL]

Construcción de caminos rurales con tecnología de mano de obra intensiva en Guatemala (Santiago, PREALC), June 1979 (No. 172).* [GTM]

Expectativas migratorias de la juventud campesina (Santiago, PREALC), Oct. 1979 (No. 178). [CHL]

Reconstrucción de un camino rural con uso intensivo de mano de obra y participación de la comunidad (Santiago, PREALC), Apr. 1980 (No. 185). [GTM]

Los Programas Especiales de Empleo: Algunas lecciones de la experiencia (Santiago, PREALC), Apr. 1983 (No. 225).

Los Programas Especiales de Empleo: Lecciones del Programa de Empleo Mínimo en Chile (Santiago, PREALC), July. 1983 (No. 228). [CHL]

Panamá: Programa especial de empleo en obras públicas rurales (Santiago, PREALC), May 1984 (No. 241). [PAN]

Antecedentes para el análisis del trabajo de los menores. Tres estudios: América Latina, Costa Rica y Brasil (Santiago, PREALC), Apr. 1985 (No. 262). [CRI, BRA]

Programas especiales de empleo en Panamá. 1978-1984 (Santiago, PREALC), June 1985 (No. 265). [PAN]

Bases para la formulación de un programa de empleo de emergencia. Bolivia 1985-86 (Santiago, PREALC), July 1985 (No. 268). [BOL]

El empleo y la juventud en América Latina (Santiago, PREALC), Dec. 1986 (No. 284).

Contenido, alcance y organización de un programa de empleo de emergencia para Bolivia (Santiago, PREALC), Mar. 1987 (No. 293). [BOL]

Situación y perspectivas del empleo juvenil en América Latina, 1950-1980 (Santiago, PREALC), Sep. 1987 (No. 305). [COL, CRI, PAN, PER, VEN]

- Asia

E. Costa: *An assessment of the flows of benefits generated by public investment in the Employment Guarantee Scheme of Maharashtra*, Dec. 1978 (WEP 2-24/WP.12) M. [IND]

N. Phan-Thuy: *Cost-benefit analysis of labour-intensive public works programmes: A case study of the Pilot-Intensive Rural Employment Project (PIREP) in Mangalur Block of Tamil Nadu in India*, Mar. 1978 (WEP 2-24/WP.10). M. [IND]

S. Guha: *Policies to enhance income redistributive potential and participatory character of labour-intensive rural public works programmes: Some lessons from the Maharashtra Employment Guarantee Scheme*, Dec. 1979 (WEP 2-24/WP.16). M. [IND]

M. Cain and A.B.M.K.A. Mozumder: *Labour market structure, child employment and reproductive behaviour in rural South Asia*, June 1980 (WEP 2-21/WP.89). M. [BGD]

M.R. Rosenzweig: *Household and non-household activities of youths: Issue of modelling, data and estimation strategies*, June 1980 (WEP 2-21/WP.90). M. [IND]

N. Phan-Thuy: *National youth service schemes in Sri Lanka: A survey*, Oct. 1982 (WEP 2-24/WP.20). [LKA] ISBN 92-2-103511-5.

N. Phan-Thuy: *National youth schemes in Malaysia: A survey*, June 1983 (WEP 2-24/WP.22) [MYS] ISBN 92-2-103512-3.

M. Muqtada: *Special employment schemes in rural Bangladesh: Issues and perspectives* (Bangkok, ARTEP), 1984. [BGD] ISBN 92-2-103935-8.

B. Martens: *A socio-economic impact study of the Bhorletar irrigation scheme*, May 1986 (WEP 2-24/WP.23). [NPL] ISBN 92-2-105517-5.

R. Thamarajakshi: *Youth employment in Asian countries* (New Delhi, ARTEP), Mar. 1987. ISBN 92-2-105771-2.

- OECD Countries

R. Breen: *The work experience programme in Ireland*, Mar. 1986 (WEP 2-43/WP.2). [IRL] ISBN 92-2-105502-7.

K.D. Grimm: *Mobilising local labour market policy: An alternative approach to youth employment in Western Europe*, Aug. 1982 (EMP 47-1/WEP.5). [USA, GBR, DEU, IRL] ISBN 92-2-103230-2.

J.M. Mesa: *Short-time working as an alternative to layoffs: The case of Canada and California*, July 1982 (WEP 2-24/WP.19). M. [CAN, USA]

Los programas especiales de empleo en Gran Bretaña (Santiago, PREALC), May 1984 (No. 242). [GBR]

- East European Countries

V.N. Yagodkin: *How child labour was eradicated in the USSR: Integrating school and society*, July 1981 (WEP 2-21/WP.109). M. [SUN] ISBN 92-2-102845-3.

ILO works published by commercial and non-profit-making publishers

- General

U. Teichler, D. Hartung and R. Nuthmann: *Higher education and the needs of society*. English version prepared by V. Ward. (Windsor, Berkshire, NFER Publishing Company, 1980), 142 pp. ISBN 0-85633-209-7.

N. Phan-Thuy, R.R. Betancourt, G.C. Winston and M. Kabaj: *Industrial capacity and employment promotion: Case studies of Sri Lanka, Nigeria, Morocco and over-all survey of other developing countries* (Farnborough, Hampshire, Gower, 1981), x+394 pp. [LKA, NGA, MAR] ISBN 0-566-00433-X.

M.D. Leonor (ed.): *Unemployment, schooling and training in developing countries. The United Republic of Tanzania, Egypt, The Philippines and Indonesia* (London, Croom Helm, 1985), 289 pp. [TZA, EGY, PHL, IDN] ISBN 0-7099-1329-X.

- Latin America and the Caribbean

M. Carnoy in collaboration with J. Lobo, A. Toledo and J. Velloso: *Can educational policy equalise income distribution in Latin America?* (Farnborough, Hampshire, Saxon House/Teakfield Ltd., 1979). [MEX, BRA, CHL, CUB] ISBN 0-566-00255-8.

- Asia

D.P. Chaudhuri: *Education, innovations and agricultural development. A study of North India (1961-72)* (London, Croom Helm, 1979), vii+130 pp. [IND] ISBN 0-85664-826-4.

P.J. Richards and M.D. Leonor: *Education and income distribution in Asia* (London, Croom Helm, 1981), 190 pp. [IND, LKA, THA, PHL] ISBN 0-7099-2201-9.

Notes:

1 Also appeared as chapter in: N. Phan-Thuy, R.R. Betancourt, G.C. Winston and M. Kabaj: Industrial capacity and employment promotion (Farnborough, Hampshire, Gower, 1981).

2 Also appeared as an article in the International Labour Review, Vol. 120, No. 4, July-Aug. 1981.

Structural adjustment and the international division of labour

ILO publications

Books and reports

- **General**

R. Plant: *Industries in trouble* (Geneva, ILO, 1981), vi + 178 pp.   Sw. frs. 20. E, S.   ISBN 92-2-102679-5.

Report to a symposium on employment, trade adjustment and North-South co-operation, 1-4 October 1985   (Geneva, ILO, 1985),   94 pp. Sw. frs. 17,50.   E, F, S.   ISBN 92-2-105147-1.

Background document, WEP 2-46-04-03 (Doc. 2). High-Level Meeting on Employment and Structural Adjustment (Geneva, ILO, 23-25 Nov. 1987), 55 pp. E,F,S,G. ISBN 92-2-106236-8.

Report of the meeting, WEP 2-46-04-03 (Doc. 3). High Level Meeting on Employment and Structural Adjustment   (Geneva, ILO, 23-25 Nov. 1987), 52 pp. E,F,S,G.   ISBN 92-2-106351-8.

Working document, WEP 2-46-04-03 (Doc. 1). High-Level Meeting on Employment and Structural Adjustment (Geneva, ILO, 23-25 Nov. 1987), 10 pp.   E,F,S,G.   ISBN 92-2-106237-6.

World recession and global interdependence. Effects on employment, poverty and policy formation in developing countries (Geneva, ILO, 1987), xi + 139 pp. Sw. frs. 20.   ISBN 92-2-105608-2.

A. Pereira, A. Ulph and W. Tims: *Coping with the oil shocks* (Geneva, ILO, 1987), 62 pp. E,F. ISBN 92-2-105933-2.

- **Africa**

Patterns of industrialisation and impact on employment and incomes in African countries: The case of Ethiopia   (Addis Ababa, JASPA, 1983),   vii + 101 pp.   [ETH]   ISBN 92-2-103788-6.

Patterns of industrialisation and impact on employment and incomes in African countries: The case of Kenya   (Addis Ababa, JASPA, 1983),   ix + 181 pp.   [KEN]   ISBN 92-2-103792-4.

Patterns of industrialisation and impact on employment and incomes in African countries: The case of Nigeria (Addis Ababa, JASPA, 1983),   vii + 141 pp.   [NGA]   ISBN 92-2-103787-8.

Patterns of industrialisation and impact on employment and incomes in African countries: The case of Sierra Leone (Addis Ababa, JASPA, 1983),   vi + 61 pp.   [SLE]   ISBN 92-2-103645-6.

Politique et stratégie d'industrialisation en Afrique. Effets sur l'emploi et la distribution des revenus: Le cas du Burundi (Addis Ababa, JASPA, 1983), vi+92 pp. Annexes. [BDI] ISBN 92-2-203801-1.

Politique et stratégie d'industrialisation en Afrique. Effets sur l'emploi et la distribution des revenus: Le cas du Rwanda (Addis Ababa, JASPA, 1983), viii+111 pp. [RWA] ISBN 92-2-203798-7.

Politique et stratégie d'industrialisation en Afrique. Effets sur l'emploi et la distribution des revenus: Le cas du Togo (Addis Ababa, JASPA, 1983), vi+68 pp. [TGO] ISBN 92-2-203799-5.

Josué Sandjiman Mamder: *Crise et pauvreté en Afrique. Les effets de la récession sur les économies africaines: Le cas du Congo* (Addis Ababa, JASPA, 1983), 73 pp. [COG] ISBN 92-2-203794-4.

A.A. Aboagye: *Impact of recession on African countries. Effects on the poor: The case of Liberia* (Addis Ababa, JASPA, 1984), 54 pp. [LBR] ISBN 92-2-103647-2.

G.M. Hamid, G.A. Aryee and I. Ahmed: *The impact of the recent world recession on the Zambian economy* (Lusaka, SATEP, 1984), iv+87 pp. [ZMB]

Pattern of industrialization: Impact of employment and incomes in six selected African countries (Addis Ababa, JASPA, 1985), iv+128 pp. [ETH, GHA, KEN, LBR, NGA, SLE] ISBN 92-2-105409-8.

Patterns of industrialization and impact on employment and incomes in African countries: The case of Ghana (Addis Ababa, JASPA, 1985), iii+89 pp. [GHA] ISBN 92-2-210364-4.

Patterns of industrialization and impact on employment and incomes in African countries: The case of Liberia (Addis Ababa, JASPA, 1985), v+44 pp. [LBR] ISBN 92-2-103789-4.

Patterns of rural development and impact on employment and incomes (A comparative sub-regional study): The case of Malawi (Addis Ababa, JASPA, 1985), iv+84 pp. [MWI] ISBN 92-2-105035-1.

Politique et stratégie d'industrialisation en Afrique. Effets sur l'emploi et la distribution des revenus: Le cas du Sénégal (Addis Ababa, JASPA, 1985), v+47 pp. Annexes. [SEN] ISBN 92-2-203800-2.

The impact of the recession in African countries. Effects on the poor: The case of the United Republic of Tanzania (Addis Ababa, JASPA, 1985), ii+55 pp. [TZA] ISBN 92-2-103782-7.

A.A. Aboagye: *Impact of recession on African countries. Effects on the poor: The case of Sierra Leone* (Addis Ababa, JASPA, 1985), ii+65 pp. [SLE] ISBN 92-2-103646-4.

K.M. Gozo and A.A. Aboagye: *Impact of the recession in African countries. Effects on the poor. Synthesis report* (Addis Ababa, JASPA, 1985), v+147 pp. Tables. [COG, GAB, CIV, LBR, SLE, TZA, TGO] ISBN 92-2-105045-9.

K.M. Gozo: *Crise et pauvreté en Afrique: Les effets de la récession sur les économies africaines. Le cas de la Côte d'Ivoire* (Addis Ababa, JASPA, 1985), iv+84 pp. [CIV] ISBN 92-2-203648-4.

K.M. Gozo: *Effets de la recession sur l'économie togolaise. Evolution récente et perspectives de croissance économique et de l'emploi à moyen terme* (Addis Ababa, JASPA, 1985), 50 pp. Annexe. [TGO]

K.M. Gozo: *Politique et stratégie d'industrialisation en Afrique: Effets sur l'emploi et la distribution des revenus. Cas de la Côte d'Ivoire* (Addis Ababa, JASPA, 1985), vi+81 pp. [CIV] ISBN 92-2-203648-4.

Structural readjustments and Zambia's self-reliance in farm equipment. Papers and proceedings of a national workshop on farm tools and equipment technology, basic needs and employment, Lusaka, 26-28 November 1985 (Geneva, ILO, 1987), vii + 135 pp. Sw. frs. 20. [ZMB] ISBN 92-2-105483-7.

The role of the African labour force in recessed economies. Report of the ARLAC-JASPA Workshop held in Harare, Zimbabawe, 15-27 June 1987 (Harare, JASPA/ARLAC, 1987), 32 pp.

- Latin America and the Caribbean

Salarios, precios y empleo en coyunturas de crisis externa. Costa Rica 1973-75. Investigation on Employment No. 16 (Santiago, PREALC, 1979). [CRI]

P. Wilson: *Efectos de la política exterior sobre el empleo en algunas ramas industriales (Chile-Periodo 1974-1977).* Monograph No. 12 (Santiago, PREALC, May 1979). [CHL]

R. Lagos: *Comercio, empleo y proteccionismo: Las relaciones de América Latina y los países desarrollados.* Monograph No. 22 (Santiago, PREALC, Sep. 1981).*

Políticas de estabilización y empleo en América latina. Investigation on Employment No. 22 (Santiago, PREALC, 1982).

R. Lagos and V.E. Tokman: *Monetarismo global, empleo y estratificación social.* Occasional papers No. 47, Rev. 1. (Santiago, PREALC, July 1982) [ARG, CHL]

N.E. García and M. Valdivia: *Crisis externa, ajuste interno y mercado de trabajo. República Dominicana 1980-83.* Monograph No. 49 (Santiago, PREALC/ECIEL, June 1985). [DOM]

M. Pollack and A. Uthoff: *Costa Rica: Evolución macroeconómica 1976-1983.* Monograph No. 50 (Santiago, PREALC/ECIEL, July 1985). [CRI]

M. Pollack and A. Uthoff: *Dinámica de salarios y precios en períodos de ajuste externo. Costa Rica 1976-1983.*[1] Monograph No. 52 (Santiago, PREALC/ECIEL, Aug. 1985). [CRI]

M. Pollack and A. Uthoff: *Wages and price dynamics in Costa Rica 1976-1983.* Monograph No. 51 (Santiago, PREALC/ECIEL, July 1985). [CRI]

Ajuste y deuda social. Un enfoque estructural (Santiago, PREALC, 1987), xiv + 144. US$ 5. S,E. ISBN 92-2-305895-3.

Ajuste, empleo e ingresos. Informe final de la V[a] Conferencia regional de responsables de la planificación del empleo en América latina y el Caribe, Buenos Aires del 4 al 7 de noviembre de 1986 (Santiago, PREALC, 1987), xxv + 388 pp.

- Asia

Export-led industrialisation and employment (Bangkok, ARTEP, 1980), 50 pp. US$3. [KOR, HKG] ISBN 92-2-102370-2.

R. Amjad (ed.): *The development of labour intensive industry in ASEAN countries* (Bangkok, ARTEP, 1981), viii + 338 pp. Sw. frs. 17.50. [PHL, IDN, MYS, SGP, THA] ISBN 92-2-102751-1.

E. Lee (ed.): *Export-led industrialisation and development* (Bangkok, ARTEP, 1981), viii + 204 pp. Sw. frs. 17.50. [KOR, TWN, SGP, HKG, PHL, IDN, JPN] ISBN 92-2-102424-5.

M.K. Datta-Chaudhuri: *The role of free trade zones in the creation of employment and industrial growth in Malaysia* (Bangkok, ARTEP, 1982), iv + 42 pp. [MYS] ISBN 92-2-102746-5.

Employment and structural change in Pakistan: Issues for the eighties. A report for the Pakistan Planning Commission for the Sixth Five Year Plan (1983-88) (Bangkok, ARTEP, 1983), xxvi + 296 pp.* [PAK]

E. Lee (ed.): *Export processing zones and industrial employment in Asia* (Bangkok, ARTEP, 1984), 266 pp. Sw. frs. 17.50. [MYS, SGP, PHL, LKA] ISBN 92-2-103683-9.

L. Lim and Pang Eng Fong: *Trade, employment and industrialisation in Singapore*. Employment, Adjustment and Industrialisation, 2 (Geneva, ILO, 1986), xi + 110 pp. Sw. frs. 25. [SGP] ISBN 92-2-105231-1.

Structural adjustment: By whom, for whom. Employment and income aspects of industrial restructuring in Asia (New Delhi, ARTEP, 1987), 97 pp. US$ 5. [PHL, LKA, PAK] ISBN 92-2-105773-9.

A.K. Bagchi: *Public intervention and industrial restructuring in China, India and Republic of Korea* (New Delhi, ARTEP, 1987), 162 pp. US$ 8. [CHN, IND, KOR] ISBN 92-2-105774-7.

M. Muqtada: *Structural change, adjustment and employment: Some policy issues*. Paper prepared for the Second Meeting of Asian Employment Planners, 24-26 November 1987, New Delhi (New Delhi, ARTEP, 1987), 55 pp.

- OECD Countries

S. Mukherjee with C. Feller: *Restructuring of industrial economies and trade with developing countries* (Geneva, ILO, 1978), viii + 110 pp. Sw. frs. 22.50. E, F. [AUS, USA, CAN, NLD, DEU, NOR] ISBN 92-2-101999-3.

G. Renshaw (ed.): *Employment, trade and North-South co-operation* (Geneva, ILO, 1981), xiv + 264 pp. Sw. frs. 27.50. E, F, S. [NLD, FRA, DEU, GBR] ISBN 92-2-102531-4.

R.P. Dore, with contributions by K. Taira: *Structural adjustment in Japan, 1970-82*. Employment, Adjustment and Industrialisation, 1 (Geneva, ILO, 1986), vii + 189 pp. Sw. frs. 30. [JPN] ISBN 92-2-105268-0.

H.P. Gray, T. Pugel and I. Walter: *International trade, employment and structural adjustment: The United States*. Employment, Adjustment and Industrialisation, 3 (Geneva, ILO, 1986), x + 108 pp. Sw. frs. 25. [USA] ISBN 92-2-105325-3.

G. Renshaw: *Adjustment and economic performance in industrialised countries: A synthesis*. Employment, Adjustment and Industrialisation, 8 (Geneva, ILO, 1986), xiv + 180 pp. Sw. frs. 30. [DEU, JPN, GBR, NLD, USA] ISBN 92-2-105510-8.

K.W. Schatz and F. Wolter: *Structural adjustment in the Federal Republic of Germany*. Employment, Adjustment and Industrialisation, 4 (Geneva, ILO, 1987), xi + 141 pp. Sw. frs. 27.50. [DEU] ISBN 92-2-106114-0.

M. Sharp and G. Shepherd, with a contribution by D. Marsden: *Managing change in British industry*. Employment, Adjustment and Industrialisation, 5 (Geneva, ILO, 1987), xv + 159 pp. Sw. frs. 27.50. [GBR] ISBN 92-2-106154-X.

Articles in the International Labour Review

- General

G. Edgren: "Employment adjustment to trade under conditions of stagnating growth", Vol. 117, No. 3, May-June 1978.

G. Edgren: "Fair labour standards and trade liberalisation", Vol. 118, No. 5, Sep.-Oct. 1979.

Y. Sabolo: "Industrialisation, exports and employment", Vol. 119, No. 4, July-Aug. 1980.

S. Watanabe: "Multinational enterprises, employment and technology adaptation", Vol. 120, No. 6, Nov.-Dec. 1981.

S.A. Kuzmin: "Structural change and employment in developing countries", Vol. 121, No. 3, May-June 1982.

G. van Liemt: "Adjusting to change", Vol. 123, No. 6, Nov.-Dec. 1984.

R. van der Hoeven: "External shocks and stabilisation policies: Spreading the load", Vol. 126, No. 2, Mar.-Apr. 1987.

- Latin America and the Caribbean

E. García D'Acuña and J. Mezzera: "The common external tariff and job creation in the Andean Group", Vol. 117, No. 2, Mar.-Apr. 1978.

V.E. Tokman: "Adjustment and employment in Latin America: the current challenges", Vol. 125, No. 5, Sep.-Oct. 1986.

L. Mertens and P.J. Richards: "Recession and employment in Mexico", Vol. 126, No. 2, Mar.-Apr. 1987. [MEX]

- Asia

A.V. Desai: "The effects of the rise in oil prices on South Asian countries, 1972-78", Vol. 120, No. 2, Mar.-Apr. 1981.

- OECD Countries

K. Inoue: "Structural changes and labour market policies in Japan", Vol. 118, No. 2, Mar.-Apr. 1979. [JPN]

Other Articles

- General

M.J.D. Hopkins, R. van der Hoeven, and J. Petit: "International development scenarios and employment", in *Labour and Society* (Geneva, IILS), Vol. 6, No. 2, Apr.-June 1981.

- Africa

V. Jamal: "Economics of devaluation: The case of the United Republic of Tanzania", in *Labour and Society* (Geneva, IILS), Vol. 11, No. 3, Sep. 1986. [TZA]

H. Tabatabai: "Economic stabilisation and structural adjustment in Ghana, 1983-86", in *Labour and Society* (Geneva, IILS), Vol. 11, No. 3, Sep. 1986. [GHA]

Working Papers

- General

A.J. Field and J.P. Sajhau: *Analysis of employment, production and trade structure in textiles and clothing in selected countries in the 1970s*, Sep. 1979 (WEP 2-36/WP.4). M.

A.J. Field and J.P. Sajhau: *Perspectives on changing production capacity and the international division of labour in the textiles clothing/sector*, Sep. 1979 (WEP 2-36/WP.5). M.

A.J. Field, in collaboration with J.P. Sajhau: *An analysis of the changing patterns of international trade in textiles and clothing 1963-1976*, Sep. 1979 (WEP 2-36/WP.3). M.

A.J. Field: *Analysis of the changing pattern of international trade in machines and equipment, 1963-1976*, Sep. 1979 (WEP 2-36/WP.6). M.

W.M. Vanegas: *United States' environment measures: Economic implications with regard to Colombian income, trade and employment*, Dec. 1980 (WEP 2-36/WP.10). [USA, COL]

C.A. Michalet and B. Madeuf: *Transfert de technologies et nouvel ordre économique international*, Apr. 1981 (WEP 2-36/WP.13). ISBN 92-2-202756-6.

R.A. Markwald: *The impact of US environmental controls on trade and employment: The case of Brazil*, Feb. 1981 (WEP 2-36/WP.11). [USA, BRA] ISBN 92-2-102676-0.

J.P. Sajhau: *Export promotion policies in developing countries*, Mar. 1981 (WEP 2-36/WP.12). [KOR, PHL, BRA, SGP, MEX] ISBN 92-2-102733-3.

H.C. Coote: *Consumer electronics: Employment, production and trade*, Apr. 1983 (WEP 2-36/WP. 22). [JPN, KOR, SGP] ISBN 92-2-103459-3.

E. Ghani: *The effects of devaluation on employment and poverty in developing countries*, Nov. 1984 (WEP 2-32/WP.57). [PER, IDN] ISBN 92-2-103976-5.

The crisis in the North and the South: The impact of the world recession on employment and poverty in developing countries, June 1985 (WEP 2-32/WP. 59). ISBN 92-2-105155-2.

G. van Liemt: *What lessons from the NIC's? The industrialisation process of Brasil, Mexico, the Republic of Korea and Singapore*, Dec. 1985 (WEP 2-36/WP.31). [BRA, MEX, KOR, SGP] ISBN 92-2-105402-0.

Stabilisation, adjustment and poverty. A collection of papers presented at an informal ILO expert group meeting (Geneva, 9-10 January 1986), July 1986 (WEP 2-46/WP.1). ISBN 92-2-105663-5.

M. Augusztinovics: *The double purchasing power parity problem*, Oct. 1986 (WEP 2-46/WP.7). ISBN 92-2-105753-4.

T. Addison and L. Demery: *The impact of liberalisation on growth and equity*, Oct. 1986 (WEP 2-46/WP.4). ISBN 92-2-105713-5.

R. Erzan: *The external account, growth and employment in Egypt and Turkey: Historical review and prospects*, Sep. 1986 (WEP 2-46/WP.5). [EGY, TUR] ISBN 92-2-105714-3.

U. Hiemenz and R.J. Langhammer: *Efficiency pre-conditions for successful integration of developing countries into the world economy*, Sep. 1986 (WEP 2-46/WP.2). ISBN 92-2-105711-9.

A.R. Roe: *Interest rates, employment and income distribution: A review of issues*, Sep. 1986 (WEP 2-46/WP.3). ISBN 92-2-105712-7.

Reestructuración productiva y respuesta interna (Santiago, PREALC), Nov. 1987 (No. 311). [DEU, JPN, BRA]

- **Africa**

J. Brossier, D. Peguin and J.L. Reiffers: *Effets de la structuration du système productif sur l'emploi en Côte-d'Ivoire*, June 1980 (WEP 2-36/WP.7). M. [CIV]

D. Gheza: *La promotion des exportations de produits manufacturiers en Tunisie: Le cas de la sous-traitance internationale*, Mar. 1982 (WEP 2-36/WP.15). M [TUN] ISBN 92-2-203044-3.

L.P. Mureithi, P.K. Kimuyu and G.K. Ikiara: *The effects of higher energy costs on the balance of payments, employment, technology choice and real incomes in Kenya*, Dec. 1982 (WEP 2-22/WP.106). [KEN] ISBN 92-2-103317-1.

R. Maex and A. Read: *A comparative analysis of local processing for exports in Niger and the Ivory Coast*, May 1982 (WEP 2-36/WP.16). M. [NER, CIV] ISBN 92-2-103117-9.

D. Pearce and R. Edwards: *The effect of oil price increases on the Egyptian economy*, Dec. 1982 (WEP 2-22/WP.108). [EGY] ISBN 92-2-103332-5.

R. Ferchiou and H. Mechri: *Emploi, commerce international et coopération Nord-Sud: Etude de cas sur la Tunisie*, June 1983 (WEP 2-36/WP. 23). [TUN] ISBN 92-2-203502-X.

G. Ngango in collaboration with P. Mandeng, A.A. Tabi and A. Tjouen: *Politique du développement industriel et commercial du Cameroun considéré du point de vue de l'emploi*, Mar. 1983 (WEP 2-36/WP. 21). [CMR] ISBN 92-2-92-2-203418-X.

V. Jamal: *Structural adjustment and food security in Uganda*, Oct. 1985 (WEP 10-6/WP.73). M. [UGA] ISBN 92-2-105293-1.

T. Mkandawire: *The impact of the recent world recession on the Zimbabwean economy* (Lusaka, SATEP), Dec. 1985. [ZWE] ISBN 92-2-105303-2

L. Beneria: *Rural development, international markets and labour appropriation by sex: A case study of l'Oulja region, Morocco*, Sep. 1986 (WEP 10/WP.43) [MAR] ISBN 92-2-105662-7.

H. Tabatabai: *Economic decline, access to food and structural adjustment in Ghana*, July 1986 (WEP 10-6/WP.80). [GHA] ISBN 92-2-105641-4.

R.E. Ubogu and J.U. Umo: *Impacts of the external sector on employment and equity: The case of Nigeria and Ghana*, Oct. 1986 (WEP 2-46/WP.6). [NGA, GHA] ISBN 92-2-105754-2.

M. Ndulo and M. Sakala: *Stabilisation policies in Zambia: 1976-85*, May 1987 (WEP 2-46/WP.13). [ZMB] ISBN 92-2-106086-1.

R. van der Hoeven and J. Vandemoortele: *Kenya: Stabilisation and adjustment experiences (1979-84) and prospects for future development*, Jan. 1987 (WEP 2-46/WP.11). [KEN] ISBN 92-2-105876-X.

- **Latin America and the Caribbean**

R. Trajtenberg and B.S.S. Roman: *El empleo y las exportaciones de frutas y legumbres de México, 1960-1975*, July 1978 (WEP 2-36/WP.2). [MEX]

A. Foxley: *Stabilisation policies and stagflation: The cases of Brazil and Chile*, Dec. 1979 (WEP 2-23/WP.81). M. [BRA, CHL]

Efecto en la generación de empleo de las exportaciones de productos industriales de América Latina y el Caribe a los países desarrollados (Santiago, PREALC), Apr. 1981 (No. 200).

Una aproximación a la estimación del efecto empleo de la fabricación de bienes de capital en los países en desarrollo (Santiago, PREALC), June 1981 (No. 208).

V. Kehl: *Los efectos ocupacionales de la exportación de materias primas y de sus manufacturas: El caso del algodón peruano*, May 1981 (WEP 2-36/WP.14). [PER] ISBN 92-2-302818-3.

Ajuste externo, empleo y salarios en América latina y el Caribe (Santiago, PREALC), Nov. 1982 (No. 220). E, S.

Desequilibrio externo y empleo en Brasil (Santiago, PREALC), Sep. 1982 (No. 218). [BRA]

R.E. Looney: *Trade, employment and industrialisation in Mexico*, Oct. 1982, (WEP 2-36/WP.20). M. [MEX] ISBN 92-2-103258-2.

Una nota sobre la generación de divisas y empleo en la producción de alimentos en Chile, (Santiago, PREALC), Dec. 1984 (No. 254). [CHL]

Una nota sobre tasa de inflación, márgenes de ganancia y tasa de interés (Argentina 1970-1983) [1] (Santiago, PREALC), Oct. 1984 (No. 252). [ARG]

R.L.F. Werneck: *Industrial growth, foreign trade and economic policy: Some aspects of the rise of Brazil as a NIC (1965-80)*, Apr. 1984 (WEP 2-36/WP.28). [BRA] ISBN 92-2-103778-9.

Ajuste externo e interno en Brasil (Santiago, PREALC), May 1985 (No. 263). [BRA]

Ajuste estructural y deuda social (Santiago, PREALC), Sep. 1986 (No. 282). S, E.

Ajuste y empleo: Los desafíos del presente (Santiago, PREALC), Dec. 1986 (No. 287).

Fuentes del cambio en la estructura del sector industrial Chileno: 1967-1982 (Santiago, PREALC), Mar. 1986 (No. 274). [CHL]

Reactivación y transformación en el cono Sur (Santiago, PREALC), Dec. 1986 (No. 286).

Una nota sobre el impacto de la liberalización y apertura financiera sobre el sector manufacturero Chileno: 1974-1982 (Santiago, PREALC), Apr. 1986 (No. 275). [CHL]

R. Cortázar: *Employment, real wages and external constraint: The case of Brazil and Chile*, Oct. 1986 (WEP 2-46/WP.8). [BRA, CHL] ISBN 92-2-105752-6.

L. Mertens: *Employment and stabilisation in Mexico*, Dec. 1986 (WEP 2-46/WP.10). [MEX] ISBN 92-2-105846-8.

Brasil: Ajuste estructural y distribución de ingreso (Santiago, PREALC), Oct. 1987 (No. 308). [BRA]

Chile: Ajuste estructural y deuda social (Santiago, PREALC), May 1987 (No. 297). [CHL]

Crisis, ajuste económico y costo social (Santiago, PREALC), Mar. 1987 (No. 291).

Desempleo estructural en Chile: Un análisis macroeconómico (Santiago, PREALC), July 1987 (No. 302). [CHL]

El ajuste frente a la crisis y sus efectos sobre el empleo en America Latina (Santiago, PREALC), Feb. 1987 (No. 290).

La caída del empleo manufacturero: Chile 1979-83 (Santiago, PREALC), May 1987 (No. 298).

- Asia

Douglas Paauw: *Frustrated labour-intensive development: The case of Indonesia* (Bangkok, ARTEP), 1979. [IDN]

M.K. Datta-Chaudhuri: *Industrialisation and foreign trade: An analysis based on the development experiences of the Republic of Korea and the Philippines* (Bangkok, ARTEP), 1979. [KOR, PHL]

R. Hsia: *Technological change, trade promotion and export-led industrialisation* (Bangkok, ARTEP), 1979. [HKG, KOR]

I.M.D. Little: *The experiences and causes of rapid labour-intensive development in Korea, Taiwan, Hong Kong and Singapore and the possibilities of emulation* (Bangkok, ARTEP), 1979. [KOR, TWN, SGP]

Yung Chul Park: *Export-led development: The Korean experience 1960-78* (Bangkok, ARTEP), June 1980. [KOR]

S.H. Jo: *The impact of the raw materials sector on employment generation in the process of South Korea's industrial growth (1955-1978)*, Aug. 1980 (WEP 2-36/WP.9). M. [KOR]

G. van Liemt: *The employment effects of the fruit and vegetable processing sector in the Republic of Korea*, June 1980 (WEP 2-36/WP.8). M. [KOR]

Chia Siow Yue: *Export processing and industrialisation: The case of Singapore* (Bangkok, ARTEP), Oct. 1982. [SGP] ISBN 92-2-103181-0.

H. Ali Khan: *Energy, employment and balance of payments: Implications of technology choice in the energy and textile sectors in the Republic of Korea*, Nov. 1982 (WEP 2-22/WP.103). [KOR] ISBN 92-2-103319-8.

J.S. Castro: *The Bataan export processing zone* (Bangkok, ARTEP), Sep. 1982. [PHL] ISBN 92-2-103179-9.

G. Edgren: *Spearheads of industrialisation or sweatshops in the sun? A critical appraisal of labour conditions in Asian export processing zones* (Bangkok, ARTEP), Aug. 1982. ISBN 92-2-103178-0.

L. Lim and Pang Eng Fong: *Trade, employment and industrialisation in Singapore,*[2] June 1982 (WEP 2-36/WP.17). M. [SGP] ISBN 92-2-103157-8.

D. Ramanayake: *The Katunayake investment promotion zone: A case study* (Bangkok, ARTEP), Sep. 1982. [LKA]

G.M. Jurado, R.D. Ferrer and E.F. Esguerra: *Trade policy, growth and employment: A study of the Philippines*, Oct. 1983 (WEP 2-36/WP.25). M. [PHL] ISBN 92-2-103602-2.

P. Yungchul: *South Korea's experience with industrial adjustment in the 1970's* (Bangkok, ARTEP), Aug. 1983. [KOR] ISBN 92-2-103285-X.

R. Islam: *Recession, employment and poverty in the developing countries of Asia*[3] (Bangkok, ARTEP), 1984. ISBN 92-2-103685-5.

D. Lim: *Industrial restructuring in Singapore* (Bangkok, ARTEP), 1984. [SGP]

E. Lee: *World recession and the developing economies in Asia* (Bangkok, ARTEP), 1984. ISBN 92-2-103936-6.

T.B. Lin and Y.P. Ho: *Industrial restructuring in Hong Kong* (Bangkok, ARTEP), 1984. [HKG] ISBN 92-2-103937-4.

T. Michell: *The Republic of Korea: Employment, industrialisation and trade*, July 1984 (WEP 2-36/WP.29). [KOR] ISBN 92-2-103887-4.

A. Singh: *The world economy and the comparative economic performance of large semi-industrial countries: A study of India, China and the Republic of Korea* (Bangkok, ARTEP), Sep. 1985. [IND, CHN, KOR] ISBN 92-2-103943-9.

I. Islam and C.H. Kirkpatrick: *Wages, employment and income distribution in a small open economy: The case of Singapore* (New Delhi, ARTEP), Mar. 1986. [SGP] ISBN 92-2-105476-4.

A. Singh and J. Ghosh: *Import liberalisation and the new industrial strategy: An analysis of their impact on output and employment in the Indian economy* (New Delhi, ARTEP), Dec. 1987. [IND] ISBN 92-2-106106-X.

- OECD Countries

The General Trading Companies of Japan and export-led industrialisation (Bangkok, ARTEP), Jan. 1980. [JPN]

H.P. Gray, T. Pugel and I. Walter: *International trade, employment and structural adjustment: The case of the United States,*[4] July 1982 (WEP 2-36/WP.18). M. [USA] ISBN 92-2-103204-3.

K.W. Schatz and F. Wolter: *International trade, employment and structural adjustment: The case study of the Federal Republic of Germany,*[5] Oct. 1982 (WEP 2-36/WP.19). M. [DEU] ISBN 92-2-103257-4.

G. de Groot and B. Evers: *Adjustment in a small open economy: The case of the Netherlands*, Dec. 1983 (WEP 2-36/WP.27). [NLD] ISBN 92-2-103668-5.

R. Dore, with contributions by K. Taira: *Flexible rigidities. Industrial policy and structural adjustment in the Japanese economy: 1970-80*,[6] July 1983 (WEP 2-36/WP.24). [JPN] ISBN 92-2-103532-8.

M. Sharp, G. Shepherd and D. Marsden: *Structural adjustment in the United Kingdom manufacturing industry*,[7] Dec. 1983 (WEP 2-36/WP.26). [GBR] ISBN 92-2-103650-2.

G. Renshaw: *Adjustment and economic performance in industralised countries: A synthesis*,[8] Aug. 1984 (WEP 2-36/WP.30). [DEU, USA, JPN, GBR, NLD] ISBN 92-2-103921-8.

R.S. Belous: *Flexibility and American labour markets: The evidence and implications*, June 1987 (WEP 2-43/WP.14). [USA] ISBN 92-2-106102-7.

J.J. Chanaron and D.A. Spagni: *The UK car industry in the 1980s*, Oct. 1987 (WEP 2-46/WP.15). [GBR] ISBN 92-2-106312-7.

K. Jones: *Structural adjustment in the United States steel industry: A North-South perspective*, Oct. 1987 (WEP 2-46/WP.14). [USA] ISBN 92-2-106315-5.

- East European Countries

O. Kovac and L. Madzar: *Employment policies in the programme of structural adjustment of the Yugoslav economy*, Nov. 1986 (WEP 2-46/WP.9). [YUG] ISBN 92-2-105842-5.

Z. Bekker: *Adjustment patterns and problems in Eastern European countries: An international comparison*, May 1987 (WEP 2-46/WP.12). ISBN 92-2-106085-3.

ILO works published by commercial and non-profit-making publishers

- General

A.J. Field: *Trade and textiles. An analysis of the changing international division of labour in the textile and clothing sector, 1963-78* (Quezon City, New Day Publishers, 1984), xii + 217 pp.

Related books and articles

- General

Y. Sabolo: "Ocupazione e disocupazione: Prospettive per l'Anno 2000", in *Affari sociali internazionali* (Milano), 1979.

Notes:

1 Also published in *Política salarial, inflación y restricción externa* (Santiago, PREALC, 1987).

2 Also published as a book: L. Lim and Pang Eng Fong: *Trade, employment and industrialisation in Singapore* (Geneva, ILO, 1986).

3 Published in: R. Islam: *Rural industrialisation and employment in Asia* (New Delhi, ARTEP, 1987), 327 pp.

4 Also published as a book: H.P. Gray, T. Pugel and I. Walter: *International trade, employment and structural adjustment: The United States* (Geneva, ILO, 1986).

5 Also published as a book: K.W. Schatz and F. Wolter: *Structural adjustment in the Federal Republic of Germany* (Geneva, ILO, 1987).

6 Also published as a book: R.P. Dore, with contributions by K. Taira: Structural adjustment in Japan, 1970-82 (Geneva, ILO, 1986).

7 Also published as a book: M. Sharp and G. Shepherd, with a contribution by D. Marsden: Managing change in British industry (Geneva, ILO, 1987).

8 Also published as a book: G. Renshaw: Adjustment and economic performance in industrialised countries: A synthesis (Geneva, ILO, 1986).

Women

ILO publications

Books and reports

- **General**

Women in rural development: Critical issues (Geneva, ILO, 1980; 3rd impression, 1984), iv + 52 pp. Sw. frs. 12,50. [YUG, POL, BGD, CHN, GHA, COL] ISBN 92-2-102388-5.

R. Anker: *Research on women's roles and demographic change: Survey questionnaries for households, women, men and communities with background explanations*. (Geneva, ILO, 1980; 2nd edition, 1981), vi + 314 pp. ISBN 92-2-102817-8.

M.F. Loutfi: *Rural women: Unequal partners in development* (Geneva, ILO, 1980; 6th impression (with modifications), 1987), iv + 82 pp. Sw. frs. 15.   E and Thai.   ISBN 92-2-102389-3.

L. Goldschmidt-Clermont: *Unpaid work in the household: A review of economic evaluation methods*. Women, Work and Development, 1 (Geneva, ILO, 1982; 2nd impression, 1983), xi + 137 pp. Sw. frs. 17.50. ISBN 92-2-103085-7.

Women, work and demographic issues. Report of an ILO/UNITAR seminar held in Tashkent, USSR, 11-19 October 1983 (Geneva, ILO, 1984), 159 pp. Sw.frs 20. [IND, BGD, EGY, CYP, MUS, NGA, GHA, COL, SUN, CUB, PAK, HUN] ISBN 92-2-103886-6.

Resources, power and women. Proceedings of the African and Asian inter-regional workshop on strategies for improving the employment conditions of rural women, Arusha, the United Republic of Tanzania, 20-25 August 1984 (Geneva, ILO, 1985), ix + 82 pp. Sw. frs. 10. ISBN 92-2-105009-2.

E. Cecelski: *The rural energy crisis, women's work and basic needs: Perspectives and approaches to action* (Geneva, ILO, 1985; 2nd impression, 1987), revised version of working paper WEP 10/WP. 35, xviii + 84 pp. ISBN 92-2-105091-2.

R. Dixon-Mueller: *Women's work in Third World agriculture. Concepts and indicators*. Women, Work and Development, 9 (Geneva, ILO, 1985), xi + 151 pp. Sw. frs. 20. ISBN 92-2-105107-2.

S. Malick: *Planning income and employment generation for rural woman - The marketing approach* (Islamabad, ILO, 1985), 35 pp. ISBN 92-2-105398-8.

S. Muntemba (ed.): *Rural development and women: Lessons from the field*. Technical co-operation report on the ILO/DANIDA Project on identification of successful projects for improving the employment conditions of rural women (Geneva, ILO, 1985), 2 vols. [BWA, ZMB, TZA, LKA, IDN, IND, ETH, LSO, CMR, KOR, SLE, MYS, ZWE, BGD, PAK, SWZ] ISBN 92-2-105154-4.

C. Oppong and K. Abu: *A handbook for data collection and analysis on seven roles and statuses of women* (Geneva, ILO, 1985), 134 pp. E,F. ISBN 92-2-105354-7.

Guides anthropologiques et questionnaires pour l'étude des changements démographiques et des rôles des femmes. Publié sous la direction de R. Anker and C. Hein (Geneva, ILO, 1986), v + 129 pp. ISBN 92-2-205601-9.

Inégalités entre hommes et femmes sur les marchés urbains du travail dans le tiers monde. Publié sous la direction de R. Anker et C. Hein (Geneva, ILO, 1986), v + 136 pp. F,S. ISBN 92-2-205602-7.

Vers la mesure des activités économiques des femmes. Publié sous la direction de R. Anker et C. Hein (Geneva, ILO, 1986), v + 147 pp. F,S. ISBN 92-2-205600-0.

Linking energy with survival. A guide to energy environment and rural women's work (Geneva, ILO, 1987), 31 pp.

The rural energy crisis, women's work and basic needs. Proceedings of an international workshop co-sponsored by the ILO and the Institute of Social Studies, The Hague, 21-24 April 1986 (Geneva, ILO, 1987), iv + 79 pp. [PER, IDN, GHA] ISBN 92-2-105802-6.

L. Goldschmidt-Clermont: *Economic evaluations of unpaid household work: Africa, Asia, Latin America and Oceania*, Women, Work and Development, 14 (Geneva, ILO, 1987), 213 pp. Sw. frs. 27.50. ISBN 92-2-105827-1.

- Africa

Employment problems of rural women in Kenya. Report of a technical mission submitted to the Government of Kenya by JASPA and the ECA/ILO/SIDA (Addis Ababa, JASPA, 1981). [KEN]

M.A. Savané: *Les projets pour les femmes en milieu rural au Sénégal.* Coopération technique. Rapport d'évaluation (Geneva, ILO, 1983), 140pp. [SEN] ISBN 92-2-203394-9.

Improved village technology for women's activities. A manual for West Africa. Prepared by the ILO and the Government of Norway joint Africa regional project on technological change, basic needs and the condition of rural women (Geneva, ILO, 1984), vi + 292 pp. Sw. frs. 27.50. [GHA, SLE] ISBN 92-2-103818-1.

Rural development and women in Africa (Geneva, ILO, 1984; 2nd impression, 1986), v + 157 pp. Sw. frs. 20. E, F. [SLE, GHA, CIV, SEN, NGA, MAR, LBY, ZAF] ISBN 92-2-103633-2.

P.D. Lynch with H. Fahmy: *Craftswomen in Kerdassa, Egypt. Household production and reproduction.* Women, Work and Development, 7 (Geneva, ILO, 1984), vii + 91 pp. Sw. frs. 15. [EGY] ISBN 92-2-103625-1.

P. van den Oever-Pereira: *Programmes de Travaux Publics et distribution du temps de travail des femmes: Le cas de Burkina Faso (anc. Haute Volta)* (Geneva, ILO, 1984), 106 pp. [BFA]

L'emploi des femmes à Madagascar. Une étude comparative du PECTA. Rapport soumis au Gouvernement de la République de Madagascar (Addis Ababa, JASPA, 1985), iii + 57 pp. [MDG] ISBN 92-2-205195-5.

L'emploi des femmes au Bénin. Une étude comparative du PECTA. Rapport soumis au Gouvernement de la République populaire du Bénin (Addis Ababa, JASPA, 1985), iv + 76 pp. [BEN] ISBN 92-2-205192-0.

L'emploi des femmes au Cameroun. Une étude comparative du PECTA. Rapport soumis au Gouvernement de la République du Cameroun (Addis Ababa, JASPA, 1985), iii + 81 pp. [CMR]

L'emploi des femmes au Sénégal. Une étude comparative du PECTA. Rapport soumis au Gouvernement de la République du Sénégal (Addis Ababa, JASPA, 1985), iii + 92 pp. [SEN] ISBN 92-2-205196-3.

L'emploi des femmes au Togo. Une étude comparative du PECTA. Rapport soumis au Gouvernement de la République du Togo (Addis Ababa, JASPA, 1985), 83 pp. [TGO] ISBN 92-2-205197-1.

L'emploi des femmes en Afrique. Rapport de synthèse dans 6 pays francophones (Bénin, Cameroun, Côte d'Ivoire, Madagascar, Sénégal et Togo) (Addis Ababa, JASPA, 1985), 128 pp. [BEN, CMR, CIV, MDG, SEN, TGO] ISBN 92-2-205198-X

L'emploi des femmes en Côte d'Ivoire. Une étude comparative du PECTA. Rapport soumis au Gouvernement de la République de Côte d'Ivoire (Addis Ababa, JASPA, 1985), iv + 60 pp. [CIV] ISBN 92-2-205194-7.

R. Wéry: *Profil socio-économique des femmes de Bamako* (Geneva, ILO, 1985), 43 pp. [MLI]

Women's employment patterns, discrimination and promotion of equality in Africa. The case of Ethiopia (Addis Ababa, JASPA, 1986), iii + 62 pp. [ETH] ISBN 92-2-105532-9.

Women's employment patterns, discrimination and promotion of equality in Africa. The case of Kenya (Addis Ababa, JASPA, 1986), xvi + 217 pp. [KEN] ISBN 92-2-105533-7.

Women's employment patterns, discrimination and promotion of equality in Africa. The case of Sierra Leone (Addis Ababa, JASPA, 1986), iii + 128 pp. [SLE] ISBN 92-2-105540-X.

Women's employment patterns, discrimination and promotion of equality in Africa. The case of the United Republic of Tanzania (Addis Ababa, JASPA, 1986), iii + 182 pp. [TZA] ISBN 92-2-105531-0.

Women's employment patterns, discrimination and promotion of equality in Africa. The case of Zambia (Addis Ababa, JASPA, 1986), iii + 170 pp. [ZMB] ISBN 92-2-105534-5.

Women's employment patterns, discrimination and promotion of equality in Africa. The case of Zimbabwe (Addis Ababa, JASPA, 1986), iii + 63 pp. [ZWE] ISBN 92-2-105536-1.

Control and management of technology by rural women of Ghana. Report of the joint ILO/Netherlands/Ghana National Council on Women and Development Project ILO/NETH/80/GHA/1 (Geneva, ILO, 1987), xiii + 169 pp. [GHA] ISBN 92-2-106216-3.

C. Oppong and K. Abu: *Seven roles of women: Impact of education, migration and employment on Ghanaian mothers*, Women, Work and Development, 13 (Geneva, ILO, 1987), xi + 127 pp. Sw. frs. 20. [GHA] ISBN 92-2-105858-1.

- Latin America and the Caribbean

Participación laboral femenina y diferencia de remuneraciones según sexo en América Latina. Investigation on Employment No. 13 (Santiago, PREALC, 1978).

C.D. Deere and M. León de Leal: *Women in Andean agriculture: Peasant production and rural wage employment in Colombia and Peru*. Women, Work and Development, 4 (Geneva, ILO, 1982; 2nd impression, 1985), xii + 172 pp. Sw. frs. 20. [COL, PER] ISBN 92-2-103106-3.

La mujer y el desarrollo rural en América latina y el Caribbe. Informe y conclusiones del seminario regional tripartito latino-americano de la OIT sobre la mujer y el desarrollo rural, Patzcuaro, Mexico, del 24 al 28 de Agosto de 1981 (Geneva, ILO, 1983), viii + 82 pp. Sw. frs. 15. S, E. [MEX, COL, PER] ISBN 92-2-303472-8.

T. de Barbieri: *Las unidades agrícola-industriales para la mujer campesina en México: Dos estudios de caso. Charo, Michoacan y Viesca, Coahuila*. Cooperación técnica. Informe de evaluación (Geneva, ILO, 1983), 96 pp. [MEX] ISBN 92-2-303515-5.

M.I. Evans: *Stove programmes in the framework of improved cooking practices: A change in focus with special refence to Latin America* (Geneva, ILO, 1987), vii + 56 pp. [MEX, PER] ISBN 92-2-106081-0.

- **Asia**

E. Croll: *Women in rural development: The People's Republic of China* [1] (Geneva, ILO 1979; 2nd impression, 1980), x + 62 pp. Sw. frs. 15. E and Thai. [CHN] ISBN 92-2-102054-1.

Women in the Indian labour force. - Papers and proceedings of a workshop in Trivandrum, India, 24-25 July 1980 (Bangkok, ARTEP, 1981), 137 pp.* [IND] ISBN 92-2-102428-8.

Rural development and women in Asia. Proceedings and conclusions of the ILO Tripartite Asian Regional Seminar, Mahabaleshwar, India, 6-11 Apr. 1981 (Geneva, ILO, 1982), viii + 88 pp. Sw. frs. 15. ISBN 92-2-102944-1.

Rural women workers in Asia. Development strategies and action at the local, national and international levels. Report on a workshop at the ILO International Centre for Advanced Technical and Vocational Training, Turin (Italy), 30 Nov.-4 Dec. 1981 (Geneva, ILO, 1982), x + 106 pp.* US$10. [BGD]

R. Kurian: *Women workers in the Sri Lanka plantation sector: An historical and contemporary analysis.* Women, Work and Development, 5 (Geneva, ILO, 1982), xiv + 138 pp. Sw. frs. 20. E. and Tamil. [LKA] ISBN 92-2-102992-1.

P. Phongpaichit: *From peasant girls to Bangkok masseuses.* Women, Work and Development, 2 (Geneva, ILO, 1982; 2nd impression, 1985), xii + 80 pp. Sw. frs. 15. [THA] ISBN 92-2-103013-X.

L. Gulati: *Fisherwomen on the Kerala coast. Demographic and socio-economic impact of a fisheries development project.* Women, Work and Development, 8 (Geneva, ILO, 1984), xi + 156 pp. Sw. frs. 20. [IND] ISBN 92-2-103626-X.

E. Croll: *Women and rural development in China. Production and reproduction.* Women, Work and Development, 11 (Geneva, ILO, 1985), viii + 172 pp. Sw. frs. 20. [CHN] ISBN 92-2-105217-6.

M. Mies assisted by Lalita K. and K. Kumari: *Indian women in subsistence and agricultural labour.* Women, Work and Development, 12 (Geneva, ILO, 1986), x + 158 pp. Sw. frs. 20. [IND] ISBN 92-2-105397-0.

- **OECD Countries**

D. Werneke: *Microelectronics and office jobs. The impact of the chip on women's employment* (Geneva, ILO, 1983; 3rd impression, 1985), 102 pp. Sw. frs. 17,50. [GBR, FRA, AUS] ISBN 92-2-103278-7.

G. Berik: *Women carpet weavers in rural Turkey: Patterns of employment, earnings and status.* Women, Work and Development, 15 (Geneva, ILO, 1987), xiii + 112 pp. Sw. frs. 20. [TUR] ISBN 92-2-106004-7.

- **East European Countries**

B. Barta, A. Klinger, K. Miltényi and G. Vukovich: *Fertility, female employment and policy measures in Hungary.* Women, Work and Development, 6 (Geneva, ILO, 1984), viii + 88 pp. Sw. frs. 15. [HUN] ISBN 92-2-103624-3.

V. Bodrova and R. Anker (eds.): *Working women in socialist countries: The fertility connection* (Geneva, ILO, 1985), xvi + 234 pp. Sw. frs. 27.50. [HUN, BGR, SUN, CUB, CSK, POL] ISBN 92-2-103910-2.

- **Middle East**

M. Molyneux: *State policies and the position of women workers in the People's Democratic Republic of Yemen, 1967-77.* Women, Work and Development, 3 (Geneva, ILO, 1982; 2nd impression, 1984), viii + 87 pp. Sw. frs. 17.50. [YMD] ISBN 92-2-103144-6.

W.J. House: *Cypriot women in the labour market. An exploration of myths and reality.* Women, Work and Development, 10 (Geneva, ILO, 1985), 141 pp. Sw. frs. 17.50. [CYP] ISBN 92-2-105108-0.

Articles in the International Labour Review

- General

D. Werneke: "The economic slowdown and women's employment opportunities", Vol. 117, No. 1, Jan.-Feb. 1978.

Z. Ahmad: "The plight of rural women: Alternatives for action", Vol. 119, No. 4, July-Aug. 1980.

I. Ahmed: "Technology and rural women in the Third World", Vol. 122, No. 4, July-Aug. 1983.

R. Anker: "Female labour force participation in developing countries: A critique of current definitions and data collection methods", Vol. 122, No. 6, Nov.-Dec. 1983.

Z. Ahmad: "Rural women and their work: Dependence and alternatives for change", Vol. 123, No. 1, Jan.-Feb. 1984.

R. Anker and C. Hein: "Why Third World urban employers usually prefer men", Vol. 124, No. 1, Jan.-Feb. 1985.

- Africa

C. Hein: "Jobs for the girls: Export manufacturing in Mauritius", Vol. 123, No. 2, Mar.-Apr. 1984. [MUS]

- Middle East

W.J. House: "Occupational segregation and discriminatory pay: The position of women in the Cyprus labour market", Vol. 122, No. 1, Jan.-Feb. 1983. [CYP]

Other Articles

- General

I. Ahmed: "Rural women and technical change: Theory, empirical analysis and operational projects", in *Labour and Society* (Geneva, IILS), Vol. 10, No. 3, Sep. 1985.

Working Papers

- General

Participación laboral y condiciones salariales de la mujer en América Latina, Estados Unidos y Canadá (Santiago, PREALC), Mar. 1978 (No. 121).* [USA, CAN]

I. Ahmed: *Technological change and the condition of rural women: A preliminary assessment,* Oct. 1978 (WEP 2-22/WP.39). M.

R. Anker: *Demographic change and the role of women: A research programme in developing countries,* Nov. 1978 (WEP 2-21/WP.69).

L. Beneria: *Reproduction, production and the sexual division of labour,* July 1978 (WEP 10/WP.2). M.

A. Bhaduri: *Technological change and rural women. A conceptual analysis,*[2] Jan. 1979 (WEP 2-22/WP.46).

E. Jelin: *Women and the urban labour market,* Sep. 1979 (WEP 2-21/WP.77). M.

C. Oppong: *Family structure and women's reproductive and productive roles: Some conceptual and methodological issues,* Sep. 1979 (WEP 2-21/WP.79). M.

C. Oppong: *A synopsis of seven roles and status of women: An outline of a conceptual and methodological approach,* Sep. 1980 (WEP 2-21/WP.94). E, F. M.

L.C. Robinson and S.P. Stephenson Jr.: *Labour policies, female labour force participation and fertility: A research design,* Jan. 1980 (WEP 2-21/WP.83).

G.M. Farooq: *Concept and measurement of human reproduction in economic models of fertility behaviour,* Mar. 1981 (WEP 2-21/WP.102). M. ISBN 92-2-102716-3.

C. Oppong and K. Church: *A field guide to research on seven roles of women: Focused biographies,* May 1981 (WEP 2-21/WP.106). M. ISBN 92-2-102806-2.

C. Oppong: *Familial roles and fertility: Some labour policy aspects,* Dec. 1982 (WEP 2-21/WP.124). M. ISBN 92-2-103321-X.

C. Oppong: *Maternal role rewards, opportunity costs and fertility,* Oct. 1982 (WEP 2-21/WP.120). M. ISBN 92-2-103269-8.

R. Anker: *Effect on reported levels of female labour force participation in developing countries of questionnaire design, sex of interviewer and sex/proxy status of respondent: Description of a methodological field experiment,* July 1983 (WEP 2-21/WP.137). M. ISBN 92-2-103545-X.

R. Anker: *Female labour force activity in developing countries: A critique of current data collection techniques,* July 1983 (WEP 2-21/WP.136). M. ISBN 92-2-103543-3.

E. Cecelski: *The rural energy crisis, women's work and family welfare: Perspectives and approaches to action,* June 1984 (WEP 10/WP.35)*. M. ISBN 92-2-103913-7.

N.H. Youssef and C.B. Hetler: *Rural households headed by women: A priority concern for development,* Mar. 1984 (WEP 10/WP.31)*. M. ISBN 92-2-103763-0.

R. Anker and C. Hein: *Employment of women outside agriculture in Third World countries: An overview of occupational statistics,*[4] Mar. 1985 (WEP 2-21/WP. 147). M. ISBN 92-2-105092-1.

R.E. Bilsborrow and D.K. Guilkey: *Community and institutional influence on fertility: Analytical issues,* Mar. 1987 (WEP 2-21/WP.157). ISBN 92-2-105969-3.

- **Africa**

R. Anker and J.C. Knowles: *A micro analysis of female labour force participation in Kenya,* Jan. 1978 (WEP 2-21/WP.62). [KEN]

G.M. Farooq: *Household fertility decision-making in Nigeria,* July 1979 (WEP 2-21/WP.75). [NGA]

M. Carr: *Technology and rural women in Africa,*[2] July 1980 (WEP 2-22/WP.61). M.

R. Longhurst: *Rural development planning and the sexual division of labour: A case study of a Moslem Hausa village in northern Nigeria,* June 1980 (WEP 10/WP.10)*. [NGA]

C. Hein: *Employment of women in Mauritian industry: Opportunity or exploitation?,*[4] Dec. 1981 (WEP 2-21/WP.114). M. [MUS] ISBN 92-2-102969-7.

A. Whitehead: *A conceptual framework for the analysis of the effects of technological change on rural women,*[2] June 1981 (WEP 2-22/WP.79).* ISBN 92-2-102814-3.

E. Date-Bah: *Sex inequality in an African urban labour market: The case of Accra-Tema,* Nov. 1982 (WEP 2-21/WP.122). M. [GHA] ISBN 92-2-103293-0.

C. Hein: *Factory employment, marriage and fertility: The case of Mauritian women,* June 1982 (WEP 2-21/WP.118). M. [MUS] ISBN 92-2-103171-3.

O.N. Muchena: *Women's participation in the rural labour force in Zimbabwe* (Lusaka, SATEP), Nov. 1982. [ZWE]

C. Oppong: *Reproduction and resources: Some anthropological evidence from Ghana,* Dec. 1982 (WEP 2-21/WP.123). M. [GHA] ISBN 92-2-92-2-103321-8.

R. Pittin: *Documentation of women's work in Nigeria: Problems and solutions,* Dec. 1982 (WEP 2-21/WP.125). M. [NGA] ISBN 92-2-103338-4.

V. Ventura-Dias: *Technological change, production organisation and rural women in Kenya,*[2] Nov. 1982 (WEP 2-22/WP.101). [KEN] ISBN 92-2-103306-6.

P.D. Lynch with H. Fahmy: *Craftswomen in Kerdassa, Egypt: Household production and reproduction,*[5] Feb. 1983 (WEP 2-21/WP.126). [EGY] ISBN 92-2-103343-0.

C. Oppong: *Paternal costs, role strain and fertility regulation: Some Ghanaian evidence,* May 1983 (WEP 2-21/WP.134). M. [GHA] ISBN 92-2-103491-7.

L.A. Adeokun, A. Adepoju, F.A. Llori, A.A. Adewuyi and J.A. Ebigbola: *The Ife labour market: A Nigerian case study,* Mar. 1984 (WEP 2-21/WP.144). [NGA] ISBN 92-2-103759-2.

C. Oppong and K. Abu: *The changing maternal role of Ghanaian women: Impacts of education, migration and employment,* Feb. 1984 (WEP 2-21/WP.143). [GHA] ISBN 92-2-103702-9.

E. Ardayfio: *The rural energy crisis in Ghana: Its implications for women's work and household survival,* Feb. 1986 (WEP 10/WP.39). [GHA] ISBN 92-2-105444-6.

L. Beneria: *Rural development, international markets and labour appropriation by sex: A case study of l'Oulja region, Morocco,* Sep. 1986 (WEP 10/WP.43). [MAR] ISBN 92-2-105662-7.

S. Urdang: *Rural transformation and peasant women in Mozambique,* Apr. 1986 (WEP 10/WP.40). [MOZ] ISBN 92-2-105443-8.

M. Vaughan and G.H.R. Chipande: *Women in the estate sector of Malawi: The tea and tobacco industries,* May 1986 (WEP 10/WP.42). [MWI] ISBN 92-2-105463-2.

S. Tomoda in collaboration with H. Myovela and I.G.M. Muijsers: *Women and special public works programmes: A case study of the Mto wa Mbu irrigation (Arusha) and the water supply (Rukwa) projects, the United Republic of Tanzania,* Aug. 1987 (WEP 2-24/WP.25). [TZA] ISBN 92-2-106226-0.

E. Gordon: *The women left behind: A study on the wives of the migrant workers of Lesotho*[3] Dec. 1978 (WEP) 2-26/WP.35) M. [LSO]

- Latin America and the Caribbean

Participación femenina en la actividad económica en América Latina (análisis estadístico) (Santiago, PREALC), Nov. 1978 (No. 161).

G. Standing: *Labour commitment, sexual dualism and industrialisation in Jamaica,* May 1978 (WEP 2-21/WP.64). [JAM]

G. Standing: *Migration, labour force absorption and mobility: Women in Kingston, Jamaica,* Oct. 1978 (WEP 2-21/WP.68). [JAM]

M.H. de Cunha Rato: *Female labour force participation and the production system in Brazil,* July 1979 (WEP 2-21/WP.76). M. [BRA]

C.D. Deere and M. León de Leal: *Women in agriculture: Peasant production and proletarianisation in three Andean regions,*[11] 1980 (WEP 10/WP.13).* [COL, PER]

G.B. Rodgers with assistance from D. Viry: *Female labour force participation in Peru: An analysis using the world fertility survey,* Sep. 1980 (WEP 2-21/WP.96). [PER]

S. Lund Skar with the assistance of N. Aris Samanez and S. García Cotarma: *Fuel availability, nutrition and women's work in Highland Peru. Three case studies from contrasting Andean communities,* Jan. 1982 (WEP 10/WP.23). [PER] ISBN 92-2-102991-3.

A. Farnos, F. Gonzalez and R. Hernandez: *The role of women and demographic change in Cuba,* Aug. 1983 (WEP 2-21/WP.138). M. [CUB] ISBN 92-2-103552-2.

Panamá: Situación y perspectivas del empleo femenino (Santiago, PREALC), Mar. 1984 (No. 234). [PAN]

E. Alántara, M. dela Peña, M. Abuhadba and D. Flores: *Crisis de energia rural y trabajo femenino en tres areas ecológicas del Perú.* Nov. 1985 (WEP 10/WP.38). [PER] ISBN 92-2-305445-1.

M.I. Evans: *Change in domestic fuel consumption in central Mexico and its relation to employment and nutrition,* Sep. 1986 (WEP 10/WP.44). [MEX] ISBN 92-2-105760-7.

M. García Castro: *Mujeres pobres como jefes de hogar y como esposas en el proceso de reproducción en Bogotá: Identidad y heterogeneidades,* Feb. 1987 (WEP 2-21WP.156). [COL] ISBN 92-2-305883-X.

- **Asia**

Z. Bhatty: *Economic role and status of women: A case study of women in the beedi industry in Allahabad,*[6] Dec. 1980 (WEP 10/WP.15)*. [IND]

M. Mies: *Housewives produce for the world market: The lace makers of Narsapur,*[7] Dec. 1980 (WEP 10/WP.16).* [IND]

G. Standing: *Analysing women's labour force activity with the WFS: Insights from Sri Lanka,* Mar. 1980 (WEP 2-21/WP.85). [LKA]

B. Agarwal: *Agricultural modernisation and Third World women: Pointers from the literature and an empirical analysis,* May 1981 (WEP 10/WP.21)*. M. [IND] ISBN 92-2-102778-3.

N.H. Fan: *A preliminary study of women rubber estate workers in Peninsular Malaysia,* Feb. 1981 (WEP 10/WP.19). M. [MYS] ISBN 92-2-102681-7.

R. Kurian: *The position of women in the plantation sector in Sri Lanka,*[8] Feb. 1981 (WEP 10/WP.18). [LKA] ISBN 92-2-102636-1.

N.L. Peluso: *Survival strategies of rural women traders or a women's place is in the market. Four case studies from North-Western Sleman in the special region of Yogakarta,* Jan. 1981 (WEP 10/WP.17)*. [IDN] ISBN 92-2-102633-7.

The struggle towards self-reliance of organised resettled women in the Philippines, Feb. 1982 (WEP 10/WP.26). [PHL] ISBN 92-2-103036-9.

R.X. Desai: *Migrant labour and women: The case of Ratnagiri,* Oct. 1982 (WEP 10/WP.28). [IND] ISBN 92-2-103273-6

M. Nag, R. Anker and M.E. Khan: *A guide to anthropological study of women's roles and demographic change in India (Operations Research Group/ILO study in Uttar Pradesh),* Mar. 1982 (WEP 2-21/WP.115). M. [IND] ISBN 92-2-103084-9.

C. Colfer: *On circular migration. From the distaff side: Women left behind in the forests of East Kalimantan,* May 1983 (WEP 2-21/WP.132). M. [IDN] ISBN 92-2-3465-8.

L. Gulati: *Women in fishing villages on the Kerala coast: Demographic and socio-economic impacts of a fisheries development project,*[9] Mar. 1983 (WEP 2-21/WP.128). [IND] ISBN 92-2-103400-3.

T.S. Papola: *Women workers in an Indian urban labour market,*[4] Sep. 1983 (WEP 2-21/WP.141). M. [IND] ISBN 92-2-103582-4.

E. Croll: *Changing patterns of rural women's employment, production and reproduction in China,* Mar. 1984 (WEP 10/WP.33). [CHN] ISBN 92-2-103764-9.

R. Chatterji: *Marginalisation and the induction of women into wage labour: The case of Indian agriculture,* Mar. 1984 (WEP 10/WP.32). M. [IND] ISBN 92-2-103765-7.

E. Eisold: *Young women workers in export industries: The case of the semiconductor industry in Southeast Asia,* Mar. 1984 (WEP 10/WP.30)*. ISBN 92-2-92-2-103744-4.

M. Mies assisted by Lalita K. and K. Kumari: *Indian women in subsistence and agricultural labour,*[12] May 1984 (WEP 10/WP.34). [IND] ISBN 92-2-103328-9.

G.M. Farooq and M. Irfan with the assistance of T. LeGrand: *A micro empirical analysis of fertility behaviour in Pakistan,* June 1985 (WEP 2-21/WP. 150). [PAK] ISBN 92-2-105205-2.

Rural women and social structures in change: A case study of women's work and energy in West Java, Indonesia, Feb. 1986 (WEP 10/WP. 41). [IDN] ISBN 92-2-105448-9.

N. Heyzer: *Women workers in South-East Asia: Problems and strategies* (New Delhi, ARTEP), May 1987. [IDN, PHL, BUR, LAO, VNM, MYS] ISBN 92-2-106007-1.

A.V. Jose: *Employment and wages of women workers in Asian countries: An assessment* (New Delhi, ARTEP), Sep. 1987. ISBN 92-2-105777-1.

M.E. Khan, R. Anker, S.K. Ghosh and S. Bairathi: *Inequalities between men and women in nutrition and family welfare services: An in-depth enquiry in an Indian village,* June 1987 (WEP 2-21/WP.158). [IND] ISBN 92-2-106134-5.

G. Sen and L. Gulati: *Women workers in Kerala's electronic industry,* Mar. 1987 (WEP 10/WP.45). [IND] ISBN 92-2-105924-3.

- **East European Countries**

B. Barta, A. Klinger, K. Milténvi and G. Vukovich: *Interdependence between female employment and fertility in Hungary,*[10] Mar. 1983 (WEP 2-21/WP.129). M. [HUN] ISBN 92-2-103421-6.

- **Middle East**

H.T. Azzam: *The participation of Arab women in the labour force: Development factors and policies,* Oct. 1979 (WEP 2-21/WP.80). M.

H.T. Azzam and D. Shaib: *The women left behind: A study of the wives of Lebanese migrant workers in the oil rich countries of the region* (Beirut, LPME), 1980 (WP. 3), 56 pp. [LBN] ISBN 92-2-102503-9.

O. Dahhan: *An examination of the literature on Jordanian women* (Beirut, LPME), 1981 (W.P.8), ii, 146 pp. [JOR] ISBN 92-2-102582-9.

W.J. House: *Patterns and determinants of female labour force participation in Cyprus,*[4] Apr. 1982 (WEP 2-21/WP.116). M. [CYP] ISBN 92-2-103108-X.

G.B.S. Mujahid: *Female labour force participation in the Hashemite Kingdom of Jordan* (Beirut, LPME), Apr. 1982 (WP. 12). [JOR] ISBN 92-2-103099-7.

G.B.S. Mujahid: *Female and status of women in the labour force in the Arab world, with particular reference to the role of women in Syria* (Beirut, LPME), 1983 (WP. 14). (Arabic) [SYR]

I. Lorfing and M. Khalaf: *The economic contribution of women and its effect on the dynamics of the family in two Lebanese villages*, May 1985 (WEP 2-21/WP. 148). [LBN] ISBN 92-2-105122-6.

ILO works published by commercial and non-profit-making publishers

- General

R. Anker, M. Buvinic and N.H. Youssef (eds.): *Women's roles and population trends in the Third World* (London, Croom Helm Ltd., 1981), 288 pp. [IND] ISBN 0-7099-0508-4.

L. Beneria (ed.): *Women and development: The sexual division of labour in rural societies* (New York, Praeger Publishers, 1982), xxviii + 260 pp. [NGA, MEX, ETH, CHN, MYS, SGP] ISBN 0-03-061802-9.

G.M. Farooq and G.B. Simmons (eds.): *Fertility in developing countries. An economic perspective on research and policy issues* (London, Macmillan, 1985), xxiv + 533 pp. [KEN, NGA, CRI, MEX, IND, TUR, YUG] ISBN 0-333-36972-6.

R. Anker and C. Hein (eds.): *Sex inequalities in urban employment in the Third World* (London, Macmillan, 1986), xx + 378 pp. [CYP, IND, LKA, GHA, MUS, PER, NGA] ISBN 0-333-41298-2.

C. Oppong (ed.): *Sex roles, population and development in West Africa. Policy-related studies on work and demographic issues* (London, James Currey Ltd., 1987), x + 242 pp. ISBN 0-85255-400-1.

D. Werneke: *La microelectrónica y los puestos de trabajo en oficinas*. La importancia del circuito integrado en el empleo feminino (Madrid, Centro de Publicaciones, Ministerio de Trabajo y Seguridad Social, 1987), 119 pp. ISBN 84-734-377-1.

- Africa

R. Anker and J.C. Knowles: *Fertility determinants in developing countries: A case study of Kenya* (Liège, Belgium, Ordina Editions, 1982), x + 222 pp. [KEN] ISBN 2-87040-025-X.

I. Ahmed (ed.): *Technology and rural women* (London, George Allen and Unwin, 1985), xvi + 383 pp. [KEN, GHA, NGA, SLE] ISBN 0-04-382043-3.

- Latin America and the Caribbean

G. Standing: *Unemployment and female labour - A study of labour supply in Kingson, Jamaica* (London, Macmillan Press Ltd., 1981), xii + 364 pp. [JAM] ISBN 0-312-83266-4.

- Asia

Z. Bhatty: *The economic role and status of women in the beedi industry in Allahabad, India*, Vol. 63 - Social science studies on international problems. Edited by Prof. Dr. D. Breitenbach (Saarbrücken, Verlag Breitenbach Publishers, 1981), viii + 98 pp. [IND] ISBN 3-88156-192-7.

T.A. Abdullah and S.A. Zeidenstein: *Village women of Bangladesh: Prospects for change* (Oxford, Pergamon Press, 1982), xx + 246 pp. [BGD] ISBN 0-08-026795-5.

M. Mies: *The lace makers of Narsapur: Indian housewives produce for the world market* (London, Zed Press, 1982), xii + 196 pp. [IND] ISBN 0-86232-032-1.

- Middle East

J. Abu Nasr, N.F. Khoury and H.T. Azzam (eds.): *Women, employment and development in the Arab world* (Berlin, Mouton Publishers, 1985), 143 pp. [YEM, LBN, JOR, EGY, KWT] ISBN 90-279-3380-4.

Related books and articles

- General

R. Anker: "An analysis of fertility differentials in developing countries", in *Review of Economics and Statistics* (Amsterdam), Vol. LX, No. 4, 1978.

Z. Ahmad and M. Loutfi: "Decently paid employment - Not more drudgery", in *Ceres* (Rome), July-Aug. 1983.

- Africa

G. Sheehan and G. Standing: "A note on economic activity of women in Nigeria", in *Pakistan Development Review* (Karachi), Vol. XVII, No.2, Summer 1978. [NGA]

G.M. Farooq: "More education leads to higher fertility for rural Nigerian women", in *International Family Planning Perspectives* (New York), Vol. 6, No. 4, Dec. 1980. [NGA]

- Asia

R. Anker and M. Anker: *Reproductive behavior in households of rural Gujarat: Social, economic and community factors* (New Delhi, Concept Publishing Company, 1982), xii + 140 pp. [IND]

- Middle East

W.J. House: *Socio-economic determinants of fertility in Cyprus* (Republic of Cyprus, Department of Statistics and Research, Ministry of Finance, 1981), 30 pp. [CYP]

Notes:

1 A revised version is published in E. Croll: Women and rural development in China. Production and reproduction (Geneva, ILO, 1985).

2 Published in I. Ahmed (ed.): Technology and rural women: Conceptual and empirical issues (London, George Allen and Unwin, 1985).

3 Also published in W.R. Böhning (ed.): Black migration to South Africa. A selection of policy-oriented research (Geneva, ILO, 1981).

4 Also published in R. Anker and C. Hein (eds.): Sex inequalities in urban employment in the Third World (London, Macmillan, 1986).

5 Also published as P.D. Lynch with H. Fahmy: Craftswomen in Kerdassa, Egypt. Household production and reproduction (Geneva, ILO, 1984).

6 Also published as Z. Bhatty: The economic role and status of women in the beedi industry in Allahabad, India (Saarbrücken, Verlag Breitenbac Publishers, 1981).

7 Also published as M. Mies: The lace makers of Narsapur: Indian housewives produce for the world market (London, Zed Press, 1982).

8 Also published as R. Kurian: Women workers in the Sri Lanka plantation sector: An historical and contemporary analysis. (Geneva, ILO, 1982).

9 Also published as L. Gulati: Fisherwomen on the Kerala coast. Demographic and socio-economic impact of a fisheries development project (Geneva, ILO, 1984).

10 Also published as A. Barta, A. Klinger, K. Milténуi and G. Vukovich: Fertility, female employment and policy measures in Hungary (Geneva, ILO, 1984).

11 Also published as C.D. Deere and M. León de Leal: Women in Andean agriculture. (Geneva, ILO, 1982).

12 Also published as M. Mies assisted by Lalita K. and K. Kumari: Indian women in subsistence and agricultural labour (Geneva, ILO, 1986).

Author Index

Abate, A. 49, 50
Abdel Gadir Ali, A. 35
Abdel-Fadil, M. 5
Abdel-Fattah Nassef 5
Abdullah, T.A. 115
Aboagye, A.A. 35, 82, 96
Abu, K. 106, 108, 112
Abu Nasr, J. 116
Abuhadba, M. 113
Addison, T. 100
Addo, N.O. 63
Adelman, I. 26, 32, 71
Adeokun, L.A. 112
Adepoju, A. 112
Adewuyi, A.A. 112
Adler, S. 63, 65
Agarwal, B. 48, 113
Agourram, A. 11
Ahmad, A. 30
Ahmad, N. 53
Ahmad, Q.K. 53, 54
Ahmad, Z. 110, 116
Ahmed, A. 84
Ahmed, B. 8
Ahmed, I. 25, 47, 48, 56, 58, 80, 96, 110, 115, 116
Ahmed, Iq. 44, 45
Ahmed, M. 30
Alagh, Y. 46
Alailima, P. 30
Alailima, P.J. 29
Alántara, E. 113
Alfthan, T. 25, 26, 28
Ali, I. 83
Ali, Md.E. 54
Ali Khan, H. 103
Allal, M. 2, 34, 76
Allen, B.T. 86
Amer, M.H. 82
Amjad, R. 17, 19, 97
Andersson, P-A. 92
Aninat, E. 31
Anker, M. 116

Anker, R. 37, 42, 61, 70, 72, 73, 106, 107, 109-111, 113-116
Antolinez, P. 61, 63, 64
Applebaum, L. 49
Arda, M. 49
Ardayfio, E. 112
Arellano, J.P. 31
Arif, M. 8
Aris Samanez, N. 113
Aristy, J. 83
Arndt, H.W. 64
Arriaga, E. 60
Aryee, G.A. 81, 92, 96
Asiama, S.O. 60
Augusztinovics, M. 100
Avramov, T. 20
Azzam, H.T. 13, 20, 41, 65, 72, 114, 116
Bachrach, M. 51
Baffoe, F. 11
Bagchi, A.K. 82, 85, 98
Bairathi, S. 72, 114
Balan, J. 64
Balkenhol, B. 38, 82, 91, 92
Ball, N. 10, 13
Bandyopadhyaya, N. 55
Bandyopahyay, D. 55
Banerjee, D. 85
Bangasser, P. 37, 48
Banguero, H. 28, 32, 33
Banugire, F.R. 34
Barampama, A. 39, 83
Bardhan, K. 46, 53, 54
Bardhan, P.K. 46, 53
Barnett, T. 35
Baron, C.G. 79-81, 87
Barta, B. 109, 114
Barwell, I. 56, 80, 87
Barwell, I.J. 43
Bautista, G.M. 55
Baytelman, D. 44
Beckerman, W. 24, 30, 31

Bekker, Z. 104
Belous, R.S. 104
Benachenhou, A. 62
Benavente, D. 24
Beneria, L. 100, 110, 112, 11.
Benyoussef, A. 14
Bequele, A. 25, 50
Berik, G. 109
Bernstein, H. 63
Bérouti, L. 14
Berrios, R. 84
Berry, A.R. 56
Bessat, C. 27, 63, 92
Betancourt, R.R. 94
Beyazov, T. 20
Bhadurai, A. 46
Bhaduri, A. 49, 53, 56, 58, 11
Bhagwati, J. 2
Bhalla, A.S. 2, 54, 75, 80, 81, 87, 88
Bhalla, G.S. 46
Bhatia, R. 85, 86
Bhatt, A.P. 30
Bhatty, I.Z. 14, 41, 56
Bhatty, Z. 14, 41, 56, 113, 115, 116
Biggs, S.D. 49
Bilsborrow, R.E. 59, 62, 66, 68, 111
Birch, D.R. 81
Birks, J.S. 60, 62, 65, 67
Biswas, A.K. 81
Blandy, R. 71
Blardone, G. 72
Bluestone, B. 41
Boardman, J. 75
Bock, C. 64, 72
Bodrova, V. 109
Böhning, W.R. 2, 59, 61, 62, 65-68, 116
Boissen, H. 79
Boon, G.K. 87
Bose, A.N. 41, 57
Bot, C. 53, 54

Bourguignon, F. 28
Bozhilov, Y. 20
Bragança, S.L. 70
Breen, R. 94
Bresson, Y. 82
Broadfield, R. 1
Bromberger, N. 62
Brossier, J. 100
Bruggink, J.C. 83
Bunge, C. 28
Burle de Figueiredo, J.B. 70
Burton, H.J. 81
Buttari, J.J. 7
Buvinic, M. 115
Cain, M. 93
Capt, J. 35, 75, 83
Carle, I. 92
Carnoy, M. 31, 94
Carr, M. 111
Carrizo, A. 39
Carton, M. 38, 39
Caspar, M.-L. 19
Castillo, L. 51
Castillo, M. 23
Castro, J.S. 41, 103
Castro, M.G. 66
Castro de Rezende, G. 52
Cecelski, E. 106, 111
Célestin, J-B. 18
Chanaron, J.J. 104
Chandra Mishra, S. 55
Chatterji, R. 114
Chatterji, S. 30
Chau, L. 25, 31
Chaudhuri, D.P. 94
Chayaputi, P. 8
Chee Peng Lim 54, 84
Chekir, H. 65
Chia Siow Yue 103
Chipande, G.H.R. 50, 112
Chiswick, C.U. 30
Chowdhury, A. 19
Chowdhury, T.K. 30
Church, K. 111
Chuta, E. 34, 37, 41, 48, 50, 58, 82
Clark, J.A. 14
Clarke, D.G. 62

Clay, E.J. 49
Cline, W.R. 56
Cohen, S.I. 18, 32
Colclough, C. 19, 50
Colfer, C. 113
Collier, P. 50, 51, 56
Commander, S. 52, 64
Conyers, D. 19
Coote, H.C. 100
Córdova, J. 29
Cornelisse, P.A. 32, 61, 63
Cornu, P. 72
Correa Fleury, A.C. 84
Cortázar, R. 42, 102
Costa, E. 91, 93
Croll, E. 109, 114, 116
Crouch, L. 18
Curtis, D. 26
da Cunha Rato, M.H. 70, 71
Dahhan, O. 114
Danilov, A.V. 1
Dario Uribe E. J. 83
Das, P.K. 14
Date-Bah, E. 112
Datta-Chaudhuri, M.K. 97, 102
Davey, K. 26
Davies, O. 84
Davis, C. 84
Dawson, A. 48
de Barbieri, T. 108
de Bragança, S.L. 70, 71
de Cunha Rato, M.H. 112
de Groot, G. 104
de Janvry, A. 52
de Labastida, E. 63
de Veen, J. 44, 56, 75, 78, 87
de Villamil, A. 32
de Vletter, F. 62, 63
Deere, C.D. 52, 108, 113, 117
dela Peña, M. 113
Demery, L. 100
Demol, E. 34, 35, 37-39, 42
Deolalikar, A.B. 85
Desai, A.V. 84, 85, 99
Desai, R.X. 113
Dey, J. 35
di Mare, A. 84

Diouf, M. 18
Diskin, M. 52
Dixon-Mueller, R. 106
Djeflat, A. 51
Dore, R. 104
Dore, R.P. 98, 105
Dorling, M.J. 50, 56
Douglas Paauw 102
Drewer, S. 81
Duiker, P. 15
Dumont, R. 44
Dunkel, P.W. 57
Dunne, J.P. 13
Dupré, E. 23
Durán, H. 23
Dutta, S.Ch. 84
Ebigbola, J.A. 112
Echeverría, R. 7
Edgren, G. 8, 19, 98, 103
Edmonds, G.A. 48, 56, 75, 78, 79, 81, 87, 88
Edquist, C. 51
Edwards, R. 82, 100
Efremov, A. 10
Egger, P. 48
Eisold, E. 114
El Karanshawy Mohamed Sakr, H. 82
El Neima, A.M. 50
El Salmi, A. 5
El-Bagir, I. 35
El-Hawary, M.A. 49
El-Issawy, I.H. 5
El-Reedy, T.Y. 49
Elek, A. 71
Elliot, Ch. 50
Elliott, J.W. 83
Elton, C. 52
Emmerij, L. 1
Engelgardt, K. 9
Enos, J.L. 81
Enrietti, A. 86
Entzinger, H. 61
Errington, A. 49
Erzan, R. 100
Esguerra, E.F. 103
Evans, M.I. 108, 113
Evers, B. 104

Fafchamps, M. 45, 50
Fahmy, H. 107, 112, 116
Fallon, P. 50
Fals Borda, O. 57
Fan, N.H. 113
Fapohunda, O.J. 38, 59
Farbman, M. 58
Farnos, A. 113
Farooq, G.M. 69, 70, 111, 114-116
Farooq-i-Azam 64
Feller, C. 98
Fels, G. 1
Ferchiou, R. 77, 100
Fergany, N. 26, 65
Ferrer, R.D. 103
Ferri, P. 86
Field, A.J. 99, 100, 104
Figueroa, A. 52
Findley, S.E. 64
Fine, S.M. 29
Flores, D. 113
Fluitman, A.G. 79
Fluitman, F. 49, 81
Fong Chan Onn 84, 85
Forsyth, D.J.C. 47, 79, 81, 83, 84
Fowler, D.A. 38
Foxley, A. 31, 42, 100
Fransman, M. 82
Freedman, D.H. 4, 9, 10, 13, 18, 25, 48
Freeman, D. 50
Fulton, O. 15
Fundaçao Instituto Brasileiro de Geografia e Estatistica 73
Ganesan, S. 85
García, A. 7, 23
García, N.E. 6, 7, 13, 16, 23, 36, 97
García Castro, M. 113
García Cotarma, S. 113
García D'Acuña, E. 6, 9, 46, 99
García-Huidobro, G. 40
Garland, G. 84
Garnier, P. 89
Garson, J.P. 65

Garzuel, M. 9, 24, 27, 29
Gaude, J. 60, 61, 63, 64, 67, 68, 91, 92
Germidis, D. 21
Gern, J.M. 35
Ghai, D. 1, 21, 25, 43, 44, 49-51, 56, 57
Ghani, E. 27, 100
Gheza, D. 100
Ghose, A.K. 49, 53-56
Ghosh, J. 35, 103
Ghosh, S.K. 72, 114
Glisman, H.H. 1
Godfrey, M. 21
Goldschmidt-Clermont, L. 106, 107
Gomez, S. 51
Gonzalez, F. 113
González, R. 7
Gooneratne, W. 24, 29, 33, 47
Gordon, A. 15
Gordon, E. 112
Gothoskar, S. 53
Gozo, K.M. 35, 96
Gray, H.P. 98, 103, 104
Greene, G. 69
Greer, J. 46
Gregory, S. 2
Griffin, K. 30, 47
Grimm, K.D. 94
Guérin, L. 89
Guerrero, B. 32
Guha, S. 91, 93
Guichaoua, A. 48, 63, 91
Guilkey, D.K. 111
Gulati, L. 109, 114, 117
Gupta, A.P. 29, 30
Gupta, D.B. 53
Gupta, R.B. 37
Gupta, S. 71
Gutiérrez, A. 24, 79
Gutkind, E. 30
Haan, H.C. 36, 39
Hakam, A.N. 82
Hallak, J. 92
Hamid, G.M. 2, 11, 96
Handoussa, H.A. 5
Hansen, B. 5, 9

Hara, Y. 46
Harrison, B. 41
Hart, G. 54, 55
Hartung, D. 94
Harvey, C. 56
Haywood, B. 86
Healey, D.T. 1
Heap, A. 79
Hein, C. 37, 42, 106, 107, 110-112, 115, 116
Herath, H.M.G. 54
Herman, B. 2
Hernandez, R. 113
Herrera, A. 81
Hetler, C.B. 111
Hewavitharana, B. 30
Heyzer, N. 114
Hideshima, , K. 85
Hiemenz, U. 60, 100
Hihn, J.M. 71
Hill, J. 86
Hintermeister, A. 46, 52
Hirashima, S. 47, 48
Hirschhorn, L. 86
Ho, Y.P. 103
Höpfner, K.H. 61
Hoffman, K. 82
Hollister, R.G. 19
Holtsberg, C.P. 25, 29, 30
Homem de Melo, F. 52
Hopkins, M.J.D. 1, 9, 10, 12, 14, 18, 21, 25-28, 31, 32, 72, 73, 99
Hossain, M. 53, 54
Hossein, M. 54
House, W.J. 14, 39, 41, 50, 51, 67, 71, 82, 88, 110, 114, 116
Howe, J.D.G.E. 43, 49, 56, 80, 87
Hsi Huang Che 53
Hsia, R. 25, 31, 102
Hsieh, D. 24
Huber, M. 61
Hugh Jones, J. 49
Hughes, A. 26
Huq, M. 8
Hurst, C. 82, 85
Hussain, M.I. 80, 88

ICEM 2
Ichimura, S. 84, 85
Ikiara, G.K. 100
Infante, R. 40
Inoue, K. 99
International Council on Social Welfare 32
Irfan, M. 114
Ishikawa, S. 47, 85
Islam, I. 19, 103
Islam, K.Md.N. 54
Islam, R. 8, 47, 48, 55, 58, 84, 103, 104
Jabbar, M.A. 55
Jacobs, J. 56
Jaisaard, P. 8
Jamal, V. 11, 21, 27, 50, 99, 100
James, D. 87, 88
James, J. 26, 32, 81-83, 87, 88
Jannisar, M. 8
Jarvis, L. 7
Jeanrenaud, C. 61, 67
Jelin, E. 111
Jo, S.H. 102
Johnston, B.F. 50
Join-Lambert, L. 25
Jondoh, C. 37, 38
Jones, K. 104
Jong-goo Park 21
Jose, A.V. 70, 114
Joshi, B. 30
Joshi, B.K. 85
Josué Sandjiman Mamder 96
Jourdain, R. 37, 38
Juarez, A. 83
Jurado, G.M. 41, 103
Jurvelius, M. 87
Kabaj, M. 92, 94
Kamya, A. 39, 83
Kaneko, D. 82
Kanhere, V. 53
Kaplinsky, R. 77
Karlsson, L.S. 75, 79
Kasryno, F. 55
Katouzian, H. 56
Kay, C. 51
Keddeman, W. 44

Kehl, V. 100
Keyder, C. 56
Khai, A. 84
Khalaf, M. 115
Khan, A.R. 8, 47, 53, 56, 57
Khan, M.E. 37, 72, 113, 114
Khan, M.H. 53
Khoju, M.R. 85
Khomelyansky, B.N. 70
Khoury, N. 72
Khoury, N.F. 65, 116
Kilby, P. 1, 48
Killick, T. 50
Kimuyu, P.K. 100
Kinsey, B.H. 48, 50, 56, 58
Kirkpatrick, C.H. 19, 103
Kirloskar Consultants 41
Kiros, F.G. 50
Klein, E. 6, 7, 16, 18, 36
Klinger, A. 109, 114, 117
Knowles, J.C. 72, 73, 111, 115
Knowles, M. 90
Kondratiev, V. 10, 18, 20
Korayem, K. 27
Koti, R.K. 85
Kovac, O. 104
Krishna, M.A. 88
Krishnayya, J.G. 30, 85
Krongkaew, M. 30
Kueh, Y.Y. 19
Kulkarni, S. 53
Kumar, M.S. 79
Kumari, K. 109, 114, 117
Kurian, R. 109, 113, 116
Kurihara, E. 82
Kutscher, R.E. 13
Kuwahara, Y. 86
Kuyvenhoven, A. 26, 81
Kuzmin, S.A. 10, 26, 99
Laarman, J.G. 25, 80, 87
Lachaud, J-P. 39
Lagos, R. 97
Laite, J. 64
Lakhoua, F. 77
Lal, D. 79
Lalita K. 109, 114, 117
Lamb, G. 56, 81
Langhammer, R.J. 100

Larhed, T. 30
Le Boterf, G. 42, 63
Leblond, B. 89
Lecaillon, J. 21, 25
Lee, E. 8, 43, 47-50, 56, 58, 97, 98, 103
Lee, E.H. 53
LeGrand, T. 114
Lehmann, D. 36, 51
Leibenstein, H. 31
León de Leal, M. 108, 113, 117
Leonor, M.D. 21, 26, 31, 94
Leroy, M.Ch. 72
Levy, B. 81
Lieberman, S.S. 72
Liedholm, C. 37, 41
Lim, D. 103
Lim, L. 98, 103, 104
Lim Teck Ghee 54
Lin, T.B. 103
Linsu Kim 85
Lira, E.A. 64
Lisk, F. 11, 21, 25, 31
Little, I.M.D. 102
Livingstone, I. 5, 27
Lizano, E. 84
Llori, F.A. 112
Lobo, J. 31, 94
Londoño de la C. J.L. 83
Longhurst, R. 111
Looney, R.E. 100
Lorfing, I. 115
Loutfi, M. 116
Loutfi, M.F. 106
Lubell, H. 32, 59, 60
Lucángeli, J. 84
Lund Skar, S. 113
Luu, N.N. 54
Lwoga, C. 63
Lydall, H. 27
Lynch, P.D. 107, 112, 116
Mach, E.P. 25
Mackillop, A. 81
Macura, M. 70, 72
Madeuf, B. 100
Madzar, L. 104
Maeda, J. 43

Maex, R. 100
Mahmood, R.A. 53
Mahmud, S. 55
Mahmud, W. 55
Maillat, D. 61, 66, 67
Maitra, T. 8
Majeres, J. 48
Maldonado, C. 35, 39, 63
Malick, S. 106
Mandeng, P. 35, 100
Marfán, M. 16, 36
Marga Institute 42, 84
Markwald, R.A. 100
Marsden, D. 44, 98, 104, 105
Martens, B. 92, 93
Mason, W. 15
Mathur, R.S. 84
Maton, J.G. 29, 31, 86
Mayer, J.P. 2, 9, 10, 18
Mazoyer, M. 44
Mbali, F. 39
McCallum, D. 60
Mechri, H. 100
Mehta, F.A. 1
Meller, P. 36
Mercado, A. 83
Merchant, N.P. 85
Mertens, L. 99, 102
Mesa, J.M. 10, 94
Mezzera, J. 6, 9, 37, 99
Mhlanga, E.M. 11
Michalet, C.A. 100
Michell, T. 103
Mies, M. 109, 113, 114, 116, 117
Miles, D.W.J. 87
Miles, N. 50
Miller, M.J. 65
Miltényi, K. 109, 114, 117
Minami, R. 74
Mishra, G.P. 27, 81
Mitra, A. 19
Mkandawire, T. 39, 100
Moir, H. 41, 42
Molapi Sebatane, E. 62
Molina, V. 30
Molyneux, M. 109
Mongi, M.A.F. 5

Mora y Araiyo, M. 51
Moreland, R.S. 72, 73
Moreland, S. 18, 71-73
Morice, A. 92
Morrison, D. 84
Morrisson, C. 21
Moujabber, C.E. 14
Mouly, J-P. 1, 26
Mozumder, A.B.M.K.A. 93
Mramba, B.P. 50
Mubin, A.K.A. 84
Muchena, O.N. 112
Muchri, G. 50
Muhammed Muqtada 85
Muijsers, I.G.M. 112
Mujahid, G.B.S. 114, 115
Mukherjee, C. 70
Mukherjee, S. 98
Mukhopadhyay, S. 54, 64
Mulina, T. 70
Mulwila, J.M. 39
Muntemba, S. 106
Muqtada, M. 48, 54, 93, 98
Murad, M.J. 65
Mureithi, L.P. 100
Mushota, R.K. 39
Musillo, I. 65
Mustafa Alam, M. 54
Mutlu, S. 56
Myovela, H. 112
Nag, M. 113
Nair, K.N.S. 30, 85
National Council of Applied Economic Research 53, 55
Ndlela, D.B. 83
Ndulo, M. 100
Ng Gek-Boo 29, 52, 53
Ngango, G. 100
Nihan, G. 34, 37-39, 42
Niitsu, K. 85
Nilsson, B. 79
Norbye, O.D.K. 10, 26
Norcliffe, G. 50
North, D.S. 65
Nurul Amin, A.T.M. 37
Nuthmann, R. 94
Oakley, P. 44

Oberai, A.S. 4, 49, 53, 59, 61, 62, 64, 66-68, 70
Ocampo, R.B. 54
Ofori, G. 82
Olavarría, C. 46
Olsson, U.K. 39
Ono, A. 74
Oppong, C. 106, 108, 111, 112, 115
Orlansky, D. 51
Otero, D. 84
Ourabah, M. 27
Panditrao, Y.A. 41
Pang Eng Fong 98, 103, 104
Papola, T.S. 30, 55, 84, 85, 114
Paranjape, P.V. 53
Paredes, C.E. 84
Parisot, G. 72
Paukert, F. 21, 29, 31, 33
Pearce, D. 82, 100
Pease, J.W. 51
Peek, P. 51, 52, 59-63, 66, 67
Peguin, D. 100
Peiris, G.H. 47
Pelley, D. 49
Peluso, N.L. 113
Penouil, M. 39
Pereira, A. 79, 80, 87, 95
Perez-Sainz, J.P. 64
Pernia, E.M. 64, 69
Petit, J. 10, 99
Petruccelli, J.L. 70
Phan-Thuy, N. 91-94
Phaneendhrudu, V. 30
Philips-Howard, K.D. 51
Phongpaichit, P. 8, 109
Pickford, J. 27
Pieris, G.H. 30
Piña, C. 36
Pingle, G. 27, 81
Pinnock, R. 52
Piriyarangsan, S. 8
Pittin, R. 112
Plant, R. 2, 95
Pollack, M. 97
Pommier, P. 10
Pontoni, A. 84

Popovic, B. 20, 72
Prasad, K.K. 82
Prasad, P.H. 54, 71
Prinz, F.A. 62
Pugel, T. 98, 103, 104
Pyo, H.K. 86
Raabe, C. 52
Rachidi, E.G. 11
Rada, J. 75
Rada, J.F. 82, 87
Radwan, S. 5, 9, 25, 26, 43, 44, 49, 50, 56
Rahman, K.M. 54
Rahman, Md.A. 44, 47, 49, 55-57, 84
Rahman, R.I. 85
Rahn, R.J. 86
Raj, K.N. 53
Rajaraman, I. 55
Ramanayake, D. 103
Ramírez, M. 84
Rammanohar Reddy, C. 55
Ramos, J. 36
Rao, V.M. 47
Rao Maturu, N. 25
Rasevic, M. 70
Rato, M.H. 70
Ray, S. 55
Read, A. 100
Reboul, C. 44
Reddy, A.K.N. 49, 80
Reddy, V.R. 55
Reiffers, J.L. 100
Reijmerink, J. 59
Rempel, H. 14, 67
Renshaw, G. 98, 104, 105
Reppy, J. 10
Richards, P.J. 1, 9, 21, 24-26, 31, 33, 49, 56, 94, 99
Richter, L. 15, 17, 18, 20, 57
Rietschin, R. 27
Rincon, A. 84
Ringor, O. 30
Rivera, F.F. 30
Roberto, E.L. 85
Robinson, L.C. 111
Robinson, S. 32
Roca, S. 51

Rodgers, G.B. 29, 32, 38, 54, 58, 61, 62, 66, 69-73, 89, 91, 92, 113
Rodgers, J. 58
Rodriguez, J. 24
Roe, A.R. 100
Rogers, J.D. 45, 46
Roman, B.S.S. 100
Ropert, M.A. 36
Rosen-Prinz, B.D. 62
Rosenberg, N. 82
Rosenzweig, M.R. 93
Royer, J. 9, 10
Rudra, A. 24, 53, 54
Rugege, S. 62
Rush, H. 82
Ruttan, V.W. 49
Rydzewski, J.R. 81
Saavedra, N. 60
Sabolo, Y. 9, 80, 99, 104
Sadoulet, E. 52
Sagasti, F.R. 84
Saith, A. 30, 47, 55, 64
Sajhau, J.P. 99, 100
Sakala, M. 100
Santikarn Kaosa-ard, M. 86
Sanyal, B. 27
Sathe, N. 53
Savané, M.A. 107
Schaffer, B. 56
Schatz, K.W. 60, 98, 103, 104
Schultz, T.P. 71
Schwartz, J. 39
Scolnik, H. 1
Sehgal, J.M. 69
Sen, A.K. 26, 31, 32
Sen, G. 114
Servat, J. 51
Sethuraman, S.V. 27, 32, 34, 37, 38, 42, 57, 58, 66
Shah, S.M. 30
Shaib, D. 114
Sharma, A.N. 71
Sharma, B. 71
Sharma, S.N. 84
Sharp, M. 98, 104, 105
Shaw, R.P. 60, 61, 72
Sheehan, G. 21, 26, 32, 69,

116
Shepherd, A. 26
Shepherd, A.W. 50
Shepherd, G. 98, 104, 105
Sicherl, P. 31
Sidibé, H. 38
Sigurdson, J. 53
Siha, S.P. 27
Silva, F. 86
Silva, M.M. 31
Simmons, G.B. 115
Sinclair, C.A. 60, 62, 65, 67
Singh, A. 26, 30, 103
Singh, H.K.M. 49, 53, 61, 64, 66, 67
Sinha, J.N. 65
Sinha, R.C. 27, 30, 53, 81, 85
Sinha, S.P. 81
Siregar, M. 55
Skolka, J. 27, 29, 31, 33
Skorov, G.E. 1
Sladen, J. 82
Smith, C.A. 52
Smith, D.V. 82
Smith, J.D. 54
Smith, L. 50
Smith, L.D. 57
Soza, S. 23
Spagni, D.A. 104
Srivastava, R.K. 27
Stahl, C.W. 62, 63
Stallmann, J.I. 51
Standing, G. 9, 10, 23, 33, 37, 38, 59-63, 66-69, 73, 89, 91, 92, 112, 113, 115, 116
Starr, G. 5
Stavenuiter, S. 13
Stephenson Jr. S.P. 111
Stern, J.J. 1
Stevens, Y. 87
Stewart, F. 2, 80
Strassman, W.P. 88
Stretton, A. 37, 61
Suckling, J. 83
Suhartono, R.B. 85
Suleta J. L.A. 83
Suliman, A.A. 39
Sundaram, A.K. 85

Svejnar, Z. 44
Swann, J. 86
Szal, R.J. 21, 23-28, 32, 51, 57, 66
Szretter, H. 24
Tabatabai, H. 51, 99, 100
Tabi, A.A. 34, 35, 39, 100
Taira, K. 98, 104, 105
Tamblay, J. 7
Tan Phaik Leng 54
Tapinos, G. 65
Tauile, J.R. 84
Taylor, L. 18
Teichler, U. 94
Teklu, T. 49
Teng-Hui Lee 53
Thamarajakshi, R. 19, 93
Tharakan, M. 53
the Institute of Rural Development Planning in Dodoma 92
Thee, M. 9
Thobani, M. 85
Thomas, P.K. 49
Thomson, A.M. 31, 33
Thorbecke, E. 21, 32, 46
Thorsson, I. 9
Tiedt, F. 64, 72
Tilakaratna, S. 54, 55
Tilakaratne, S. 47
Tims, W. 87, 95
Tjouen, A. 100
Tokman, V.E. 7, 10, 23, 36, 42, 79, 97, 99
Toledo, A. 31, 94
Tomíc, B. 7, 16, 23, 46
Tomoda, S. 112
Touraine, A. 37
Trajtenberg, R. 100
Trouvé, J. 27, 50, 63, 92
Turok, M. 27
Ubogu, R.E. 100
Ulph, A. 87, 95

Umar, I.S. 85
Umo, J.U. 100
UNCTAD 2
Urdang, S. 112
Urmeneta, R. 7
Uthoff, A. 23, 36, 69, 70, 97
Vaidya, K.K. 85
Vaidyanathan, A. 46
Valdivia, M. 97
van den Oever-Pereira, P. 107
van der Hoeven, R. 10, 14, 25-28, 31, 32, 99, 100
van Dijk, M.P. 59
van Dijk, T. 92
van Gent, V. 92
van Ginneken, W. 9, 21, 24-26, 28, 31, 33, 87, 88
Van Kempen, C. 91
van Liemt, G. 99, 100, 102
Vandemoortele, J. 18, 28, 100
Vanegas, W.M. 100
Vargas, V. 23
Vasuprasat, P. 8
Vaughan, M. 112
Velloso, J. 31, 94
Ventura-Dias, V. 112
Versluis, J. 92
Vinod Kumar, T.M. 29
Virtanen, K. 87
Viry, D. 38, 39, 113
Vukovich, G. 109, 114, 117
Vyas, V.S. 30
Wachi, Y. 85
Wagner, A. 35, 56
Wahiduddin Mahmud 85
Walter, I. 98, 103, 104
Wangwe, S. 56
Wangwe, S.M. 83
Watanabe, S. 58, 80, 84, 86-88, 99
Weitz, R. 49
Wells, J. 8

Werneck, R.L.F. 102
Werneke, D. 79, 87, 109, 110, 115
Werth, M. 65
Wéry, R. 17, 32, 67, 71-73, 108
Westin, A.F. 86
Wesumperuma, D. 47
WFP 2
White, J. 81
Whitehead, A. 111
Whittle, P. 26
Wickramasekara, P. 8, 55
Widmer, J.-Ph. 61, 66, 67
Wilcock, D. 48
Wilcox, L. 52
Wilke, P. 11
Williams, G. 15
Wilson, P. 97
Winsbury, R. 81
Winston, G.C. 94
Woillet, J.C. 39, 63, 76, 77
Wolter, F. 98, 103, 104
Wong, J. 19
Wood, R.H. 48
Woods, W.M. 62
Wulf, H. 11
Wun'gaeo, S. 85
Wurgaft, J. 7, 24
Yagodkin, V.N. 94
Yalcintas, N. 65
Yamada, S. 47
Yamba, F.D. 83
Yamlinfung, P. 85
Yeres, D.J. 65
Youssef, N.H. 111, 115
Yueh-eh-Chen 53
Yung Chul Park 102
Yungchul, P. 103
Zachmann, R. 9, 11
Zeidenstein, S.A. 115
Zottos, S. 2

Country and Area Index

Afghanistan [AFG] 14, 60, 87
Algeria [DZA] 9, 27, 51, 60, 62, 63, 65
Angola [AGO] 45
Antigua [ATG] 16
Argentina [ARG] 12, 29, 34, 36, 37, 40, 42, 46, 51, 64, 84, 92, 97, 102
Australia [AUS] 24, 79, 86, 98, 109
Bahrain [BHR] 60, 65
Bangladesh [BGD] 8, 17, 25, 31, 37, 43, 47-49, 53-57, 79, 81, 84, 85, 87, 93, 106, 109, 115
Barbados [BRB] 87
Belgium [BEL] 24, 86
Belize [BLZ] 16
Benin [BEN] 4, 5, 16, 22, 78, 90, 107, 108
Bolivia [BOL] 7, 11, 12, 16, 28, 36, 40, 46, 51, 93
Botswana [BWA] 2, 27, 44-46, 49, 50, 56, 62, 77-79, 90, 91, 106
Brazil [BRA] 7, 8, 11-13, 15, 19, 27, 28, 31, 34, 36, 37, 40, 44, 46, 51, 52, 56, 64, 66, 70, 71, 73, 79, 80, 83, 84, 87, 93, 94, 100, 102, 112
Bulgaria [BGR] 20, 109
Burkina Faso (formerly Upper Volta) [BFA] 5, 16, 22, 27, 34, 39, 44, 48, 60, 63, 77, 78, 87, 90, 107
Burma [BUR] 17, 114
Burundi [BDI] 16, 27, 60, 63, 78, 91, 96
Byelorussian SSR [BYS] 18, 20
Cameroon [CMR] 4, 16, 22, 34, 35, 37-39, 46, 60, 63, 77, 90, 92, 100, 106-108
Canada [CAN] 9, 10, 13, 30, 31, 65, 86, 94, 98, 110
Cape Verde [CPV] 16, 44, 70
Central African Republic [CAF] 16
Chad [TCD] 35
Chile [CHL] 7, 8, 12, 13, 16, 18, 19, 23, 24, 28, 29, 31, 35, 36, 39-42, 46, 48, 51, 52, 56, 60, 66, 69, 70, 79, 83, 92-94, 97, 100-102
China [CHN] 17, 19, 26, 29-31, 34, 43, 44, 47-49, 52-56, 79, 84, 85, 87, 98, 103, 106, 109, 114, 115
Colombia [COL] 7, 11, 12, 14, 21, 23, 27-29, 32, 40, 46, 49, 56, 57, 60, 66, 69, 75, 83, 84, 87, 93, 100, 106, 108, 113
Comoros [COM] 90
Congo [COG] 16, 22, 34, 90, 96
Costa Rica [CRI] 7, 12, 16, 23, 29, 36, 37, 40-42, 52, 64, 69, 71, 84, 87, 93, 97, 115
Côte d'Ivoire [CIV] 16, 21, 22, 25, 28, 44, 50, 77, 82, 90, 96, 100, 107, 108
Cuba [CUB] 31, 51, 56, 66, 94, 106, 109, 113
Cyprus [CYP] 41, 106, 110, 114-116
Czechoslovakia [CSK] 109
Djibouti [DJI] 9, 35
Dominican Republic [DOM] 8, 13, 51, 97
Ecuador [ECU] 7, 11, 12, 18, 24, 29, 35, 37, 46, 52, 61, 63, 64, 66, 67, 69, 79
Egypt [EGY] 5, 9, 13, 27, 49, 56, 60, 62, 67, 81-83, 87, 94, 100, 106, 107, 112, 116
El Salvador [SLV] 7, 11, 12, 23, 29, 35, 36, 42, 52, 69
Ethiopia [ETH] 31, 44, 45, 49, 50, 56, 57, 77, 87, 91, 95, 96, 106, 108, 115
Fiji [FJI] 47, 79
France [FRA] 9, 13, 19, 65, 72, 77, 79, 87, 98, 109
Gabon [GAB] 16, 21, 45, 78, 90, 96
Gambia [GMB] 34, 44, 77, 90
Germany, Fed. Rep. [DEU] 9, 13, 17, 26, 60, 64, 65, 72, 94, 98, 100, 103, 104
Ghana [GHA] 22, 44, 45, 50, 63, 69, 77, 81, 82, 87, 90, 96, 99, 100, 106-108, 112, 115
Greece [GRC] 30
Grenada [GRD] 16
Guatemala [GTM] 8, 13, 19, 29, 36, 37, 40, 42, 46, 51, 52, 71, 92, 93
Guinea [GIN] 16
Guyana [GUY] 16, 23, 56, 63, 66
Honduras [HND] 11, 12, 29, 36, 40, 42, 51, 52
Hong Kong [HKG] 17, 21, 25, 31, 88, 97, 102, 103
Hungary [HUN] 106, 109, 114
India [IND] 1, 2, 5, 8, 15, 17, 21, 24, 27, 29-32, 34, 37, 41, 43, 44, 46-49, 53-58, 61, 64, 66, 67, 71-73, 75, 79, 84-88, 92-94, 98, 103, 106, 109, 113-116
Indonesia [IDN] 13, 17, 27, 29, 34, 37, 41, 47, 54, 55, 64, 66, 71, 79, 84, 85, 94, 97, 100, 102, 106, 107, 113, 114
Iran, Islamic Rep. of [IRN] 29, 31, 56, 87
Iraq [IRQ] 9
Ireland [IRL] 31, 94
Italy [ITA] 16, 30, 65, 86, 87
Jamaica [JAM] 8, 16, 35, 51, 84, 112, 115
Japan [JPN] 2, 17, 46-48, 55, 74, 77, 86, 87, 97-100, 103, 104
Jordan [JOR] 9, 56, 60, 114, 116
Kenya [KEN] 5, 14, 21, 22, 25, 27, 28, 31, 34, 35, 44-46, 50, 56, 61, 66, 67, 72, 73, 75, 77, 78, 79, 82, 87-91, 95, 96, 100, 107, 108, 111, 112, 115
Korea, Rep. of [KOR] 17, 26, 29, 31, 48, 49, 53, 55, 56, 58, 64, 75, 85-88, 97, 98, 100, 102, 103, 106
Kuwait [KWT] 9, 60, 65, 116
Lao People's Dem. Rep. [LAO] 8, 48, 70, 114

Lebanon [LBN] 9, 114-116
Lesotho [LSO] 2, 4, 5, 11, 22, 59, 60, 62, 77, 106, 112
Liberia [LBR] 4, 22, 45, 77, 89, 90, 96
Libyan Arab Jamahiriya [LBY] 60, 65, 67, 107
Madagascar [MDG] 16, 21, 35, 45, 51, 107, 108
Malawi [MWI] 35, 44, 45, 50, 56, 77, 91, 92, 96, 112
Malaysia [MYS] 17, 19, 29-31, 43, 54-57, 64, 66, 75, 79, 84, 85, 87, 93, 97, 98, 106, 113-115
Mali [MLI] 5, 16, 21, 22, 35, 38, 39, 42, 63, 77, 78, 83, 90, 108
Mauritania [MRT] 9, 16, 21, 37-39, 63, 72, 77, 90, 91
Mauritius [MUS] 81, 91, 106, 110-112, 115
Mexico [MEX] 6, 7, 10-12, 24-26, 28, 29, 31, 35, 36, 40, 42, 48, 52, 57, 64, 66, 69, 75, 81, 83, 87, 94, 99, 100, 102, 108, 113, 115
Morocco [MAR] 11, 16, 92, 94, 100, 107, 112
Mozambique [MOZ] 27, 44, 112
Namibia [NAM] 11, 28, 44, 45
Nepal [NPL] 8, 17, 24, 44, 47-49, 56, 57, 66, 79, 84, 85, 93
Netherlands [NLD] 9, 98, 104
New Zealand [NZL] 17
Nicaragua [NIC] 11, 19, 29, 36, 42, 46, 52, 56, 57, 100, 102
Niger [NER] 4, 16, 38, 77, 78, 100
Nigeria [NGA] 6, 18, 21, 22, 27, 34, 38, 44, 45, 50, 51, 56, 59, 66, 69, 87, 90, 92, 94-96, 100, 106, 107, 111, 112, 115, 116
Norway [NOR] 13, 24, 98
Oman [OMN] 60, 65
Pakistan [PAK] 8, 17, 34, 47, 48, 53, 55-57, 60, 64, 84, 85, 87, 88, 92, 98, 106, 114
Panama [PAN] 7, 12, 13, 23, 28, 29, 36, 40, 42, 51, 52, 83, 92, 93, 113
Papua New Guinea [PNG] 19, 37, 56, 61, 69
Paraguay [PRY] 46
Peru [PER] 8, 11-13, 16, 23, 25-28, 31, 36, 40, 41, 46, 51, 52, 56, 63, 64, 66, 84, 92, 93, 100, 104, 107, 108, 113, 115
Philippines [PHL] 17, 21, 23, 25, 28-31, 34, 37, 41, 47, 48, 54-57, 61, 64, 67, 69, 71-73, 79, 80, 84, 85, 87, 88, 94, 97, 98, 100, 102, 103, 113, 114
Poland [POL] 66, 106, 109
Portugal [PRT] 9, 31, 32, 87
Qatar [QAT] 60, 65
Rwanda [RWA] 6, 16, 39, 83, 91, 92, 96
Saint Christopher and Nevis [KNA] 16
Saint Lucia [LCA] 16
Saint Vincent and the Grenadines [VCT] 16
Samoa [WSM] 56, 87
Saudi Arabia [SAU] 13, 41, 60, 65
Senegal [SEN] 5, 16, 18, 21, 22, 26, 31, 32, 34, 38, 44, 77, 78, 90, 96, 107, 108, 114
Sierra Leone [SLE] 4, 5, 22, 25, 34, 37, 38, 41, 45, 77, 82, 83, 90, 95, 96, 106-108, 115
Singapore [SGP] 17, 69, 77, 88, 97, 98, 100, 102, 103, 115
Somalia [SOM] 4, 6, 9, 11, 21, 22, 27, 44-46, 50, 72, 77, 89-91
South Africa [ZAF] 2, 11, 39, 59, 62, 63, 107
Spain [ESP] 60, 87
Sri Lanka [LKA] 8, 17, 24, 29-31, 34, 37, 42, 47-49, 54, 55, 57, 64, 66, 69, 79, 84, 85, 87, 93, 94, 98, 103, 106, 109, 113, 115
Sudan [SDN] 6, 9, 35, 39, 44-46, 50, 51, 56, 60, 62, 69, 71, 72, 78, 79, 82, 92
Suriname [SUR] 5, 16, 18, 34, 35, 38, 45, 50, 65, 66, 83, 89, 96, 100, 102, 107
Swaziland [SWZ] 2, 59, 62, 77, 106
Sweden [SWE] 2, 13
Switzerland [CHE] 53, 61, 65, 67
Syrian Arab Rep. [SYR] 9, 13, 60, 65, 115
Taiwan, China [TWN] 47, 48, 53, 55, 64, 97, 102
Tanzania, United Rep. of [TZA] 4-6, 22, 27, 31, 34, 35, 43, 45, 46, 49, 50, 56, 57, 63, 66, 75, 77-80, 83, 87, 89, 90, 92, 94, 96, 99, 106, 108, 112
Thailand [THA] 8, 17, 19, 25, 29-31, 47-49, 53-56, 64, 69, 75, 79, 84-87, 94, 97, 109
Togo [TGO] 16, 22, 35, 37-39, 44, 63, 90, 96, 107, 108
Trinidad and Tobago [TTO] 16
Tunisia [TUN] 9, 13, 16, 60, 65, 77, 100
Turkey [TUR] 56, 60, 65, 72, 100, 109, 115
Uganda [UGA] 34, 45, 50, 56, 100
United Arab Emirates [ARE] 55, 60, 65
United Kingdom [GBR] 10, 13, 24, 26, 37, 77, 79, 86, 87, 94, 98, 104, 109
United States [USA] 10, 13, 24, 41, 61, 65, 77, 86, 87, 94, 98, 100, 103, 104, 110
Uruguay [URY] 7, 12, 40
USSR [SUN] 1, 10, 70, 94, 103, 106, 109
Venezuela [VEN] 8, 11, 12, 23, 28, 29, 37, 40, 41, 46, 63, 69, 83, 93
Viet Nam [VNM] 49, 53, 54, 56, 57, 114
Yemen [YEM] 9, 60, 65, 116
Yemen, Democratic [YMD] 9, 72, 109
Yugoslavia [YUG] 20, 31, 64, 69, 70, 72, 104, 106, 115
Zaire [ZAR] 6, 16, 35, 78, 90
Zambia [ZMB] 4, 18, 21, 22, 25, 27, 34, 39, 44, 45, 50, 56, 77-79, 83, 89-92, 96, 97, 100, 106, 108
Zimbabwe [ZWE] 39, 45, 62, 77, 80, 83, 100, 106, 108, 112